ORDINARY WHITES IN APARTHEID SOCIETY

ORDINARY WHITES IN APARTHEID SOCIETY

Social
Histories of
Accommodation

Neil Roos

INDIANA UNIVERSITY PRESS

This book is a publication of

Indiana University Press
Office of Scholarly Publishing
Herman B Wells Library 350
1320 East 10th Street
Bloomington, Indiana 47405 USA

iupress.org

© 2023 by Neil Roos

All rights reserved
No part of this book may be reproduced or utilized in any form or by any means, electronic or mechanical, including photocopying and recording, or by any information storage and retrieval system, without permission in writing from the publisher. The paper used in this publication meets the minimum requirements of the American National Standard for Information Sciences—Permanence of Paper for Printed Library Materials, ANSI Z39.48-1992.

Manufactured in the United States of America

First printing 2023

Library of Congress Cataloging-in-Publication Data

Names: Roos, Neil, author.
Title: Ordinary whites in apartheid society : social histories of accommodation / Neil Roos.
Other titles: Social histories of accommodation
Identifiers: LCCN 2023044858 (print) | LCCN 2023044859 (ebook) | ISBN 9780253068026 (hardcover) | ISBN 9780253068033 (paperback) | ISBN 9780253068040 (adobe pdf)
Subjects: LCSH: White people—South Africa—Social conditions—20th century. | Apartheid—South Africa—History—20th century. | South Africa—Race relations—History—20th century. | BISAC: HISTORY / Africa / South / Republic of South Africa | SOCIAL SCIENCE / Anthropology / Cultural & Social
Classification: LCC DT1768.W55 R66 2024 (print) | LCC DT1768.W55 (ebook) | DDC 305.809068—dc23/eng/20230925
LC record available at https://lccn.loc.gov/2023044858
LC ebook record available at https://lccn.loc.gov/2023044859

For Sheila

CONTENTS

Foreword ix

Preface xiii

Acknowledgments *xvii*

1 Compliance and Defiance in the Making of White Apartheid Society *1*

2 Whites and South African History *20*

3 The Delicacy of Teacups *38*

4 *Insluipers*, Geoffrey Cronjé, and Social Policy *57*

5 Work and Ideology in the Apartheid Public Service *77*

6 Women, the Labor Market, and the Domestic Economy *105*

7 Nationalism, Whiteness, and Consumption *131*

8 Alcohol and Social Engineering *161*

9 The End *186*

Notes *191*

Bibliography *217*

Index *231*

FOREWORD

The Choice of the Ordinary

In his classic study of the Haitian Revolution, Trinidadian historian C. L. R. James formulated matters in a way that insisted on subtle appreciation of the fact that two things that we too often regard as being at odds can both operate in tandem, and be supportive of each other. James wrote, "The race question is subsidiary to the class question in politics, and to think of imperialism in terms of race is disastrous. But to neglect the racial factor as merely incidental is *an error only less grave* than to make it fundamental."[1] James Baldwin, the great American essayist and novelist, insisted on a similar way of dialectical seeing in his 1984 *Essence* magazine article, "On Being White and Other Lies," still the best four pages to read for anyone wishing to confront the costs of whiteness to whites. Baldwin's piece described the decision to adopt and treasure white identities by poorer European immigrants to the US as "absolutely a moral choice" and, in only seeming contradiction, as a decision structured by "a vast amount of coercion."

The ability to understand contradiction is one great virtue of the provocative book that you hold. In this brief foreword I want to think about how the deft use of the word *ordinary* underpins such an accomplishment. *Ordinary* runs through Neil Roos's important scholarship on race in consistent and important ways. His influential 2005 study of white South Africans who fought in World War Two carries the title *Ordinary Springboks*, and this ambitious volume gives us the history of "ordinary whites" more generally.

Though separated from mine and from the foundational post-1990 US works in the critical study of whiteness by just one scholarly generation—and an ocean—Roos's evocation of the ordinary differs dramatically from at least the earliest incarnations of my own writing on working people in the US. The advantages of his starting point ensure that he can often produce more patient and mature analyses than many US writers on whiteness have done. My generation—the New Left and just after—was trained to suspect a word like *ordinary* and its cousin, *common*. Talk about the "common people" launched us into praises of how *uncommonly* brave, excellent, creative, and effective working-class people and organizations had been. When I was in graduate school, the most widely read account of the importance of the *ordinary* was the Welsh Marxist Raymond Williams's brilliantly crafted 1958 provocation, "Culture Is Ordinary." Williams argued that daily practices of workers and farmers both treasured cultural values and had in critical ways defined British culture. The *ordinary* was *extraordinary*, certainly in its impact and in its virtues as well.

Those of us seeking to raise questions about the disfiguring impact of white supremacy—a system and ideology ordinary in the history of the US—on politics and social relations eventually needed to bump up against totalizingly romantic views regarding the working majority of society. At least, we had to emphasize that some of the downtrodden also trod on those further below. Inheriting a certain kind of Marxism, we tended to concentrate on the whiteness of the working class and particularly of immigrants within it.

One easy way to dismiss critical whiteness studies in the US came to hinge on the charge that the scholarship too flattened whiteness, not registering differences. Another charge asserted that the field of critical whiteness studies blamed those who were white for a system not of their making. Without overly crediting that charge—clearly the effort of critical whiteness studies has been to discuss the particular appeals of whiteness to workers and immigrants, and thus not to homogenize whites—it can be granted that at least in my case, treatment of differences among the working class was attenuated and attention to what came in the twentieth century to be called the "middle class" was inadequate.

More complicated still is the related critique that US historians on the left studying whiteness deny the presence of "good whites" as they "blame" non-elite whites for racism. On the one hand, it would be hard to find more enthusiastic admirers of the white fighter against white supremacy, John Brown, than the late and great critical whiteness studies scholars Joel Olsen, Theodore Allen, and Noel Ignatiev, for example. But on the other hand, they and others of us do stand with Baldwin in insisting that identifying one's interests as white was and remains a disastrous moral choice. We do reject the notion that the presence of a Brown, or for liberals, an Abraham Lincoln, overrides the larger pattern of white supremacy.

Roos likewise struggles to balance the ways in which identification with whiteness, and with apartheid, was coerced and accepted, but with more success than we in the US have had. He too learned the historians' craft from those doing some variant of a "history from below"—mostly white, largely radical, and working inside and outside universities in South Africa. They sought to rescue what US historians called a "useable past" of resistance, partly via a search for white participation in heroic struggles. But Roos's moment of arrival was past the crest of such a tendency, which in South Africa always had to be treated with a certain astringency in part because of the marginal role of white trade unions in anti-apartheid campaigns. The most sustained treatment of a, in some ways, heroic and visionary radical struggle, Jeremy Krikler's account of the Rand Revolt, describes from its title forward the tragedy of a "white rising." Roos also benefits from the experience of a transition from white rule in his lifetime, from a Truth and Reconciliation process (and left critiques of it) encouraging national reflection on complicity and guilt, and from demographics that make it clear that a critique of whiteness does not indict the people of South Africa in their majority.

Even with such advantages, what Roos achieves in this book is remarkable, in no small matter due to his theorizing of the *ordinary*. Beginning with so broad a category as "ordinary whites" forces disaggregation almost immediately, when he writes of that group as itself, "made up of people from the working class, whites who broke their way into the 'middle class,' the destitute and those separated from the mainstream of *ordentlike* (respectable) white society, and it included Afrikaans speakers . . . as well as English speakers." Happily, examples from his own family, so deftly woven into this story that when they disappear for a stretch we miss them, provide examples from all of these categories. Roos is not uninterested in exemplary anti-racist whites—they appear frequently in *Ordinary Springboks*, for example—but a sense of proportion keeps them away from the center of the important histories that Roos probes.

Its longer roots and recent past make *ordinary* an apt choice to focus attention on questions of agency, structure, and responsibility. Descending from Latin and Old French, the *ordinary* had from earliest (circa 1400) usages connoted both "belonging to the usual order or course" and reflections of "rank." The *ordinary* as an individual was in England either the figure of immediate clerical authority (a bishop or archbishop) or a judge. The specific references by Roos to recent work take us to Nazi terror and complicity with it, especially via Christopher Browning's important *Ordinary Men: Reserve Police Battalion 101 and the Final Solution in Poland* and, more controversially, Daniel Goldhagen's *Hitler's Willing Executioners: Ordinary Germans and the Holocaust*. *Ordinary* as the quotidian and as the power-wielding are usefully counterposed.

Roos adds the specific dimension of complicity among the subaltern, themselves policed and surveilled. He details a post-1948 South African state project bent on actively securing a full place within white society for all defined as members of the club. The project emphasized as its subjects poorer Afrikaners whose failures to thrive according to the state's view had previously attracted harsher measures, but now deployed more bureaucratic and biopolitical methods of watching and ranking. The enormous role of government employment and of jobs in parastatal enterprises made the white-making processes literally state-sponsored, even as the production of race was mediated by modernizing academic experts who commandeered what it meant to be a modern and good Afrikaner, South African, and white.

Resistance was certainly not absent. Government workers deployed strategies very much resembling the infrapolitical weapons found among subalterns everywhere in contesting the race-based management of the dominant race. But the fact that the racial state did uplift poorer and urbanizing whites, both in absolute terms and within the chasm separating them from Africans, foreclosed reaching toward political expressions of grievance. The refusals by ordinary whites of full incorporation into the ranks of the successfully surveilled and judged and into effective enthusiastic participation in the National Party were often desperate ones, as in the recalcitrant patterns of what Roos wonderfully discusses as "white drinking." Sometimes, he tragically shows, the weapons of the advantaged weak were literally suicidal.

David Roediger
Foundation Professor of American
Studies, University of Kansas

PREFACE

Just as I began research for this book, I was invited to deliver a talk to a group of white retirees in Bloemfontein, South Africa. They asked me to talk about aspects of South African history, and I thought that the social history of ordinary white people in South Africa in the 1950s, 1960s, and 1970s might be of interest to an audience who had lived and worked under apartheid and witnessed the negotiated settlement in 1994. This, I thought, would present them with connection points to the past and a historical commons for telling and sharing stories of their own. How wrong I was. When I put my idea to the conveners, some expressed acute discomfort while others were openly hostile to the idea.

The chair, a retired professor from the local university, asked if I could not instead speak of something "apolitical" like the history of the African National Congress (ANC), once one of South Africa's major liberation movements and, since the formal end of apartheid in 1994, South Africa's governing party. No praise-singer of official histories (and certainly, in some South African circles, the ANC's history is assuming the mantle of a national history), I proposed a compromise where I would talk about some of the perspectives on the South African past that have been opened up by the social history movement in South Africa. This allowed me to introduce a number of episodes from the history of working class and other non-elite whites, some of which feature in this book: work colonies, the "white yogi," the *moederkunde* program, and motor racing at the speedway.

What stuck most in my mind about that talk, and what puzzled me, was the disaffection that my proposed topic invoked. I was struck that they considered a history that included them to be "political" and therefore not an appropriate topic for polite conversation, while the history of the ANC was considered "apolitical." Could it be, I speculated, that opening a window onto their past left them feeling uneasily close to apartheid's history? And that once they acknowledged being part of white apartheid society, this left them aligned, in their own minds at least, with a racist state, apartheid's ideologies and the worst of its excesses? The ANC's history, on the other hand, was plausibly more distant and safer. By the second decade of the millennium, this history had largely settled into a recitation of a canon of nation building, where the cadence and directness of its telling avoid difficult questions of complicity, participation, and moral ambiguity.

If this is indeed the case, then the committee's resistance to my suggestion might be characterized as something akin to active forgetting. Among whites in contemporary South Africa, active forgetting (often bustled along with declaimers that "what I did isn't interesting or historical" or "that is all in the past now, let's leave it") must take its place alongside whitewashing ("we were opposed to apartheid all along") or apologia ("it wasn't all bad"). All of these strategies may be discerned in various permutations among white South Africans—those who came of age under apartheid, as well as younger ones—and they serve to create some distance from apartheid and the racialized privilege it bequeathed to a postapartheid generation of young white people. It is far easier, historically and morally, to divert responsibility to apartheid's ideologues, politicians, and brutal police and military.

Yet it is precisely these questions of how whites were connected to apartheid society that this book seeks to address. It is not meant to categorize people as good whites or bad, those on the right side of history and those on the wrong. Rather, it seeks to tease out the complex ties that bound whites into apartheid society, the contestations which these provoked, and implications of these struggles, which varied in scale, intensity, and geography, for the shape of the apartheid social order as a whole.

Autobiography is often woven into the fabric of historical scholarship. An earlier book that I wrote, *Ordinary Springboks*, centered on the social history of white men who served in South Africa's Union Defence Force during the Second World War. That book was inspired by my father's history as he enlisted as a seventeen-year-old volunteer. Questions that particularly intrigued me were how, during the war and after, he and other men like him went about staking their claims in segregated South African society. How their whiteness hollowed out the anti-fascist mobilization they participated in during the early 1950s. Despite the entry point to *Ordinary Springboks* provided by my father's life and times as a soldier and then as a veteran, this history was, in effect, a generation removed from my own experience. *Ordinary Whites*, on the other hand, is set in the world I grew up in. Or, more accurately, the people whose stories feature most prominently in this volume were people I grew up with, people I knew over a long period. I make no great claims to the personal importance of these people for the apartheid project, and none occupied powerful or influential positions in apartheid society. For the purposes of this book, their significance lies in what their history tells us about that society and, I will argue furthermore, that their history is essential to understanding the dynamics of the apartheid social order.

My proximity to the life, times, and foibles of some of the people I write about, along with my familiarity with particular fragments of their history, has come with both benefits and costs. Although I cannot and do not propose to speak for broad swaths of white society, this knowledge coupled with my roots in a poorer white working-class family did guide me as I combed the sources for white society's routines, codes, aspirations, and modes of indocility and transgression, as well as the limits to these. This is an ethnographic position of both advantage and privilege, but the closeness that allowed me to peer into some of the unspoken, hidden, obscured, and taken-for-granted reaches of white life also prompted questions and doubts. Was I misinterpreting what I had seen and heard? Was I forcing anecdotes and other observations into preconceived arguments? My direct use of these anecdotes is thus quite limited, even as they provide a lens into some of the book's major arguments.

Midway through writing *Ordinary Whites*, the decolonization movement flooded through sections of South African society, driven largely by university students. Turning their attention to what featured in South African university curricula, student activists were critical not only of the content of their courses but also of the conventional chronologies and disciplinary divisions that organized the knowledge which they were taught. Among many other claims, they demanded a reconsideration of histories of colonialism, racism, and whiteness. The students' insistence was hardly surprising, since the abiding legacies of these interconnected systems were everywhere apparent in their daily lives. These young people repudiated explanations of racism that equated it with the chronologies of the colonial, segregationist, and apartheid states in South Africa. Their strident dissatisfaction served as a rallying call for fresh, bold, and unashamedly political approaches to whiteness since routine answers simply fail to account for the resilience of racism, or what whiteness means historically or contemporaneously. These questions demand fine-grained investigation into the evolving, malleable ways of whiteness in its historical complexity.

Whiteness does moreover beg introspection on the part of whites. To borrow a rather evocative claim made by Rick Turner, an anti-apartheid intellectual murdered in 1978 probably by apartheid agents, such introspection may help whites to "decolonize" and thus reimagine their place in South African society. As it explores the history of ordinary whites in the early years of apartheid, these are the ideals to which *Ordinary Whites* aspires.

Neil Roos
Alice, Eastern Cape
February 2022

ACKNOWLEDGMENTS

This book has been long in the framing, imagining, thinking, writing, and revising. As may be expected of such a long project, its list of acknowledgments is lengthy as well. But that's not the main reason why the list of those whom I must thank is extensive. The length of this list reflects far less the scope of my undertaking than it does the great generosity of my colleagues and friends. To paraphrase fellow historian and friend Betsy Esch (herself paraphrasing a novelist whom she admired): "everyone we work with is smart. Thus, the challenge is not to be smart, the challenge is to be kind." And I have been the recipient of kindness and generosity in buckets. There have been occasions of unkindness too, but buried beneath these were sometimes observations that were generative and insightful.

The germ of this book lay in questions that were raised, but not answered, during my writing of an earlier work, *Ordinary Springboks: White Servicemen and Social Justice in South Africa, 1939–1961*. However, it was during a Fulbright fellowship at the Chicago Center for Contemporary Theory and the Department of Anthropology at the University of Chicago that this book began to take shape in earnest. There I learned the historiography, the comparative and theoretical work, and the methodological range that have guided this book. Participants at the university's workshops in African studies and social theory encouraged me to write a history that, while firmly rooted in African studies, was about white people. White people are part of the continent's history and, as several protagonists in the Social Theory Workshop, steeped in the lineage of the Frankfurt School, pointed out, it is inconceivable to fathom the history of an oppressive society, or of a racial state, *only* from the perspective of its victims.

At the University of Pretoria, Charles van Onselen cajoled and encouraged me. He regularly reminded me of the value of history—social history in particular—and warned me of the dangers of the nationalist historiographies that became such a potent force in millennial South African history-writing. Geoff Eley of the University of Michigan and Dipesh Chakrabarty of the University of Chicago—both of whom, like van Onselen, are among the world's most influential social historians—were tolerant, kind, collegial, and supportive as I posed questions to them about some of the dead ends and dismissals that the project of social history faced in the 2000s, as well as about possibilities for a new, insurgent social history fitted to the political and intellectual climate of the second and third decades of the millennium.

At the University of the Free State, the International Studies Group (ISG), headed by Ian Phimister, gave me an intellectual home. At ISG seminars, in the university corridors, and over coffee (or more often, beer), I had several years of collegial, friendly, and interested conversation with the ISG's wonderful cohorts of doctoral students and postdoctoral fellows. Ian himself, as well as Kate Law, Lazlo Passemiers, Rory Pilossof, and Tinashe Nyamunda, all engaged particularly closely and critically, and over a long period, with the work that eventually cohered as *Ordinary Whites*. I also thank David Patrick, who provided common sense, calm, and a perspective from outside the field of African studies, and Richard Pithouse, who undertook a reading of the entire manuscript at a critical time.

I was hosted at many seminars and workshops both within and outside of South Africa during my time writing this book. These directed me to many of the blind spots, contradictions, and ambiguities that were present in my text, and also helped me tease out issues for further development and elaboration. I must also thank archivists and librarians across South Africa—most notably, those at the Archive for Contemporary Affairs at the University of the Free State; the State Archives; the Strange Collections at the Johannesburg Public Library; the Kweekskool at the University of Stellenbosch; and the Killie Campbell Africana Collections at the University of Kwazulu-Natal. But most of all I thank Hesma van Tonder from the University of the Free State library, who was always ready to assist me with my frequent, broad and, I suspect, often esoteric search queries.

Fulbright funded the early part of this work; the bulk of the funding came from the National Research Foundation and the University of the Free State. There were also smaller awards from the African Studies Workshop at Harvard and the Miller Center for Historical Studies at the University of Maryland.

I reserve my most substantial gratitude for last. To my colleague and friend Jackie du Toit, who has guided and supported me through the intellectual and emotional labor required to bring this book to fruition, I am especially indebted: for her advice, encouragement, and good sense when I contemplated, and then undertook, a major rewrite of the manuscript. And, finally, to M, endlessly patient, supportive, and kind from the outset of this project to its final fruition.

ORDINARY WHITES IN APARTHEID SOCIETY

COMPLIANCE AND DEFIANCE IN THE MAKING OF WHITE APARTHEID SOCIETY

1

A Kind of Madness

"These bloody Nats!" was the repeated refrain of my 1960s South African childhood. "Nats" was shorthand for the ruling pro-apartheid National Party (NP), and "The bloody Nats!" was my mother's go-to pronouncement for everything wrong in her world. Sheila Roos was probably the most class-conscious person I knew, and it was not only the NP that attracted her distaste. As a boy I learned to distrust creatures called managers and bosses and lawyers (although I hardly knew what any of these characters were). Even worse were those who drove Mercedes-Benz cars. Her ingrained understanding of class did, however, stop at the frontiers of South Africa's racial order, and she never considered any type of fraternity, any common ground, with other working people who were not white. She was more educated than my father who had only a few years' schooling. He was unable to secure the kind of work that white men aspired to in the 1960s, and my mother's job as a legal secretary meant that she was the economic stabilizer in a household where the veneer of patriarchy had to be maintained for the outside world. Yet in 1960, when the NP announced a referendum to declare a republic, she took unpaid leave from her job—courtesy of a boss who shared her political persuasions—to mobilize white electoral support against the NP's plans. Every afternoon and every evening she campaigned, knocking on doors up and down Durban streets.

Sheila's scorn for the NP operated on a wide front and at one level probably included an element of ethnic chauvinism. An English speaker, Durban born and raised, she was not particularly fond of Afrikaners, at least those who identified with the NP. She also warned me against playing with the "railway children," a coded phrase referring to working-class Afrikaans children. During the 1960s when the NP was rolling out its plans for "grand apartheid"—its macro-scale ambitions to use territorial segregation to "resolve" the race question once and for all—she called the NP "quite mad" and regularly wrote letters to the press, an uncommon sort of intervention for a working-class woman. Despite her opposition to grand apartheid and the republic, she shared much of the NP's belief in segregation, and certainly as a lower-working-class family, we benefited materially from the racial privileges NP rule guaranteed. For instance, we lived in subsidized housing, and I went to good schools. She was one of those whom an NP politician in the 1950s once scornfully described as preferring their apartheid "enunciated with honey in the voice."[1]

Besides her almost visceral political sense, Sheila had another great interest: horse racing. For her it wasn't about the glamour of the track but rather about figuring out small wagers to place with the bookie or the off-course totalizator. Horse races took place on Wednesdays and Saturdays, so she would spend Tuesday and Friday evenings in the living room with friends we'll call Mrs. G and Mrs. N, drinking tea, smoking, and debating the form of particular race horses. Under South Africa's race laws, neither Mrs. G nor Mrs. N was classified as white, yet these three friends met regularly to figure out how to beat the odds, their time together was convivial, and their relationships included favors and exchanges well beyond the scope of horse racing. Under the emerging apartheid social order, these friendships also represented little acts of defiance, and humble, mostly unnoticed enactments of history across the color line.

These shards of experience from my mother's life, and the belonging, loathing, indifference, and defiance that they demonstrate, arguably offer important keys to understanding the history of white people under apartheid. Their lives cannot be read as more prosaic versions of the big histories of apartheid or peeled off from its official ideologies. Sheila's history was more complicated than this, and while the political and gender roles she assumed did make her in some respects atypical, her life offers a parable: that the history of whites in apartheid South Africa could and did contain contradictory impulses. Among these was the capacity to simultaneously challenge parts of the apartheid project while accepting other parts of it quite uncritically, generally unaware of any tension. When setting out to write this book on the lives of ordinary whites under apartheid, I thought that this relationship between opposition and acquiescence was the key to understanding histories of white life under apartheid. It is the main theme here, but there are others.

While I was doing archival work for this book, the state's seriousness in policing, controlling, and reforming people in the lower reaches of white society during the 1950s was brought home in a very personal way. This stratum of "ordinary whites" was a heterogenous mix: people from the working class, whites who broke their way into the middle class, the destitute, and those separated from the mainstream of *ordentlike* (respectable) white society. It also included Afrikaans speakers, who formed a substantial component of the NP's constituency, as well as English speakers. While scrolling through lists of men collected by the Durban Men's Home for committal to a work colony in the early 1950s, it was something of a shock to come across the names of my father, Dick, and his brother, Vic. Work colonies were institutions with a long history in South Africa of incarcerating idle but not-quite-criminal white men. By the beginning of the Second World War, work colonies had fallen into disuse, and most had closed down, but in the late 1940s they were modernized and reinstituted under the new apartheid government.[2] A bureaucracy was created to work closely with welfare organizations to identify white men to assign to work colonies. These men were generally those who, in the opinion of apartheid's social workers, did not look after their families, were drunks, or were destitute and unable to maintain a lifestyle appropriate for whites. Occasionally, magistrates would substitute detention in a work colony for criminal conviction, particularly in the cases of young men.

These ethnographic snapshots from my family's past raise themes that must feature front and center for anyone trying to make sense of the history of whites in the early apartheid years. They may also be of interest to those looking to South African history for insights into race-making, especially the historical processes by which whites and the idea of whiteness are transformed and contested, just as other material and ideological forces are changed and disputed. These family anecdotes may also draw the attention of those with a curiosity about everyday life in an authoritarian-type society. This book focuses not on the experience or the trauma of those populations who were the direct victims of an authoritarian regime (in South Africa, these were Black people) but those who were significant beneficiaries of it, whether or not they may be described as primary perpetrators of evil.

Transactions between white elites and whites in the lower echelons of white society form the spine of this volume, although, as with any history of South Africa, it is inconceivable that Black people are not integral to and present in the stories told here. In the mind's eye of white elites, Blacks sometimes featured as an abstract presence, although among ordinary whites like my mother there were real examples of friendships, alliances, and cooperation. There were also acts of racism, accompanied sometimes by violent conflict, and I introduce and discuss some of these exchanges. We already know roughly what kind of people populated the lower ranks of white society. Identifying apartheid's white subalterns—those who were subject to state

Figure 1.1 My parents, Sheila and Dick Roos. Fragments from their life prompt some of the questions that shape this book. Author's personal collection.

surveillance—is, however, by no means an exact science based on economic status or class composition. In addition to working-class people and those tenuously joining what may be described as a middle class through access to public service jobs, whole social groups were added to the mix based on Afrikaner nationalist anxieties and the social programs these anxieties activated. These included drunkards, prostitutes, and eventually even those most respectable and honored members of white Afrikanerdom: mothers.

On the other end of the socioeconomic spectrum, those considered to be white elites were NP politicians, state bureaucrats, and Afrikaner nationalist intellectuals, along with a few individuals who abided by some of apartheid's social policies but were not Afrikaners. First, I ask how and why these elites sought to engineer and manage ordinary whites, paying close attention to the tenor, variety, and gender dynamics of these interventions. Second, I ask how these ordinary whites, all some distance from the center of official power and authority, responded not only to the material opportunities and ideological blandishments of apartheid society, but also to the ways that these whites were regulated and subject to various schemata of improvement and sanction. I assess how the histories of both these opportunities and control mechanisms help us understand the everyday world of whites, at least those in the lower social classes of apartheid society. I also assess some of the diverse ways in which ordinary whites were bound into and participated in the maintenance of apartheid society, the nature of their participation in the system, and the impacts of white transgression and indocility in the face of apartheid. These are all questions about complicity, defiance, race-making, and the limits of agency in the context of an increasingly powerful, confident, and authoritarian state. They all subvert the idea of a homogenous, one-dimensional, and essentialized whiteness and thus go some way toward unmasking whiteness as an invented idea of superiority, an important consideration for any history of whites that simultaneously lays claim to being a history of race.

Both my father and uncle were veterans of the Second World War. My father had seven years of schooling and his brother a few years more. Like many veterans across the world, they were unable to find or settle into steady work. I found no traces of the circumstances that led to my kin ending up as inmates in the work colony system, nor a record of the length of their internment. But since neither had a criminal record, their detention does point to the apartheid state's ambition to manage large swaths of white society. My father never mentioned the work colony, much less his passage through it, despite spending much time during his last months reminiscing more and more about the events and people that had shaped his life—the Great Depression, the 1939–1945 war, the Comrades Marathon, his various jobs, his friends, and the seedier sides of life he witnessed (and sometimes joined in on) as a soldier during the war in North Africa and, later, back in South Africa.[3] It was as if he had erased the work colony from his memory. The shame that he clearly associated with his detention in the work colonies emphasizes something of the apartheid state's intent toward whites in the lower echelons of society. It also testifies to the ways these whites understood official attempts to reform them: the kind of rehabilitation undertaken by the state in the work colonies was not that different from a prison sentence.

Complicity in Authoritarian Society

Apartheid earned international notoriety as a system of racial oppression, and in 1984 the Security Council of the United Nations endorsed a resolution that labeled it as a "crime against humanity."[4] Apartheid spurred more than four decades of protest within South Africa, sparked outrage across the global community, and provoked an international anti-apartheid campaign. It bequeathed complex legacies to a resilient postapartheid South Africa, and it has been the subject of countless articles, books, films, and college courses. The aspect of apartheid society that did most to fuel resistance and capture horrified public imagination across the world was its systematic racism, inscribed in law. This was accompanied by the apartheid state's apparently relentless pursuit of separate development, which relied on a presumption that South Africa could be parsed into separate ethnic states—the white one dominant, of course—and the state's willingness to violently silence opposition.

After the formal end of apartheid in 1994, South African whites came under closer scrutiny. The major forum for this new and often unwelcome attention was the Truth and Reconciliation Commission (TRC), legislated into effect in 1995 as a court-like body to advance the cause of "restorative justice." Chaired by 1984 Nobel Peace Laureate Archbishop Desmond Tutu, the TRC had three branches: the Human Rights Violations Committee, with a brief to investigate human rights abuses between 1960 and 1994; the Reparation and Rehabilitation Committee, which was tasked with developing interventions to restore victims' dignity; and the Amnesty Committee, charged with considering the submissions of those who had applied for amnesty for human rights violations. The scope of the TRC's work inevitably brought into the spotlight those who had supported and maintained apartheid and who had drawn benefit from it. Volume 4 of the TRC's report addressed "the nature of the society in which gross human rights violations took place," and it asked how white people "who considered themselves ordinary, decent and God-fearing" found themselves turning a blind eye to a system that impoverished, oppressed, and violated the lives and very existence of so many of their fellow citizens.[5] Apartheid, the TRC insisted, could only have happened if large numbers of white South Africans condoned it. While it acknowledged that most white South Africans knew only "a closed world, surrounded by fences, prohibitions and some terrible assumptions about their fellow countrymen and women," the commission found it difficult to accept the defense, which became something of a refrain among whites during the late 1990s, that they knew little about the brutal realities of apartheid.[6] They could thus not be presumed responsible for the ravages that it wrought upon the majority of South Africa's population or the destabilization and violence that it brought to the southern African region, or so this line of reasoning went.

When pointing out how whites supported apartheid, tacitly or otherwise, and expressing cynicism about their pleas of innocence, the TRC opened up a Pandora's box of questions related to accommodation and complicity and how these were embedded in the everyday lives of white people. In societies marked by high levels of unfreedom, such questions represent deep moral dilemmas, and recourse to history is one way to approach and perhaps understand them.[7] The complex moral issues clustered around accommodation and complicity by citizens of authoritarian states inevitably confront and taunt historians of authoritarianism drawn to narrow and precise historical and historiographic assessments of ideology, participation (including knowledge and denial by perpetrators), and coercion—as well as of agency and its limits. Indeed, for Sir Richard Evans, one of the luminaries of German history, these moral ambiguities are central to the major questions of modern German history, especially for the Nazi period and the years leading up to it.[8] Assessing responsibility or guilt for citizens of a repressive state is equally central when considering the history of whites in apartheid society, and it represents the most compelling reason for writing this book.

Racial Rule and Periodizing Apartheid

South Africa had a long history of racial segregation before apartheid. This stretched back to British (particularly) and Dutch colonialism in the seventeenth, eighteenth, and nineteenth centuries. In 1910, the Union of South Africa was formed when the Cape and Natal, both former British colonies, united with the Transvaal and Orange Free State, both independent Boer republics until their defeat by the British in the Anglo-Boer War (1899–1902). After 1910, voting in the newly unified South Africa was reserved largely, but not exclusively, for white men.[9] The Union government mobilized itself swiftly to advance white interests, passing an early and significant piece of legislation known as the 1913 Natives Land Act, which effectively penned Blacks into 13 percent of the country. It also introduced a raft of segregationist legislation, including workplace color bars.

Against the backdrop of a society where racial segregation was already well-entrenched, apartheid began formally in May 1948, when the NP took a surprise victory in that year's general election, rallying voters with the catch-all appeal of "apartheid," that is, "apart-ness." Apartheid became official policy and remained so for more than forty years until it ended formally with the installation of the African National Congress–led Government of National Unity in April 1994 under the presidency of Nelson Mandela. While it represented a particular period of South African history, apartheid itself went through several phases. During the NP's early years, from the time it came to office under the leadership of D. F. Malan in 1948, until 1961, when Prime Minister Hendrik Verwoerd withdrew South Africa from the British Commonwealth, it did little to legislate and implement the political geography of separate development for which it would later become infamous.[10] In 1958, the NP-dominated Parliament did, however, pass the Promotion of Black Self-Government Act, which enabled the establishment of separate territorial governments in "homelands" designated for Black people. This legislation would be a cornerstone for the NP's subsequent program of "grand apartheid."

In the early stages of its occupancy of office, the NP government had more immediate priorities than implementation of apartheid. Almost as soon as they assumed office, the new occupants of the Union buildings—the seat of the South African government in Pretoria—had to contend with rising tides of resistance to racial segregation. This was part of a post–Second World War trend on the continent that had accelerated locally in the wake of a huge strike by Black gold miners in 1946.[11] The NP administration was met with wave after wave of labor and civic protest involving strikes, boycotts, mass protest marches, and passive resistance. In response to these challenges, the NP showed it had the stomach to deploy all branches of the state ruthlessly against its populace, if never entirely systematically. In 1950, it passed the Suppression of Communism Act, which defined *communism* so broadly that anyone who opposed government policy or "tried to disrupt racial harmony" risked being declared a communist. Organizations or individuals could be banned, and in addition, individuals could be jailed or tied up in lengthy judicial procedures. This legislation did little to break the spirit of protest, however, and in 1952, people from African, colored, and Indian communities came together in what was known as the Defiance Campaign to passively disobey unjust laws and make them impossible to enforce. Then, in 1955, the Congress of the People, made up of several anti-apartheid congresses, met at Kliptown near Johannesburg where they adopted the Freedom Charter, a declaration that set out a vision for a just and nonracial South Africa after apartheid.[12] In 1956 the government retaliated by arresting and placing on trial for high treason 156 leaders of the congresses in what became known as the Treason Trial. All of the accused eventually either had charges against them dismissed before the case came to trial or were acquitted, but during the legal proceedings, many congress leaders were nonetheless imprisoned or occupied with court matters for the better part of five years. The 1950s was therefore a decade that saw both resistance and repression spiraling outward.

My father's and uncle's sojourn to the work colonies points to another agenda that some members of the ruling NP and those close to it had during the early years of apartheid: the will to surveil certain classes of whites. As we shall see, measures to police white behavior predated apartheid and included laws like the 1927 Immorality Act, which prohibited sexual intercourse between Europeans (whites) and Blacks. The imperative to surveil applied equally to men and women, and it demonstrates something of the persistent historical distrust and disdain extended by Afrikaner elites to poor whites. Apartheid was at best only half a generation removed from poor whiteism, characterized by economic, cultural, and psychological ravages of land evictions, unemployment, social dislocation, and malnutrition (discussed in chap. 3). These interlocking traumas affected not only the white poor but also the middle-class custodians of Afrikaner nationalism, who feared both a dilution of the Afrikaner *volk* (people) and a blurring of lines between Black and white. In addition to these concerns, there were fairly long histories of care and welfare, albeit of a fairly authoritarian kind, associated with white poverty and urbanization. These working (or potentially working, or ought-to-be-working) classes were important for the development of apartheid society. At one level, whites, especially Afrikaners, needed to fit the *volk*-ish imagination of Afrikaner nationalism, which both emphasized and romanticized the unity of Afrikaners. At another, more practical level, there was a need for these whites to provide labor for the expanding apartheid state machinery and for racially stratifying industrial capitalism. In the late 1940s, there did not seem to be much confidence among Afrikaner nationalists in government, state departments, or universities that whites generally were up to these tasks. But by the early 1960s, labor issues as well as questions of the trustworthiness of whites were more or less resolved, and the government under Verwoerd was able to turn to matters closer to his heart, elaborating and applying the broad strokes of separate development and its legitimating ideologies.

History and South African Whites

Despite their central role in colonialism, segregation, and apartheid, historians know very little about whites in modern South Africa. Certainly, there are countless volumes on the intricacies of colonial government, administration, diplomacy, and warfare; on the Anglo-Boer War; and, after 1910, on the maneuvers and marches of party politics in the Union years. Further, in the 1980s and 1990s, there was vigorous inquiry into the lives and experiences of Black South Africans. But there was no parallel interest in the everyday histories of whites; the material, ideological, and political circumstances that shaped their lives; and the worlds that they, in turn, made. The years between the advent of apartheid in 1948 and its end in 1994 represent a particularly significant gap in historians' knowledge of these whites. It is likely that ideological and political concerns diverted the attention of historians with an interest in the period to other actors during this time.

When there are so many critical gaps in our knowledge of the African past, it is important to ask ourselves why historians should bother with this lacuna in the history of whites and whether this constitutes a legitimate subject for African studies.[13] During the late 1960s and early 1970s, in what was something of a pioneering age of Africanist scholarship for a generation of English-speaking historians who came through African, American, and British universities, the study of precolonial Africa and resistance to colonialism constituted the only genuine approach to African history. Conversely, attention to the colonial state or society risked the label of a throwback to imperial history or the accusation of a return to "historiographic colonialism."[14] Although one should be cautious about separating too distinctly African and South African history, there has been a similar discomfort and lack of interest in taking on the history of South African whites.[15]

New political winds and historiographies have changed this situation—up to a point—and the unease demonstrated by earlier generations of Africanists has diminished. Political imperatives of history-writing in and about Africa are now very different from what they were during times of primary anti-colonial struggle and fragile independence. New insights have revealed how the coherence and stability of colonial power was overestimated, while the complexities of colonial society were afforded little attention. This observation has directed historians and anthropologists of empire and imperialism to focus not only on colonial government and the lives of the colonized but also on the internal dynamics of colonial society. The same applies to studies of South Africa that claim affiliation with broader histories of colonialism. Whites in South Africa have never been homogenous. They have been colonizers, administrators, missionaries, scientists, policemen, and torturers, deeply implicated in the making of segregated society. But they have also been workers who revolted against the government of the day, opponents of segregation and apartheid, and in some cases active members of the liberation movements. Histories of whites affected those of other men and women, and the entanglements, contrariness, and, occasionally, the ironies that they deliver add texture to the way we face both the South African past and present. Whites form part of the puzzle that constitutes modern South African history. There is, however, one crucial caveat: histories of whites cannot be imagined apart from those of Blacks.

In addition to addressing the questions specific to this book, *Ordinary Whites* intervenes in debates about racial production within authoritarian and oppressive states in mid-twentieth-century societies, including the roles of bureaucracies in these historical schemata. The book represents an example of "theory from the south" that may yield different insights from other case studies due to its foundations and reference points in anti-colonial history and literature and its debts to the historiographic gains won by radical South African social history and other critical traditions, including subaltern studies and African American studies of race.[16]

A self-consciously radical history of whites, situated within a broader African historiography and framing whiteness as a central historical, political, and ethical problem, may yield political and pedagogical value and also contribute to ways that we approach histories of race. The notion of being radical as a stance in historiography is, of course, controversial and has varying meanings according to place and time. In many contexts worldwide, it has meant some affiliation with Marxism—itself a very diverse phenomenon. The same has been true for South African intellectual circles where radical history for a long time implied both historical analysis and a political vision inspired by a specific adoption of a Marxism that had emerged in the 1970s in critical dissidence toward older orthodoxies.[17] As Geoff Eley points out, however, radical history does not necessarily have to be equated with Marxist approaches. For Eley, a more useful definition of radical history involves first and foremost linking scholarly practice to a contemporary politics of social change.[18]

Any history of whites in South Africa that professes to enter debates about change (or the absence of it) must begin with race, the most ubiquitous feature of public life in contemporary South Africa. W. E. B. Du Bois wrote that the problem of the twentieth century would be the one of the color line. His prediction was quite correct, for despite more than a century of global politics grounded in anti-racist and human rights activism, the problem of the color line has never been resolved. Inequalities associated with whiteness, its resilience, the privilege it sustains, and the violence that regularly accompanies it have resurfaced in many parts of the world in the millennial years as potent political, ethical, and social points of contention. In France, the continuing marginalization and exclusion of Black French citizens from the mainstreams of French life has raised official alarm that the resulting seething discontent feeds a well of recruitment for radical jihadist Islam. In the United States, incidents of lethal police brutality unleashed against young Black men in places such as Ferguson, Baltimore, New York, and Minneapolis have manifested nationwide protests and outrage. A parallel development to this, of course, has been the emergence of the alt-right, the political mobilization of lower-middle-class whites, and the rise of Trump. In South Africa, we have seen a similar rise of middle-class white cultural movements and, perhaps more vividly, in mass, student-led protests around the stifling symbols of continuing white supremacy and the barrenness of postapartheid economic and social transformation.

Besides its common association with privilege, whiteness is problematic not only for those on the receiving end of its exclusion and violence but also for its beneficiaries. In African American intellectual and political circles, there has long been a recognition that whiteness extracts a toll from white as well as Black people and that the race problem is actually a white problem. Du Bois famously commented on the cost of whiteness to white workers: "It was bad enough to have the consequences of [racist] thought fall upon colored people the world over, but in the end it was even worse when one considers what this attitude did to the [white] worker. His aim and ideal was distorted.... He began to want, not comfort for all men, but power over other men.... He did not love humanity and he hated niggers."[19]

Not all hypotheses developed in the United States and elsewhere to account for the conditions and experience of whiteness are applicable in South Africa. However, in a similar vein to Du Bois's observation, there are contemporary South African examples of whiteness, or more precisely, specific iterations of what it means to be white, that serve to paralyze the capacity of whites to participate in postapartheid public life where white racial privilege is no longer ingrained in the structure and very DNA of the state. Historically, white people in South Africa, particularly Afrikaners, have been the subject of scholarly and popular Afrikaner nationalist narratives calculated to inspire, mobilize, and remove doubt about their historical, God-inspired mission in South Africa. Accounts like these approximate Leonard Thompson's "political mythologies of Afrikaner nationalism" and they script white Afrikaners as sturdy, steadfast, diligent, religious, incorruptible, Western, capable, and fundamentally homogenous. Afrikaner nationalist cultural explanations of postapartheid society sometimes paint whites as victims of postapartheid political, economic, and cultural transformations.[20] To eminent South African scholar and educator Jonathan Jansen, these historical narratives and their contemporary corollaries contribute to "bitter [racial] knowledge ... learned reliably in closed circles of influence through parents, teachers, coaches, peers, and *dominees* [ministers, usually of Dutch Reformed Churches]" and passed down the generations.[21] This bitter knowledge is founded on the identities and ideologies of apartheid, and it imprisons its community of believers in a vision of South Africa that is entirely out of step with the ethos of postapartheid society.

As an ongoing concern through this book, I will explore the extent to which a historiography that transcends the analytic boundaries of the specific blend of Marxism that crystallized in South African social history in the 1970s and 1980s can still be "radical." A radical history of whites ought to repudiate the idea of whites as homogenous. It should expose the banality, brutality, secrets, and fictions that sustained white identities and a self-consciously *white* sense of political belonging. And it must ask what pedagogical and political work a new radical history of whites might inspire. Following Du Bois's observation about whiteness, loss, and the ways that racism cut white workers adrift from Black workers, such a history should confront the invented ideas of racial superiority and racial separation and introduce some evidence of the dehumanizing effects of whiteness.[22] One of the ways that this volume seeks to demonstrate something of the loss and dehumanization that accompanied the development of apartheid-era whiteness is to tease out some of the poignancy and richness of what Nell Irvin Painter calls "history across the color line," albeit that instances of this became more strictly policed as the decade of the 1950s progressed.[23] Of course, it should not for a moment descend to the kind of cynical Afrikaner revisionism that seeks to put a human face on apartheid's beneficiaries. One way to avoid this historiographic and moral dead end is to keep in mind the privilege and immanent violence at the heart of apartheid-era whiteness, as well as the occasions when the white protagonists in this history faced particular moral junctions. Nonetheless I, like Eley, claim the optimism that proposes that while no history-writing can change the world, historical research should at least probe misleadingly familiar ideas and assumptions, clarify the present, and provide foundations for the future: "Depending on how the story is told the past provides potential sites for opposition."[24]

A Historical Ethnography of Whites in Apartheid Society

All of the chapters in *Ordinary Whites* pose questions about belonging, participation, defiance, and white everyday life in apartheid society. They also take on, as running threads through the text, questions of whiteness and authoritarianism. While *Ordinary Whites* emerges from the tradition of South African social history, most social historians from South Africa and elsewhere now accept the challenges and innovations spawned during the so-called cultural turn, namely, that histories *of* below could no longer be simply histories *from* below. Thus, given its centrality in shaping white as well as Black lives, diverse manifestations of "the state" feature across all sections of *Ordinary Whites in Apartheid Society* in ways that demonstrate its ambitions, its contradictions, its moments of doubt, and the types of power it commanded. And, above all, the ways that it made and remade the everyday.

Some of the chapters start with strands of my family history, but not all. The cast of characters who feature in these ethnographic snapshots—Grandfather

Figure 1.2 and Figure 1.3 Ordinary whites in apartheid society. Sheila (*top figure, right*) and her mother. Dick (*bottom figure, center*) visiting relatives. Author's personal collection.

L, Karel (who became Charles), Grandmother Roos, Sheila and Dick—should, however, not be seen as exemplars for the entire argument of a chapter. Rather than headlining chapters, they do their work in the text, ghosting in and out of the stories presented. Indeed, their unpredictable presence in these pages is the narrative equivalent to how they lived their lives in twentieth-century South Africa. They acceded to, even supported, segregation and apartheid, but neither benefited from it, nor conducted themselves exactly in the fashion that they were expected to by the regime or imagined to by its critics.

In the nature of any book with claims to being a serious history, this one consciously positions itself in relation to specific historical and historiographic lineages. Thus, the second chapter engages with historical scholarship on South Africa and how whites feature within this corpus. In addressing the protean and contested nature of what it meant to be white in a racist society, this chapter also affirms the value of connecting South African literature to broader scholarship on race, going right back to Du Bois. It draws on Indian social history to suggest that "subalternity" represents a useful lens for looking at non-elite whites in apartheid society. Accommodation and complicity are among the book's central concerns, and the chapter makes a case for the use of Hannah Arendt's observations, notably those she presented in *Eichmann in Jerusalem*, to comprehend the apparent contradictions of ethics and consciousness among white South Africans.[25] This chapter may be better suited to specialists in the field, and more general readers can skip this section and still retain the key arguments of *Ordinary Whites in Apartheid Society*.

Drawing explicitly on my family's generational ethnography and mythology, the third chapter sketches some of the complex and diverse trajectories of class formation among whites in the first half of the twentieth century. Like Macmillan and de Kiewiet, I emphasize that the ways in which white and Black people experience capitalist transformation cannot be disentangled or considered separately. The chapter tracks the state's evolving attitudes toward whites, especially those whom it understood to be "poor whites," and how gender and ethnic considerations were always present, reflecting the state's moral anxieties and sometimes deflecting its attention. This chapter also offers some snapshots of how the state occupied the life of those whom it deemed to be part of the poor white problem—as well as some of the ways in which these people were able to avoid or subvert its intentions. Chapter 4 takes as its central subject the life and career of Geoffrey Cronjé, leading apartheid intellectual and bureaucrat, to examine the connections between ideology, scientific knowledge, and the kinds of "rational" management that helped to organize the apartheid state. Moving easily between the university, commissions of enquiry, and institutions of state, Cronjé represented a new breed of apartheid intellectual/bureaucrat. Of all the contemporary apartheid intellectuals, Cronjé was one of those most invested in whites, and his career is thus of particular value in understanding the state's ambitions to subject white society to social engineering, as well as its limitations in doing so. I suggest that if we wish to utilize studies of figures such as Cronjé to elucidate the structure of the state and how it worked, conventional intellectual histories based on readings of his texts are inadequate. Following the subaltern historians, I argue that we need to go further: to inquire ethnographically how his ideas were advanced, transformed, and contested and how they became instantiated in the ideologies, routines, and disciplines of white everyday life. This line of investigation sheds light on some of the ways that ideology was "made real" for ordinary whites.

The following chapters revolve around work in the public service and government. By the late 1950s, the public service (*staatsdiens*) employed around 30 percent of all working whites, making it the largest single employer of white people. As it expanded through the late 1940s and 1950s, it was rapidly Afrikanerized. Chapter 5 looks at the reorganization of the public service in the 1950s, highlighting the growing traction of new strains of scientific management, borrowed from Japanese and US manufacturing and marked by commitment to quality control, efficiency, human resource management, and industrial psychology. Unlike most contemporary cases where these ideas were applied to the manufacturing industry, in the South African instance they were deployed to reorganize and manage an expanding bureaucracy. Grafted onto the ideological concerns of Afrikaner nationalism, these principles helped shape ideologies about work as well as regulations and forms of discipline and convention to which public servants were subject in the workplace. These principles also help to explain how the public service labor process enabled white public servants to perform their daily tasks without having to act in specifically racist ways or demonstrate any explicitly political partisanship. Thus, the chapter illustrates some of the terms of white public servants' incorporation into both the *staatsdiens* and apartheid society. The chapter also comments on the limits and forms of agency—and sometimes defiance—available to these *beamptes* (officials), and it makes use of particularly rich evidence of bureaucrats who confounded and obstructed the logics of the apartheid state without actually breaking its rules. Chapter 6 concentrates on the gendered dimension of work for whites in the *staatsdiens* as it examines the mass employment of white women as it expanded to meet the growing demands of the apartheid state. There was already a significant contingent of white professional women—Afrikaans- and English-speaking—employed as teachers and nurses. The late 1940s and 1950s did, however, represent the first significant movement of "respectable" white Afrikaans women into more-or-less permanent wage labor, and the chapter investigates how working women upset notions of Afrikaner femininity and in turn exposed the new female public servants to multiple forms of control and management. As women took to work, especially in the public service, their domestic life and home arrangements attracted growing attention from the Suid-Afrikaanse Vrouefederasie (SAVF), the women's wing of the Afrikaner nationalist movement. Notably, the SAVF increased the tempo of home visits by its amateur social workers to white working-class homes. During these visits, styles of housekeeping and childcare, and also the ways that white families interacted with female African domestic workers—a new phenomenon in white working-class homes from the 1950s—were subject to scrutiny.

Moving from the conditions and circumstances of employment, the seventh chapter takes as its starting point growing affluence among whites during the 1950s, most notably in the case of the new public service class. It asks in what ways affluence and particular styles of consumption bound whites into apartheid society and how, in turn, these emergent patterns of material and cultural consumption shed light on the ways that the cultural brokers of Afrikaner nationalism imagined the power of the state to redirect these material and cultural energies. Stretching back to the early years of the century, the development of a "respectable" white middle class was one of the key historical projects of Afrikaner nationalism. The success of the NP in absorbing poorer whites into stable and moderately well-paid jobs did, however, introduce certain strains. Essentially, as white Afrikaners became wealthier and more fully incorporated into global circuits of consumption and taste, they began to loosen some of the cultural tethers of Afrikaner nationalism. These contradictions did, however, help to initiate a new "nation" that partially transcended the older distinctions between Afrikaans- and English-speaking whites and that was forged on stability, prosperity, and as anti-apartheid resistance accelerated, security. Growing levels of affluence, along with increasingly credit-based lifestyles, implicated all whites. This was particularly true of public servants who had access to easier credit than those in the public sector. It demonstrated a very real material foundation for accommodation.

In chapter 8, the book turns to transgression and the history of those who challenged *ordentlikheid* (respectability), apartheid's evolving cultural orthodoxy, to elucidate some of the reforming, disciplinary, punitive, and penal components of apartheid society, and the effects of these systems on white people. Anxieties about white drinking remained intact through much of the 1950s. Taking as an entry point a panic in bureaucratic circles in the mid-1950s that alcoholism was on the rise among whites, this chapter focuses on the state's evolving approach to monitoring, managing, and reforming white society at large. It examines the circumstances that fueled this panic, the types of rehabilitation—and sometimes coercion—that it inspired, and how responses to the perceived abuse of alcohol led to new techniques for the management of whites. These methods enabled the state to observe and, where it considered necessary, intervene across a wide swath of the white population, including those who seemed at risk of excessive drinking as well as those who fell into petty crime, chronic ill health, or indigence. Those "at risk" were subject to attention by social workers, they were sometimes sent compulsorily to retreats (or, in the popular idiom of the day, *dronkplase*—drunk farms), and were subject to probation upon their release. State responses developed during the 1950s to this assumed danger included partnerships with various welfare agencies. These partnerships spread the financial burden of managing whites, just at a time when the expansion of apartheid's administrative mechanisms placed great strain on the resources of the state. This chapter also concentrates on work colonies for white men, components of apartheid society that do not feature in any other historical literature. Work colonies were reorganized in the late 1940s, again on the presumption that alcoholism among white men—or at least certain classes of white men—was on the rise, and that alcohol abuse had consequences not only for the individual, but for families, society, and the integrity of apartheid society. The chapter takes the history of these institutions to investigate the fate of those men considered by apartheid's elite in state, church, and university to be "miscreant." In so doing it emphasizes the point that anxieties about deviance and criminality are important for the formation of states. The chapter pays special attention to the role of social workers in determining who was consigned to a work colony or work corps, and how the authority for these types of confinement and incarceration slipped from the judiciary to state-appointed social workers. The history of the work colonies allows us to see glimmers of challenge, evident in oral sources and from reading state papers slightly against the grain. These signs are few and far between in the history of the apartheid-era whites, a reflection perhaps not only of acquiescence but also of the administrative orientation of the archive. Contemporarily, these glimmers of challenge did not have much impact beyond the ripples that may be seen in the archival record—but historiographically, these small and scattered acts of resistance to the cultural, moral, and disciplinary order of apartheid society were significant for the ways in which we theorize questions of accommodation, agency, and its limits in white society under apartheid. As an experiment in the management of miscreant, mainly drunken, white men, the work colonies were a failure and were finally closed in 1961. Overall, the chapter elucidates the extent, seldom recognized, to which whites featured as subjects for management, reform, and punishment under apartheid. It ends by discussing the implications of these systems for histories of whites' belonging, participation, and compliance in apartheid society.

The conclusion revolves around a middle-aged white man's suicide, which took place one morning before dawn in 1971. This fragment highlights the relentlessness as well as some of the human cost, to Black and white people, of apartheid state-formation and nation-making. It lays open the kind of moral and legal order that underpinned these large-scale social processes, and it invites reflection on the book's central themes of accommodation and complicity, as well as on how we write histories of white people in apartheid society. Not least, this fragment reminds us that the management of whites is a crucial element that needs to be incorporated into our understanding of apartheid social relations. It emphasizes, moreover, that the task of regimenting poor and working-class whites required vast political labor by elected officials, bureaucrats and academics. While seldom opposing white supremacy, whites routinely defied efforts to manage them. Occasionally, however, their transgression broke the fundamental prescriptions of apartheid society, with tragic results for themselves and others. In foregrounding themes such as these, the book may offer comparative insights for historiographies of everyday life in other societies with authoritarian features.

WHITES AND SOUTH AFRICAN HISTORY

2

Ordinary Whites in South Africa

The study of whites never cohered as a major focus within South African history, even though for much of the twentieth century, historical scholarship on South Africa was, in fact, all about whites and excluded Blacks. History-writing in South Africa has often been highly charged politically, and at times, prevailing ideological and political concerns have prompted some historians to concentrate on whites, usually with particular intellectual or political aims, while other historians have neglected this group almost entirely.

This book is motivated by questions that are also central to parts of the history and moral dilemmas of twentieth-century authoritarianism in Germany and elsewhere. These questions represent one set of reference points. In addition, the literature on South Africa offers insight but also reveals a number of blind spots that help to account for the book's specific location vis-à-vis South African historical writing and to pin it down as both a social history of race *and* as a radical history of whites.

Some of the best historical work on South African whites is found in studies of the white poor, which were produced by W. M. Macmillan and C. W. de Kiewiet in the first half of the twentieth century, well before the advent of the apartheid state, and subsequently neglected. Each of these historians drew detailed, complex pictures of white everyday life, and it is no coincidence that much of the power of their respective histories derives from the fact that both Macmillan and de Kiewiet were careful to locate analyses of the white poor within a wider examination of poverty in South Africa, its relation to capitalist transformations, and how it was racialized. Writing initially during the First World War, Macmillan drew heavily on economics and sociology to examine links between the mineral revolution, rural dispossession, and white urbanization. He described how the transition to capitalism devastated the lives of the rural poor, emphasizing the impossibility of separating the study of the white from the Black poor.[1] De Kiewiet was ahead of his time when he accounted for not only the structural, but also the affective factors inhibiting new Afrikaner immigrants from establishing themselves in cities. While convinced that being white entitled them to certain status and comfort based on their race, they could not afford a white urban lifestyle. Lacking the necessary skills and dispositions, they were largely limited to unskilled manual labor which, for the white poor, was synonymous with degrading "kaffir work." They were unwilling to "reduce" themselves to this and consequently remained unemployed.[2] As a Marxist historiography of South Africa emerged in the early 1970s, it developed in some respects against so-called liberal scholarship. Most liberal scholars in history and other disciplines tended to ascribe a progressive role to the white business classes in South Africa, arguing that capitalist development was likely to erode "irrational" racist beliefs, undermine racist legislation, and ultimately, dismantle apartheid. Marxists refused to concede to this rosy belief in capitalism's potential to transform South African society. Along with other scholars who might be described as "liberal," Macmillan and de Kiewiet were sidelined; despite their empirical richness and analytical sophistication, more recent historians seldom cite their work on early twentieth-century South Africa.

In the period between the end of the Anglo-Boer War in 1902 and the formation of the Union of South Africa in 1910, a national convention was held to negotiate a new, unified South Africa. Delegates—all white men—from the Cape, Natal, the Orange River Colony, and the Transvaal shared a belief that they faced two "race conundrums." One was obviously the color question, upon which most of these white delegates agreed: South Africa was to be a white man's country. The other race question—more pressing and immediate for the delegates in the bitter aftermath of the Anglo-Boer War—concerned relations between "Boer and Brit," the "Dutch" (Afrikaans) and English-speaking sectors of the white population.

The idea that Dutch speakers and English speakers were distinct political and cultural communities that needed either to be reconciled (the viewpoint of the majority of delegates to the National Convention) or rescued and nurtured (the viewpoint of Afrikaner nationalists) crept into dominant strands of South African history. This particular formulation of "the race question" focused on South African parliamentary politics where, in fact, the political struggles between advocates of a broad white South African nationalism (often called South Africanism) and those of a more exclusive Afrikaner nationalism commanded the stage for the first half of the twentieth century.

The presumptions of deep political differences between Afrikaans- and English-speaking South African whites is another point, and it is quite blind to the more abiding distribution of privilege, power, and discrimination in modern South Africa. This notion of difference is also host to some pernicious historical, political, and ideological errors, notably one that has been remarkably persistent in liberal historical circles: that Afrikaans speakers were fundamentally homogenous nationalists, that they were the core constituency of the NP, and that they supported apartheid (they generally did, although I shall demonstrate that there were manifest class differences in the ways that Afrikaans speakers understood what apartheid meant). English speakers, who were often alienated by the ethnic exclusivity of Afrikaner nationalism, were somehow thought to be more liberal on race matters. This was not so: the NP politician who sneered during the 1950s that "you English-speakers just like your apartheid enunciated with honey in the voice" was in fact quite perspicuous.[3]

Many years ago I wrote *Ordinary Springboks*, a social history of race, class, and masculinity among white men who served in South Africa's military during the Second World War. These men's histories emphasized that the distinction between "English" and "Afrikaans" did not always have much purchase, certainly not among soldiers who came mostly from the meaner parts of white society. They were unskilled workers, the unemployed and destitute, those living on charity and welfare. *Ordinary Springboks* did moreover reiterate the need to avoid discussing apartheid as if support for it was limited to Afrikaans speakers—and for that matter, that white sentiment against the NP dwelled only among English speakers. *Ordinary Whites in Apartheid Society* focuses on the history and experience of whites in the middle and lower classes, and from this foundation, will address histories of both English- and Afrikaans-speaking whites. As my mother's injunction not to play with the railway children suggests, there were differences between English- and Afrikaans-speaking whites, but these tended to operate as gradations of status rather than large political categories. Where they existed, such social distinctions tended to be shaped by geography and region: it would, for instance, be far more likely for an English-speaking mother like Sheila to warn her child against playing with Afrikaans-speaking children in Durban, in the province of Natal where English speakers dominated, than in cities where Afrikaans speakers were predominant, like Pretoria or Bloemfontein, in the Transvaal and Orange Free State provinces respectively. It is of course acknowledged that in some sectors of society like the *staatsdiens* (public service), most of the new class of apartheid-era public servants were Afrikaans speakers, and there was in fact a concerted effort to recruit Afrikaans speakers for these positions. Class, in other words, was produced in both ethnicized and nationalist forms.

There is very little scholarship on interracial collaborations and entanglements in South Africa similar to what United States historian Nell Irvin Painter describes in her classic work *Southern History Across the Color Line*. While historians of politics and social movements have shown alliances between Black and white anarchists, trade unionists, activists, and revolutionaries, there have been few attempts to search for and understand these kinds of relationships in the realm of the everyday.[4] Painter points out that in the American South, most historians have followed (and continue to follow) segregation's decree, writing about the South as though people of different races occupied entirely different spheres. She writes that white historians initially "made up a lily-white southern history" that included few Blacks except those who loved serving whites. After the civil rights movement, Black historians and their allies sought to address this imbalance by publishing the history of Blacks as though whites existed only as "faceless oppressors."[5] Painter's assessment rings true for South African history where there remains very little by way of histories across the color line, with the complexity and occasionally unexpected course of these relationships often under-researched and thus misunderstood.[6] Like my mother's long friendship with Mrs. G and Mrs. N, histories across the color line represent acts of defiance against the cultural, ideological, and legal codes of the day. They are also acts of historiographic insurrection against presumptions that see whites in homogenous terms and whiteness as a kind of impenetrable fortress. Despite the dehumanizing effects of whiteness as an ideology of supremacy, exclusion, and power, these women's friendship gave my mother the opportunity to reclaim something of her own humanity through acts of solidarity founded on a shared interest in horse racing, milky tea, and far too many cigarettes. As such, histories across the color line, if they exist, are small but important building blocks for a radical history of whites.

Although historical records can and do yield much about everyday racial and gender ideologies, the virtually nonexistent scholarship on histories across the color line means that we know little about the "morality of everyday."[7] More energetic exploration of everyday life at apartheid's frontiers might not only reveal where the traction of apartheid ideology, law, and surveillance was less than total, but, as apartheid was consolidated through the 1950s and 1960s, also show instances of everyday morality among whites that differed from officially sanctioned ones.

While Black scholars have written about colonialism, segregation, and apartheid and their impact upon Black people, they have also written about white people. As US historian of race David Roediger writes, some of the most compelling insights into the "souls of white folk" in America come from African Americans such as James Baldwin, W. E. B. Du Bois, and bell hooks, whose "secret" knowledge of whites comes from "seeing without being observed."[8] The same applies in South Africa, where perspectives from Black writers have much to offer those with an interest in race and the histories of white folk. Black critical commentary in South Africa goes back to at least the early part of the twentieth century, and on one level it offers a very useful starting point in understanding the role of ordinary white people in modern South Africa. For instance, in the early twentieth century, Solomon T. Plaatje, a Black South African who worked for the British colonial authorities and was himself a founder of the South African Native National Congress (later the African National Congress), identified colonialist, segregationist, and attendant racist ideologies and practices as the "white problem."[9] He hoped that Cape liberalism, which promised some amelioration to educated Africans like himself, would prevail in the new Union of South Africa. With the consolidation of the Union after 1910, however, Plaatje and others from the Black Christian elite became increasingly aware that the political struggle between Cape liberals and conservative Boers from the interior had little relevance for most Africans. He detected a fundamental consensus among these different groups on white dominance that seldom needed to be made explicit. Steve Biko, intellectual, activist, and founder of the Black Consciousness Movement, made a similar point almost fifty years later, describing an essential unity among whites, even professed liberals.[10] Moreover, based on their experience from the other side of the color line, Black writers have been able to comment authoritatively on how whiteness works in a routine, everyday kind of way. In his autobiography, *Long Walk to Freedom*, Nelson Mandela shows how Christo Brand, a white prison warder on Robben Island, exhibited at the same time *baasskap* (a belief in white supremacy) and considerable compassion to Mandela and other Black political prisoners jailed on the Island.[11] Such unexpected ambiguities, seldom visible in writing from the white side of South Africa's racial divide, are brought into relief by histories across the color line and by Black people's special capacity to observe whites, adding further layers of detail and subtlety to the ways we might understand these people's histories.

A final point is about South African social history. There is a well-established school of social history in South Africa, and *Ordinary Whites in Apartheid Society* attaches itself to this tradition—with some qualification. By the late 1980s, Marxist-inclined social history, influenced by British and North American Marxist historians like E. P. Thompson, Eric Hobsbawm, and Eugene Genovese, had made landfall in South Africa. Marxist South African social history developed around the Wits History Workshop, which was a loose amalgam of historians and other scholars brought together at the University of the Witwatersrand. Hailing from disciplines that included history, sociology, and anthropology, they were bound by a broad theoretical and methodological consensus and by old friendships. Although never quite the mainstream of South African history-writing, the workshop nonetheless stands as the most important movement within professional South African history.[12] Many of its social historians were committed intellectually and politically to the overthrow of the apartheid regime. In the popular struggles of the 1980s, they championed history as a mobilizing tool. Indeed, History Workshop events at the University of the Witwatersrand were sometimes combined with worker rallies, thus making use of the relative safety from the excesses of police brutality offered by the university campus. For the purposes of this book, though, the social historians' activist orientation tended to lead them to disregard the history of ordinary white workers, public servants, those deemed to be "good whites," and those considered "degenerate." The historians were interested in the revolutionary and potentially revolutionary classes, and the racist and reactionary character of most whites, including the white working class, seemed obvious. There were exceptions, and some social historians did take on the internal contradictions of white society and the class struggles that these spawned to write complex and sophisticated histories of white society. Generally absent from these social histories, however, is a broader account of how class-based manifestations of racial identity and racism were connected to the production, organization, and maintenance of a racist society. Indeed, the very precision and empirical focus of these studies may make it difficult for them to see their subjects not only as part of the rural poor, the "army of the unemployed," or even the "aristocrats of labor," but simultaneously as elites, bound to segregated society by the privileges of whiteness, regardless of how contested its terms often were. These studies miss the wider vistas opened up by Plaatje, Biko, and others who showed that despite other political differences, whites generally agreed on the principle of white supremacy. Despite these shortcomings, this volume anchors itself to some of the legacies of South African social history, notably its dedication to writing histories of non-elites, the ways that it carefully connected its narratives to the material lives of its subjects, the fine grain of its analysis, and, not least, the strong left-wing political sense that these social historians brought to their work.

In the late 1990s and early 2000s, the South African social history movement floundered. Not only did it buckle under a global reaction against the confident claims of Marxist theory and historiography, but its theoretical and political positions hobbled its ability to respond adequately to the challenges of history-writing in postapartheid South Africa and the historical questions that have emerged most vociferously from postapartheid society.[13] Writing in a similar vein to Eley, workshop historian and sympathizer Deborah Posel emphasizes that "dissident" history must be tied politically, theoretically, and historiographically to a project of insurgency, which in turn must address the pressing issues of the day.[14] With the more confident assertions of many forms of Marxism now undermined, it is no longer easy to tie history-writing to a grand, teleological vision. If we hope to work the eroded foundations of Marxist social history and create a new *radical* historiography of whites that is able to confront contemporary political, theoretical, and historiographic challenges, it should instead be attached to smaller-scale emancipatory ends. Above all, these goals include rendering their histories problematic or, in the case of *Ordinary Whites in Apartheid Society*, interrogating the histories of power, ideology, and state formation that in turn shaped everyday practices of accommodation, complicity, and transgression.

History in a Racial State

Without any apparent contradiction, my mother was able to support white supremacy in South Africa while opposing the NP. She was deeply opposed to the NP's emerging scheme for grand apartheid, the kind that was based on republicanism and could be represented on a map. Sheila felt strongly enough about the NP's plans to leave her job for several months in 1961. Yet she accepted the broader arrangements of the racial order, of which the NP's nascent ideological and bureaucratic framework for apartheid was the dominant one since its 1948 electoral victory. Among most whites there was no secrecy, no manufactured silence, around South Africa's system of white supremacy: it did not require any particular discussion or debate among whites, as it had been resolved much earlier in the century. Sheila's strong political opposition to the NP, along with her acceptance of the assumption that racial hierarchy lay at the heart of South Africa's social order, meant that she could claim to be "anti-apartheid." In this she was like so many whites, although it must be said that the majority lacked even the decency of token, partial defiance of the NP. This contradiction represents the major historical and moral conundrum of accommodation, complicity, and transgression that *Ordinary Whites in Apartheid Society*, like many social histories of everyday life in other authoritarian societies, seeks to illustrate and explain.

Hannah Arendt's body of work has been influential, if controversial, among historians grappling with these questions, and it sheds some light on the textures and moral circumstances of white everyday life in apartheid South Africa. Arendt developed a general theory of totalitarianism in

The Origins of Totalitarianism.[15] Then, in 1961, she traveled to Jerusalem to cover the Nazi Adolf Eichmann's trial for *The New Yorker*, and her reports were later published as *Eichmann in Jerusalem*.[16] She did not modify her theses about totalitarianism substantially in *Eichmann in Jerusalem*, which was neither a general history of the Holocaust nor an account of the Nazi regime as such. Rather, her reflections were on the moral, political, and jurisprudential bases on which the trial and sentencing of Eichmann could take place.[17] Using the idea of banal evil to describe Eichmann's role in the genocide of European Jewry, she noted the disjuncture between Eichmann's personal insignificance, the mediocrity of his life before he joined the Nazi party, and the great destructive power he was able to derive from his participation in a novel totalitarian system of government whose organizational dynamics she had analyzed in *Origins*.[18] The observations made in *Eichmann in Jerusalem* were widely debated and attracted (and continue to attract) great notoriety for Arendt.[19] Most notably, critics were outraged that she seemed to put the blame for mass murder at the door of all kinds of midlevel bureaucrats; and that Eichmann did not *intend* evil but was merely "thoughtless," and incapable of thought.[20]

Some of the ways that Arendt explained and defended her theses are of particular value for this history. Apartheid South Africa was not Nazi Germany, and some have expressed reservations about applying Arendt's formulation of the "banality of evil" to the apartheid state: "inappropriate, perhaps even tasteless."[21] Like Nazi Germany, it was an authoritarian state, but while the very existence of apartheid South Africa was premised on state racism and the exploitation of Blacks as a form of cheap labor, it did not practice genocide. As a further distinction, with some exceptions—in the 1950s and early 1960s these would have been policemen—few whites were at the murderous edge of the state, "doing" evil. In the course of their daily lives, most did neither particular good nor particular evil, although they certainly drew benefit from evil. Nonetheless, just as Arendt's work should not be read as a basis for direct comparison, parts of it are of significant value in teasing out some of the historical processes and conditions that are quite fundamental in understanding the everyday consciousness, and some of the political behavior, of whites in the apartheid state.

Most significantly, as she responded to her critics, Arendt identified a crucial moral inversion in Nazi society where, under the ideological conditions of the Reich, "normal" behavior could only be expected of those able to muster the courage to act "abnormally."[22] My mother's history suggests that a variant of this phenomenon existed among whites in South Africa under apartheid, as well as before the formal advent of the apartheid state. What they took as "normal" was a racially segregated society. In apartheid South Africa, the "abnormal" included those few whites in organizations like the Springbok Legion, the Congress of Democrats, the Communist Party, and the Liberal Party who summoned the vision and bravery to oppose white supremacy and much of what apartheid stood for. Using Arendt's approach as a form of intellectual scaffolding, there can be no space for apologia in a history of white everyday life in apartheid South Africa, but her idea of a kind of moral inversion does help us to understand the conditions in which these histories unfolded, although never to condone them.

As we shall see, thoughtlessness and the kind of mundane bureaucratic tasks noticed by Arendt were central features of the public service labor process under apartheid, but unlike in Nazi Germany, this process did not serve as a cover for mass murder. In apartheid South Africa, the banality of routine would serve different ends among white public servants. It did certainly go some ways toward inhibiting thinking and maintaining the fiction of a normal society, although material privilege was without doubt the biggest determinant in ensuring that whites remained complicit in the moral inversion represented by apartheid society. Bureaucratic routines also helped to centralize authority in the public service, keeping decisions away from a new class of public servant who were central to the development of the apartheid state, but were not entirely trusted by its political and bureaucratic leaders. While banality was certainly evident in work routines, it was perhaps more compellingly manifest in the careers of the likes of Geoffrey Cronjé, sociologist extraordinaire whom we shall meet in chapter three. Cronjé was one of apartheid's major intellectuals, and the ways that he and other Afrikaner nationalist intellectuals spoke to each other (and almost exclusively to each other) and elaborated plans for "Racial Apartheid with Justice" represented the true banality of apartheid.

Lessons from Subaltern Studies

Like any other historical actors, neither my mother nor my father were completely free to command their lives. Despite the vigor and energy with which she took on some of the perceived wrongs of her universe, Sheila was unable to escape the topsy-turvy world that she, like all whites, occupied. The very force of ideologies about segregation and racial supremacy meant that they required neither reiteration nor explanation and thus receded into the background of taken-for-granted knowledge. Dick, with his experience in the Durban Men's Home and the work colony, was subject to the apartheid state's aim to keep a vigilant eye on some sectors of white society and to reform individuals who, like Dick and his brother, were down on their luck, and deemed worthy of such attention.

Arendt's reflections on Eichmann's trial, and her responses to criticism, help us understand the moral shape of white life under apartheid. As intimated earlier, when reflecting on some of the trends in South African history-writing, however, we need to look further than South African scholarship to parse the historical textures of white everyday life and the historical processes that shaped it. Questions that need to be asked include how ordinary whites featured in the elite imagination; how they were regulated, surveilled, and policed; and, ultimately, what kinds of agency they claimed—or abdicated. With its emphasis on agency and world-making, the South African strand of social history falls short in taking on histories of whites in apartheid society where the basis of the social order was being systematically reorganized, where biologically referenced social categories were becoming more prominent, and where apartheid ideals were becoming instantiated in the basic exchanges of everyday life. It was a society, in sum, where ideology was becoming increasingly pervasive. Under these circumstances, histories of below could no longer be simply histories from below.

Subaltern studies emerged within Indian historiography in the early 1980s, and its currents, swirls, and eddies offer useful approaches to histories of whites that are cast from both above and below. The dangers of traveling theory are always imminent, and these dangers seem particularly close when trying to apply a body of historiography developed to understand the history of colonial subjects in India to apartheid-era South African whites. Nonetheless, if we avoid reading subaltern studies too literally, lessons may be drawn from its historiographic and methodological positions and from its eclecticism, bound by a common focus on subalterns. The idea of "the subaltern" lends itself to many interpretations. Like most scholars who were part of the subaltern studies collective, I define it as a condition rather than a category, and I use the term to refer to those who were somehow—or in some circumstances—subordinate in a social order. Characterizing subalternity as a condition of subordination that was dynamic and could change, often quite arbitrarily, as opposed to being more-or-less "fixed" (like a class), has particular utility for a history such as this. Of course, the caveat is that while some whites were undoubtedly subordinate within apartheid's white social hierarchy, they were in fact part of a dominant elite when considering the class and race structure of South African society as a whole. This particular understanding of subalternity allows us to pin down those whites whose representation as "problems" rendered them subordinate. It allows us to follow the tracks from ideology to policy, as such representation was inevitably followed by state intervention, sometimes bureaucratic (changes to reporting lines in the public service), sometimes penal (confinement to the work colonies), and sometimes welfarist and medical (the establishment of inebriate retreats). Drunks and the unemployed featured here, but more surprisingly, so too did those exemplars of modern Afrikaner nationalist femininity—women who could simultaneously hold down wage labor and manage their households. The idea of subalternity also directs us to the social history of those whites who were subordinate in white society. Sometimes they were specifically identified as problems within the elite discourse of the day: for example, men like my father. At other times, they were not. Here, the men and women who made up the new class of public servants spring to mind, elevated into white-collar jobs during apartheid, but never quite trusted by prominent apartheid figures like Geoffrey Cronjé or his protégé, Jannie Pieterse.

Like South African social history, subaltern studies emerged first as a politically inspired "history from below." Initially, scholars within subaltern studies were influenced by Antonio Gramsci's Marxism. They also drew theoretically and methodologically from other Marxist-oriented social histories, including that being developed in South Africa. Their intellectual agenda, at least at the beginning, was by no means a substantial break from the cultural Marxism of the day. A major difference, however, from Marxist social history, and arguably a reason for the early vitality of subaltern studies, was the redefinition of "the political" by its founding figure, Ranajit Guha. He was not willing to be bound by the primacy of class; rather, he was guided more by ethnography than theory in considering arrangements such as kinship, tradition, and friendship groups as structures and strategies invoked in colonial and postcolonial India.[23]

In a recent critique of the accounts produced by historians from the subaltern studies group, Vivek Chibber charged that their drift away from Marxist universalism and class-based analysis diluted their capacity to provide the intellectual foundations for progressive, class-based resistance.[24] This caution is pertinent for histories of South African whites, where there is a danger of writing them outside of the class structure. There is a recent interest in identities that represents another instance of decontextualization. However, these approaches fail to fully acknowledge how white cultural identities (usually Afrikaner ones) are used as a proxy for race, and how in South Africa class is fundamentally structured according to race—more so under apartheid than contemporaneously. Missing these connections means avoiding a key goal of writing histories of whites: namely, to expose the structural foundations of injustice and inequality. While retaining a commitment to class analysis, the pragmatism demonstrated by Guha remains attractive and useful for the kinds of analytic pathways that this book seeks to explore—in elucidating, for instance, what lay behind Sheila prohibiting me from playing with the railway children. As Axel Andersson commented, the tensions between class and cultural analysis are not necessarily a zero-sum affair.[25] Moreover, acknowledging "actually existing" historical conditions does not necessarily erode the foundations of Marxist analysis but may in fact render it a "living project," neither simply a discourse nor a body of academic knowledge.

From the end of the 1980s, the focus of subaltern studies shifted from the everyday lives, experiences, and consciousness of ordinary people to how people- as well as ideologies, institutions, and loci of power of the state—were represented. Its theoretical foundations moved from Gramsci to Foucault and Edward Said. This reorientation brought an increasing concentration on textual analysis and how major groups of the population were marginalized through these texts (which were written by and instrumental for those with privilege, economic means, and power).[26] In South Africa it was, of course, mainly Black people who were the subject of this kind of discursive marginalization. But in the early apartheid years, white people also featured as the focus of sociological, psychological, and criminological studies, and it was precisely this kind of intellectual work that provided the foundation for targeting certain categories of whites for surveillance, reform, and sometimes punishment.

Subalternists were always interdisciplinary, and debates among the core group of Indianists, as well as challenges from subalternists elsewhere, help to clarify what a radical history of ordinary whites under apartheid might look like. Reorientation from trying to reveal "the true form of the subaltern" to "how the subaltern is represented," with the growing ascendancy of literary theorists, prompted a reaction from some subalternists aligned to the political left.[27] Lamenting the drift toward analyses of representation and power, historian Sumit Sarkar wrote that "radical Left-Wing social history... has been collapsed into cultural studies and critiques of colonial discourse and we have moved from Thompson to Foucault and, even more, Said." The pervasiveness of the power/knowledge complex, he argued, raised the academically and politically debilitating possibility of reifying (and romanticizing) the subaltern, of robbing the subaltern of agency.[28] This pervasiveness of the power/knowledge complex does moreover raise the possibility of conflating the ambitions of intellectuals, politicians, and senior bureaucrats with the effects of the state.

Subaltern studies had always claimed not just to be the study of colonial history, but to be an enabler and informer of political practice. For Sarkar, the act of homogenizing "colonial-western" cultural hegemony (or for that matter, any type of representation or ideology, including apartheid intellectuals' ideal image of white society) and presenting it as fully pervasive and virtually irresistible meant "abandoning any quest for immanent critique through the possibility of conflict and groups taking over and using in diverse and partially autonomous ways elements from dominant structures and discourses."[29] While ideology, representation, and channels through which power operated are quite essential components for understanding white everyday life under apartheid, there was a danger, in short, of fleeing from a radical history to which social critique is inherent and reducing the intellectual foundations of political insurgency to a "dull hagiography of the subaltern." This represents quite the opposite of the type of radical historiography described by Geoff Eley, to which *Ordinary Whites in Apartheid Society* aspires. Further, as Gyanendra Pandey and Gautam Bhadra remind us, idioms of domination and subordination are always intertwined. This "contradictory complexity" must be interrogated if we are to understand something of the ways in which white consciousness was shaped and the experience of ordinary whites was enacted.[30]

Subaltern studies never pretended to offer a fully fledged alternate historiography within Indian history-writing, choosing instead to emphasize the critique of dominant views as its main objective. The intense debates and contests within subaltern studies meant that it never settled into orthodoxy which, Eley argues, encourages "a different vision of evidence, subject matters, and writing strategies."[31] Theoretical restlessness, pragmatism, and the absence of a "total" narrative are approaches appropriate not only for those interested in hidden, insurgent histories of specific groups, but for any historiography. These traits are, however, particularly useful in writing histories of apartheid-era whites where there are many deeply entrenched conventional wisdoms.

Some Notes on Angles and Archives

Ordinary Whites in Apartheid Society is concerned, above all, with the social histories of how certain sectors of white society were managed. From here the book asks more specific questions about how ordinary whites were represented in the writing of Afrikaner nationalists and other intellectuals. It seeks to elucidate some of the ways that ordinary whites were policed in a number of settings, including the workplace and the home. It looks at how white people, subject to such surveillance, negotiated not only the strictures imposed by various branches of the state, but also the contours of life in apartheid society more broadly. Not least, it attempts to identify instances of opposition and challenge among white people, including upwardly mobile public servants, itinerant construction workers, policemen, teachers, and *boemelaars* (hoboes), however muted and limited these were.

These questions are neither primarily event-related nor overtly concerned with chronologies, and they are, like earlier iterations of subaltern studies, propelled by a more "anthropological" approach to history.[32] Although the methodologies, sources, and registers vary from chapter to chapter in this book, all of these inquiries represent historical ethnographies that allow us to peer backwards and forwards in time and to think about genealogies; to ponder the significance of ironies, ambiguities, and contradictions; and to plot the connections between large-scale processes and local-scale happenings.

Historian Dipesh Chakrabarty, one of the subaltern group's leading lights, wrote that one of the features that distinguished subaltern studies from English Marxist history-from-below was a concern with knowledge, ideology, and representation.[33] So too is the case with *Ordinary Whites in Apartheid Society*. When acknowledging that everyday worlds are made as much from the top as the bottom, notably in an authoritarian society organized by racist ideologies, this is an important vector. I plot how white people featured in some major contemporary scholarly work that subsequently informed both policy towards whites and the language used to discuss them, connecting these representations to particular ideological currents. In this respect the work of sociologists Geoffrey Cronjé and Jannie Pieterse, and of psychiatrist Louis Freed, are quite significant; all of them left numerous texts, including books, academic articles, reports, and lecture notes. These texts are freely available, and I found Cronjé's books at the University of the Free State, Pieterse's published work at the University of Pretoria, and a selection of Freed's writing in the Harold Strange Library of African Studies at the Johannesburg Public Library. Cronjé also left a small but significant collection of correspondence housed at the University of Pretoria's archive. In addition to their formal content, the language and tone of these books, essays, reports, and lectures are often quite revealing of the authors' attitudes toward their white subjects—ranging, as we shall see, from suspicion and disdain to cold distance.

The state archive in Pretoria is the major repository for evidence of the transactions that are central to this book. Files from the Departments of Justice, Social Work, Health, and Labour and from the Public Service Commission were particularly germane, although material from other departments like the Treasury indicates that if the public service did represent something of an ideological and disciplinary endeavor, this endeavor was never uncontested. The apartheid state was highly bureaucratized, and it left substantial records. Apartheid's records are well maintained and well cataloged, and this thoroughness enables reading across the planes of the archive for signs of the themes, moods, anxieties, and disputes that activated senior and midlevel bureaucrats. Theses is irony, though, in the fact that most of the post-apartheid archivists tasked with curating these sources today are Black. The state and the NP were close but not synonymous, although the alignment between the two entities grew during the later apartheid years. While the state archives host the official record, the Archive for Contemporary Affairs at the University of the Free State contains important collections from the NP, including the papers of influential cabinet ministers and members of Parliament such as Eric Louw, C. R. Swart, and N. J. Diederichs. This archive represents one of South African history's great untapped resources. If the state archive yields detail on the justification and techniques used to manage whites (including evaluation of the success of such schemes), collections in the Archive for Contemporary Affairs help us understand how luminaries in the NP elaborated their understanding of apartheid, including the role of whites, how they differed from one another, and how they negotiated the demands of various NP constituencies.

Sarkar has reminded us of the political danger within aspects of subaltern studies of reifying or "fixing" the subaltern. Frederick Cooper points out the methodological stakes that this historiographic error raises. Noting empirical difficulties with the Foucauldian formulation of power, especially assumptions about how it diffuses through society, he writes that in colonial societies, "power was more arterial than capillary—concentrated spatially and socially." "Can the theorist listen?" he retorted wittily to Spivak and those subalternists inclined to textual analysis and discourses of power and representation rather than to the social history project. Indeed, he wrote, the tenuous and contested essence of power "should be a theoretical rallying point for historians: they have the tools (and often the inclination) to analyze in specific situations how power is constituted, aggregated, contested and limited, going beyond the poststructuralist tendency to find power diffused in 'modernity,' 'the post-enlightenment era,' or 'western discourse.'"[34]

Gyanendra Pandey wrote a strong defense of local analysis and what he describes as the fragment or small historical vignettes, when he commented that a historiography tracking flickers of insurgency and other instances of subaltern consciousness, agency, and action will yield at best a partial history. For historians of India, the advantage is that this approach "foreground(s) state-centered drives to homogenize and normalize the deeply contested territory of nationalism" while simultaneously demanding that the historian resist shallow homogenization and pointing to potentially new notions of "the nation" and future political communities.[35] Oral histories, ethnographic techniques, and the observation of practice all shaped the methodologies of subaltern studies. These methodologies permitted the "elaboration of a new kind of cultural essence for India ... found in the iconic residues of hidden identities, expressions of difference and misunderstood mentalities."[36] These techniques are similarly central to *Ordinary Whites in Apartheid Society*. As in Pandey's case, they not only demonstrate something of the overarching strength (and limits) of elite-driven, state-centered Afrikaner nationalism, but also demand that the very idea of "whites" under apartheid be approached with nuance and circumspection. Insurgency, defiance, and indocility are significant counterweights to the ways in which we understand processes of accommodation by white people as they negotiated their place at apartheid's table. These acts, including histories across the color line, all provide some of the building blocks for an alternate radical but by definition fragmentary history of whites. Neither the public state records nor the more private NP papers contain specific references to these ripostes and challenges. They emerge instead as shards, buried in the detail of reports, complaints, and correspondence that unwittingly opens up vistas about race-making among whites and about how whites were managed and how they resisted. For example, describing his treatment at the hands of a white male nurse, a white scientist ended his letter of complaint with the comment that he had been addressed in a tone "more suitable for a non-European labourer." This phrase was almost a non sequitur, but it speaks volumes about the scientist's understanding of racial hierarchies and the codes that he presumed should govern racial interactions. In another example, we are presented with monthly tallies of men who absconded from work colonies. These men had the status of detainees and were usually held against their will. Visitors were discouraged and few of the inmates were letter writers. In such circumstances desertion statistics become a proxy for these men's willingness and capacity to resist their incarceration.[37]

    I interviewed many people, and these discussions affirmed Pandey's point about scales of analysis and the worth of the fragment. From these interviews I learned about social difference and immanent class divisions in white society, much like those demonstrated by my mother, Sheila Roos: "those bastards in the *Broederbond*."[38] These discussions show some awareness of how whites were surveilled and the pettiness of much of this: "When I started at the Railways I wasn't allowed to drink at the Balmoral Hotel, and they wanted to know where I lived."[39] There were revelations of histories of collaboration and cooperation across the color line. Asking one family on the

KwaZulu-Natal coast about furniture credit, I learned of a remarkable history of trade credit between a community of white railway workers and a Muslim businessman: "A coolie, but you couldn't find a more thorough gentleman."[40] Fascinated, I pursued this story, which was confirmed by other people's testimony and other records. These interviews also reveal racial sentiments that, while wedded to the idea of white supremacy, had a different feel than those elaborated by the elite architects of the apartheid state. There was often a strange contradictory strand of compassion, coupled with a rather complicit recognition that it was race, not skill, that shaped the boundaries of the public service labor market. A white road worker, for example, pointed out: "We did the same work all day but they [Black workers] got paid very little." This is where we find the "souls undressed" of whites, and these grains may conceivably dent the structures of essentialized whiteness.[41] Of course, we must take seriously Bill Sewell's caution that the task of integrating large-scale social and political structures with accounts of the local and particular must be approached with care.[42] Nonetheless, while these intimate fragments on their own do not support commanding sociological claims, they do offer examples of how apartheid society worked, and they can suggest doubts, introduce intricacies and anomalies, and pose further questions.

A comment by Dipesh Chakrabarty is pertinent to methodologies of the intimate.[43] Reflecting on the history of the subaltern studies group, he raised the idea of "generative mistakes," methodological errors that nevertheless advance how questions are answered and how we understand history. For instance, in *Elementary Aspects*, Guha incorporated the archaic and the modern, humans and gods. Chakrabarty recounted Guha's statement that he had relied on his own experience and "feel" when writing this "autobiographic" work. Chakrabarty characterizes this as a "generative mistake" which gave subaltern studies much of its original analytic richness.

Can similar "generative mistakes" be found for a new radical history of ordinary whites? One springs to mind, and like Guha's "autobiographic account," it is an attempt to undertake what has been described in other contexts as "biographies of a people."[44] Here, the historian is situated differently than the conventional anonymous, unobtrusive, objective scholar. I am in a privileged position to write this sort of history, having grown up in a white working-class family during apartheid, albeit later than the period that features in this book. My parents, Sheila and Dick, manifest many of the ambiguities and ironies that I discuss, and my father, at least, was subject to the most overt, invasive kinds of reform. While they are both deceased, I am able to see retrospectively how these ethnographies played out in their lives and the lives of other white people I knew, and beyond the range of acquaintances, among white people whom I met through the archival traces that they left. This particular angle erases some of the social distance between myself and the people and places I write about, a distinction that is anyway quite arbitrarily drawn.[45] This angle does moreover squarely face an "elephant in the room" identified by anthropologist Francis Njamnjoh in his critique of postapartheid South African anthropology (and for that matter, history): with the occasional exception of "white others" who are sometimes the subject of study, white anthropologists seldom do fieldwork "at home" among people much like themselves. The consequence is that white people are left "beyond ethnographic contemplation," a position antagonistic to any history of whites that claims affinity with radical intellectual traditions by rendering whiteness strange.[46]

The degree of proximity to the lives of the people I write about does present dangers, and as a corrective against nostalgia and apologia, those twin enemies of any legitimate history of whites, one needs to relentlessly keep in mind the very reason for writing. The purpose of this book is to shed light on race-making and white everyday life in an increasingly authoritarian society, and all the evidence—archival, oral, and ethnographic—must be read from this bridgehead. Against the possibility of analytic and ethical errors and the possibility of unwarranted historical revisionism, generative mistakes associated with closeness to the subjects do offer some intuitive sense of where to look for contradiction, ambiguity, irony, and other conditions and dispositions that texture a historiography of ordinary whites.

Finally, ordinary whites in the 1940s, 1950s, and 1960s were generally not diarists, and personal letters have, so far, proven difficult to come by. Many who grew up and entered work during those decades are however still alive, making them a valuable, although challenging, source of oral history. The requirement is to simultaneously understand their world on their terms, listen to how they account for the ways they thought and lived, and avoid betraying their legitimacy while not too readily accepting retrospective justification of their actions. This methodological balancing act requires strong appreciation of and ethnographic sensitivity to the disconnect between oral history and memory studies.[47]

THE DELICACY OF TEACUPS

3

The Genealogy of Grandparents

My grandfather L beat his daughter. This was in the 1930s while he was in the thrall of alcohol-fueled rage after heavy binges, especially when he had been drinking brandy.[1] I deduced this family secret from intimations from my mother, Sheila—lessons from a mother to her son about masculinity and alcohol. For much of the twentieth century, sugar was a major pillar of the Natal regional economy, and sugar-milling villages (some of these were company towns) dotted the coastal sugar belt. My kin lived in one of these villages, and in about 1938, my mother was sent to board with relatives in Durban. It is impossible to determine whether this represented a conscious decision to remove her from the heavy drinking and possible violence to which she was exposed or whether it simply reflected the fact that in the village where her family lived, there was no schooling beyond the level of primary education. This transfer to the city had one happy consequence for her, as it gave her access to good schools. She went on to complete high school, which was uncommon for girls at the time.

Grandfather L, born in 1905, was the son of a Scottish immigrant who arrived in South Africa in 1902 to work as a stationmaster on the Natal Government Railways.[2] Although a railway official's salary would not have stretched to private tuition at Hilton College or Michaelhouse, both modeled on British public schools and established to school new generations of senior public servants, business leaders, and public figures for colonial society, he must have received a decent education from a government school.[3] By 1927, he was chief chemist with the Zululand Planters' Union, a highly skilled position that entailed analysis of the sucrose content of sugar cane that planters sent to the mills so that they would be paid appropriately. He married in 1928 and the couple's first child, Sheila, was born the next year. She was followed by a sister, who did not survive infancy, and a brother.

In the Natal sugar belt's white anglophone society, my mother's family was the epitome of probity and respectability. Her younger brother won a place at one of the best government schools for boys in the province. After he retired, my grandfather was kept on by the sugar company to manage the recreation club, a kind of subsidized country club for its white employees and a common feature of company towns in the sugar belt. "The Company" built a little cottage for him and his wife. During the brief years that I knew him, he no longer drank, then preferring tea. My grandparents represented the very pillars of white village society, models of the civility to which some English-speaking whites aspired, partially in order to distinguish themselves from Afrikaners. My grandparents had the "correct accent" without a hint of Afrikaans pronunciation. They belonged to an Anglican congregation, a denomination at the heart of the white English-speaking establishment in South Africa and other parts of the British Commonwealth. My grandfather was on the committee of the local lawn bowling club, a game quintessentially associated with the respectable middle classes across the Commonwealth. For all intents and purposes, they indeed were pillars of this enclave of white society—except for those hints of a secret buried in the 1930s.

My paternal grandfather, Karel, was born to Afrikaans-speaking parents in Richmond in the Karoo region of the Cape Colony sometime during the second half of the 1880s. His status as an Afrikaner and his experience as a poor white in the early years of the new century meant that he had a very different historical trajectory than Grandfather L, and he encountered the state and other forms of regulation and authority in markedly different ways. Richmond is sheep country. Family legend, as well as a broader reading of the marches of colonialism, capitalism, and law by which Blacks as well as whites were dispossessed of their land, suggests that Karel's family were *bywoners*, a class of whites who survived as clients of landowners, offering their labor for purposes of harvesting and shearing, in return for squatting rights.

In October 1899, the Second Anglo-Boer War broke out, and by the middle of 1900 the British had taken the capitals of the Orange Free State (OFS) and the Zuid-Afrikaansche Republiek (ZAR): Bloemfontein and Pretoria, respectively. By late 1900, generals from both the Orange Free State and ZAR had agreed to initiate mounted Boer offensives deep into Natal and the Cape Colony; the most spectacular of these was a raid led by General Jan Smuts. Hoping to initiate an uprising among Cape Afrikaners, Smuts's column, just 250 strong, left the Transvaal in August 1901. Although it operated mainly in the northern Cape, it did get to within one hundred kilometers of Cape Town. The column did not succeed, however, in sparking an uprising in the Cape. Nor did it attract significant numbers of Cape rebels. But among those

Cape Afrikaners who did throw their lot in with Smuts was the youthful Karel.

Karel's decision to join Smuts's raiders had profound consequences. Sharing the trials and hardships of Smuts's daring military campaign must have forged a bond of personal loyalty between Karel and the general; having served in Smuts's ragtag commando of civilian-soldiers, Karel followed Smuts politically for the rest of his life. He was one of those known—after J. B. M. Hertzog led a rump of nationalist-minded Afrikaners out of the ruling South African Party (SAP) to form the National Party in 1912—as a *bloedsap*, literally a "blood" supporter of the SAP. The term *bloedsap* was aimed disparagingly at those who demonstrated unwavering loyalty to Smuts, the SAP, and later in the century, the United Party (UP). Ultimately, being a *bloedsap* set Karel on a course that would lead to countless small collisions with the guardians of Afrikaner nationalism.

South Africa's Poor Whites

Karel's part in Smuts's war did not end well. He was taken as a prisoner of war and shipped abroad—as family legend has it—to Ceylon (Sri Lanka). For nearly two decades we lost sight of him, but he emerged once again in the early 1920s. By then he was married and lived in an informal shantytown west of Pretoria. He made a precarious living as a *togt* (day) laborer. As they arrived at towns and cities, poor immigrants, both Black and white (the latter group described by a commission as an "undesirable influx"), gravitated toward these settlements that were not much different from the Hoovervilles built by homeless people in the United States during the Great Depression.[4] They were usually located on the urban periphery, often just beyond the municipal boundaries, and thus escaped easy regulation. In these settlements, racial segregation was a haphazard affair, and there were pragmatic, if sporadic, interactions across the color line: Black women, for instance, commonly acted as midwives. It is also likely that there were instances of interracial sex and cohabitation. Both the state and the mainstream churches evinced a distinct "miscegenophobia" that hardened as the century unfolded and was accompanied by legislation like the Immorality Act of 1927, which proscribed sex between whites and Blacks. It is, however, unlikely that official or clerical disapproval eliminated these intimate associations. As sociologist Pierre van den Bergh dryly pointed out during the height of apartheid: "The history of miscegenation is as old as the first permanent Dutch settlement at the Cape in 1652."[5]

Poor whiteism had been "discovered" by politicians and clergy as a social problem in the 1860s. In the early 1920s, it was still one of the dominant concerns in white political, intellectual, and clerical circles, especially among those who worried about the survival of Afrikaners as a distinct cultural and racial group and about their future in an unyielding capitalist world.[6] Of course, there were whites who were poor under the agrarian and trading economies that dominated South Africa to about the mid-1860s. However, the tumultuous waves of economic, social, and political change set in motion by South Africa's mineral revolution systematically impoverished thousands more. The mineral revolution afforded some economic opportunity, and fabulous wealth to a few, but for the majority, both Black and white, it brought dislocation and upheaval and thwarted their capacity to maintain independent, agrarian livelihoods. Up until the mineral revolution, Afrikaans-speaking whites were by and large rural people, and they would constitute by far the bulk of the white poor.

Whites dispossessed of title or access to land became squatters (like Karel's father) or moved to towns where they often ended up in the kind of shanty settlements where we find Karel in the early 1920s. A rinderpest epidemic in 1896 and the effects of the Anglo-Boer War, which laid to waste much agricultural land in the Free State and Transvaal, only exacerbated the migration of whites to the towns.[7] The reason why poor whiteism caused such consternation, especially among Afrikaans-speaking intellectuals in the Cape and the Transvaal where the greatest number of poor whites were to be found, was that the new phenomenon of mass white poverty seemed to suggest that whites were "going backwards."[8] Justifying such gloomy prognoses, one described (probably with an element of exaggeration) how settlers at Mapochs Gronden in the ZAR "walked around naked" and reported that drunkenness and carousing were so bad that the local liquor outlet was closed down.[9] Among whites, most of the poor were Afrikaners and Nederduitse Gereformeerde Kerk (NGK) congregants. The Church was troubled by the extent to which the collapse of the preindustrial agrarian world and the wholesale exodus of whites from the *platteland* (countryside) threatened the destruction of white families. Furthermore, the NGK was also deeply worried that in an industrializing economy, Afrikaners were set to become "hewers of wood and drawers of water."[10]

Before South Africa's Union in 1910, the Dutch Reformed churches shouldered much of the responsibility for rehabilitating and ministering to the needs of destitute whites. Locating the problem of poor whiteism within the framework of its own practical theology, the Cape synod of the NGK asserted in 1894 that it had a duty to assist its poor and indigent congregants. Dominee (Reverend) B. P. J. Marchand, who would later head the NGK Kommissie van Arbeidskolonies (Commission on Work Colonies), characterized this component of the Church's work as an "internal mission," styled on the London missions to the poor.[11] Based on the recommendations of Marchand's Kommissie, the Church approved the establishment of church-sponsored agricultural settlements for impoverished white families.

Kakamas, beside the Orange River in the northern Cape Colony, was selected for the first—and most well-known—church-run agricultural settlement. The Kommissie agreed that each family accepted would be allocated one-and-a-half hectares of land and assisted to purchase the necessary farming implements, although in order to "protect" the settlers from the temptation to sell their land (which many tried to do), the Church would retain ownership of the settlement.[12] By July 1898, a primary school had been established, which Kakamas superintendent Dominee C. W. H. Schröder insisted that all children attend. Schröder also made it obligatory for all settlers to attend church.[13] At Kakamas, as well as at lesser-known settlements for the white poor at Olifantshoek, Wildernis, and Goedemoed, the Cape NGK eventually accommodated eight hundred families.[14] Settlements similar to that pioneered at Kakamas were established by different Church congregations in other parts of the country. In the Transvaal, for instance, the Nederduits Hervormde Kerk (NHK) established one at De Lagersdrif in 1907 to serve indigent whites in Roossenekal, part of the Middelburg district. As in the Cape settlements, the development of schools was seen as significant in the overall rehabilitation of the white poor of Roossenekal.

Both the Cape and Transvaal synods of the churches clearly believed that the discipline required of settlers would not only enable families to regroup from the disastrous effects of rural poverty, but would also endow them with some of the moral dispositions necessary for survival in the modern economy. Notably, they hoped that the healthy and wholesome routines of life in the settlement would help to dispel notions that manual labor was "kaffir work."[15] Church settlements in both the Cape and the Transvaal accepted only white families who were members of the churches, poor and of "good character." In this way they simultaneously established Calvinistic influences upon their "internal mission" and drew a distinction between the deserving poor—the righteous—and those who lacked these virtues.[16]

After South Africa's 1910 unification and the introduction of a centralized administration, the burden of addressing the causes of poor whiteism and its many social pathologies shifted from the church to the government. While in a general sense the very purpose of the fledgling SAP government was to further various white interests and foster "racial reconciliation," understood by the white political establishment as reducing the legacies of bitterness between "Boer and Brit," several more specific issues demanded its attention.

These included relations with Britain, South Africa's imperial power, and the "native question." In 1906, Chief Bambatha kaMancinza from Natal led an armed insurrection against the imposition of a poll tax. Bambatha's rebellion was quelled in a bloody battle in the Mome Gorge. The panic that it ignited among whites helped to frame the ways in which the white South African public understood the native question in the years around the formation of the Union. And of course there was the problem of the white poor, who numbered around three hundred thousand or 17 percent of the white population.[17]

The new government was less convinced than the church that restoring whites to the agrarian world was the answer to white poverty. Nonetheless, its immediate response was to try to keep as many whites on the land as possible. To this end it introduced subsidies, deployed agricultural extension officers, invested in irrigation projects, and established agricultural settlements around the Vaalharts irrigation scheme in the northern Cape and the Hartebeespoort dam in the Transvaal.[18] It also extended the provision of pensions and disability grants.

Like the church, the government believed that if white children were to escape the poverty, dislocation, and demoralization so apparent among their parents, education was the most viable pathway. By 1910, when the Union of South Africa was formed, school attendance was more or less compulsory for whites between the ages of seven and fifteen or sixteen, roughly equivalent to primary school.[19] Ordinances for compulsory primary schooling for whites had been approved in the Cape, the Orange Free State, and the Transvaal (Natal lagged behind, and only introduced its ordinance in 1911). However, not all white children of primary-school age did in fact attend school: the facts that their labor was necessary on farms and that many lived some distance from the nearest school meant that education standards were uneven. Collaborating with provincial authorities, the SAP government set about consolidating and implementing the measures envisaged by the provincial ordinances. The number of inspectors was increased, as was the number of "duly qualified teachers."[20] Between 1909 and 1921, the number of white children in school increased tremendously: in the Cape, by 76 percent; in Natal by 85 percent; in the Transvaal by 160 percent; and in the Orange Free State by 140 percent.[21]

However, it was in towns where the problems of poor whiteism imprinted themselves most visibly. Like poor people anywhere, whites who found that life in the countryside had become impossible migrated to towns and cities. They often first tried their luck in smaller country towns and then moved on to bigger cities like Johannesburg, Pretoria, Bloemfontein, Durban, Port

Elizabeth, and Cape Town. Few had either the skills or appetite that would have helped them claw their way into an industrializing urban economy. For these new townspeople, being white mattered. The conundrum of urban poverty among whites is aptly described by de Kiewiet: they were not suited for skilled work, yet they believed that their skin color elevated them above the station of manual labor.

There was also a gendered dimension to urbanization and white poverty. As the relentless pressure of capitalist transformation drove both Blacks and whites from the land, the idea of belonging to the land, of being rural people, featured powerfully in the imagination of both. The depths of these attachments are evident in a comment made to a Commission of Inquiry in 1922. As late as the 1920s, "the mass of Afrikaans mine-workers were yet only half-miners . . . still looking back to their fathers' farms, spending their savings on small-holdings to keep contact with their tradition as frontier Boers."[22] Thus, those families most vulnerable to eviction or ruin, *bywoners*, or those with small, unproductive farms, struggled to stay on the land. Growing numbers of white women sought wages to supplement family livelihoods. In 1921, there were 111,709 women on the Witwatersrand, the majority of whom worked (or sought work) in the garment industry or shops. This gender imbalance and the separation of families caused widespread fear among Afrikaans-speaking commentators that these women would succumb to sexual mixing across the color line and that the Indian shopkeepers who hired them would exploit them sexually.[23]

Almost inevitably, multiracial slums developed. Some, like those where Karel lived in the early 1920s, were informal settlements on the edges of town. Others were in more established neighborhoods like parts of Fordsburg and Bertrams in Johannesburg. The contrasting ways in which the central government and municipal authorities responded to urbanization widened the social distance between Black and white. While some Blacks lived in mixed settlements or city slums, the majority stayed in designated native "locations," as they were termed, on the outskirts of cities. Although the circumstances of their neglect varied slightly from city to city, Black people were considered by the authorities across the country as sojourners rather than permanent residents. The idea of impermanence justified city councils' unwillingness to spend much on the provision of services or infrastructure to these communities. As a newspaper critical of the then-colonial government pointed out in 1908, "under the present system, locations are looked upon rather as convenient sources of revenue than as objects of serious responsibility."[24] Pass laws completed the fiction that Blacks did not belong in cities. Through various laws and ordinances dating back to the eighteenth century and culminating in the Native (Urban Areas) Act of 1923, Black men were obliged to carry a pass proving that they were employed and entitled to temporary residence in the city. Amendments to the act made it progressively more difficult for families to settle in locations.

While most white politicians, government bureaucrats, and city officials subscribed to the myth that Blacks were merely transient residents of the cities, they acknowledged that white people—poor whites who had migrated to the city—were there to stay. Having made this distinction, the authorities initiated a variety of projects, funded by both the central government and city councils, to elevate the white poor out of the slums and types of informal settlements where Karel and people like him lived. In 1920, the Union government allocated £5 000 000 to municipalities to build houses for poor white families with incomes too small to allow them to live under "decent" housing conditions. In Cape Town, for example, the city council oversaw the development of the Good Hope Model Village, 595 cottages "sewered and built on a fair-sized plot of ground with ample space for gardening." Note how those responsible for the design and provision of housing linked particular types of housing to the cultivation of particular habits, hobbies, and aptitudes, such as gardening. As the century progressed, this would become more common. These cottages were intended for European tenants with an income of between £6.1s and £15 per month.[25]

The opening decades of the twentieth century saw a rush of young white people moving from the rural areas to cities in search of employment. Pointing out that these juveniles were usually not in a position to live in surroundings "which are desirable," Cape Town social worker O. J. M. Wagner commented that he and his peers were alert to the "danger that exposure to socially defective surroundings may result in poverty, dependency and even delinquency." Clearly, sentiments of the sort expressed by Wagner were shared by welfare agencies and those who held the strings of the public purse; in Cape Town alone, several hostels were built to house "juveniles with small incomes." These included, for instance, the Afrikaanse Christelike Vrouevereniging (ACVV) Meisies Tehuis for young women, and the Prof. de Vos Hostel for young men in the service of the South African Railways. In both cases these hostels were the outcome of collaboration between welfare agencies and the city.[26]

As poor whites were assisted into more formal housing, this came at a cost to their independence. Even those with a shared interest in social welfare were at odds as to whether white poverty was caused by economic forces or genetics. According to Sir Carruthers Beattie, vice chancellor of the University of Cape Town, poor whites were "intellectually backward . . . and there was something inherent in the Afrikaners that resulted in the phenomenon," while Dominee J. R. Albertyn, who wrote a volume of the Carnegie Commission report, declared that "the poor white was lacking in ambition, thrift and prudence, and inclined to be gullible, dishonest, deceitful, irresponsible, lazy and listless."[27] All viewed moral lapses or feebleness as alarming symptoms of poor whiteism. Moving the white poor into subsidized housing provided the authorities with an ideal opportunity to monitor them for drunkenness, illicit sexual relationships, "personal demoralization," and other social ills. In Cape Town, Wagner tells us, the city appointed two social workers who received and assessed all applications for public housing. The social workers would welcome new tenants and they would advise the City Council, when necessary, on problems of "unemployment, delinquency, and so on." As part of their contribution to family welfare, the social workers also made periodic visits to untidy homes.[28] Misgivings about the character of the white poor and intent on the part of the authorities to root out signs of delinquency and indolence were ongoing themes in the social history of ordinary whites that would recur and intensify after 1948, when the NP took office.

With large numbers of poor white people gathered in towns, many living in subsidized housing and susceptible to the attentions of the government and various welfare bodies (including, notably, social workers), all manner of conditions which had hitherto been hidden away or otherwise kept within families now became identified as social problems. Sometimes individuals who bore these conditions were cast away in institutions. We find, for instance, that in Cape Town, the "European unmarried expectant mother" could find refuge in the Cape Town Home for Friendless Girls, where she would be helped with teaching and advice until she went to a maternal home. The home doubled as a prison remand center, holding women who were awaiting trial; in other words, in the mind's eye of both state bureaucrats and welfare authorities, there was little point in making a distinction between pregnant, unmarried women and those accused of criminal transgression.[29] Also, until at least the early 1930s, epileptics, once diagnosed, were often dismissed from their employment. In Johannesburg, the Rand Epileptic Employment Association maintained a property in Craighall where European epileptics could live permanently, partly earning a living through floriculture, which they performed under the supervision of an "expert, non-epileptic horticulturalist." The Craighall property came through "munificence of the Johannesburg City Council." According to Dr. Morris Cohen, vice president of the South African National Council for Mental Hygiene, the facility provided epileptics (white male epileptics, at any rate, as the institution not only refused its services to the "non-European epileptic," but also to white women) with a "sense of protection ... from the keen competition which the average person experiences in the struggle for existence."[30]

As government departments settled and matured after Union, greater collaboration between them became possible, and by the mid-1920s, the principle of cooperation between social work officers and white schools was established. "Problem children"—and, although it was unsaid, problem families—provided the basis for interaction between these two authorities. Both were worried that "early maladjustment" might develop into "serious anti-social behavior," and schools were well placed to observe the earliest signs of maladjustment, which included "delinquency, uncontrollability and truancy." According to this arrangement, school principals were thus instructed to refer any cases of delinquency and maladjustment that could possibly relate to home circumstances to the local social welfare officer.[31]

Successive Union governments were all too aware of the potential of white poverty to erode the foundations of the racial order. Albertyn, writing as late as the 1930s, warned: "If the more privileged European grudges and refuses the poor his patronage, the latter will associate with non-Europeans if he finds no member of his own race to consort with."[32] The pervasiveness and significance of white poverty in turn animated anxieties about idleness, which was seen as a harbinger of other ills. There were gendered dimensions to this. First of all, in the imagination of contemporary Afrikaner nationalist observers, white men were supposed to work and support their families. In the Calvinistic moral reasoning that shaped the worldview of many of these elites, it followed that if men were out of work they were guilty of "idleness," which was often associated with alcohol abuse.[33] Second, elite Afrikaners feared that white families not provided for by white husbands and fathers would be exposed to mixed slums, where white women "could become spiritually lost in the city and become a burden and a curse to the *volk* ('nation'), instead of a blessing."[34] This attitude coincided with an emerging penology articulated at the 1910 International Prisons Conference in Washington, DC. At this conference, several penal principles that went well beyond simple incarceration of offenders for statutory or common-law offences gained a measure of international traction. They included principles like indefinite sentence and classification of prisoners. The conference also affirmed the society's right to "use constraint or compulsion against beggars, tramps and idlers." Delegates debated what could be done to compel such individuals to work and accepted that, in addition to imprisonment, hard physical labor should be used as a broad, group-based moral corrective. Penological approaches to drunkenness received considerable attention. Disapproving of many short sentences for alcohol-related offences, the delegates passed a resolution advocating two to three years of institutionalized treatment for chronic drinkers.[35] The new penology resonated with South Africa's Director of Prisons Jacob de Villiers Roos, and he incorporated many of the principles he had learned at the Washington conference into the 1911 Prisons and Reformatories Act.[36] Among other provisions, this act created a legal framework for work colonies designed to enable the incarceration of idle whites, forcing them to work without necessarily imprisoning them.[37] In short, it focused explicitly on the white "undeserving" who were expressly excluded from the earlier church initiatives.

The system of state work colonies was inaugurated in September 1912 when the first one was opened in Baviaanspoort in the eastern Cape—suggestively, in a prison. The Baviaanspoort-Boerederykolonie en-Dronkaardgestig (agricultural colony and alcoholics' retreat) was a combined work colony and inebriate asylum for *leeglopers* (idlers/loiterers/loafers) and men who had transgressed minor laws through drinking, and its purpose was to link hard work and strict discipline with the development of industrious habits among white males. The early history of Baviaanspoort reveals a number of contradictions in the way that this new institution engaged with the wider penal bureaucracy. Prison officials sought to distinguish between those who might be rehabilitated by the moral and physical regime of the work colony and those who could not be. And while Baviaanspoort was part of the penal system, it was intended specifically for the rehabilitation of the idle and those seen to be victims of alcohol. Yet prisoners convicted of more serious crimes were also sent there, often from the Pretoria Central Prison, prompting work colony officials to complain that "mixing drunkards, idlers and criminals was not bearing the right fruit." In 1916 it was agreed that prisoners who had more than one conviction for offenses other than the consumption of liquor could no longer be sent to Baviaanspoort. Another sentencing practice undermining the stated purpose of the Baviaanspoort project was magistrates' tendency to send homeless old men who could no longer find work to the colony: "Time and again the Director of Prisons appealed for separate regulations for these old men."

In 1916, at the Cradock Conference on poor whiteism convened by the NGK, delegates noted that the state work colony at Baviaanspoort was wholly unsuccessful in rehabilitating idlers and drunkards. Moreover, the 1911 Prisons and Reformatories Act had failed to provide appropriate guidelines for management of idlers and chronic heavy drinkers. In addition to the demands that participation in the Allied war effort placed upon the still relatively new administration, the ruling SAP was not particularly sympathetic to the plight of the poorest of the Afrikaner poor, which meant that little was ultimately done to address the shortcomings of Baviaanspoort.

In 1924, the influential Cape synod of the NGK again petitioned Parliament to develop a more systematic and comprehensive framework to address white male idleness. By that time the SAP had fallen from power, replaced by the National / Labour Party Pact government, in which Afrikaner nationalists were very much the senior partner. The political environment was much more favorable to the *dominees'* appeal for stronger measures to address white idleness, and the government responded with the 1927 Work Colonies Act. The new act made provision for the founding and management of compulsory state work colonies, and it specified which persons ought to be there. It also specified under what conditions they should be detained and released. The new act retained the idea of hard labor as a tool of moral correction, but it sought to tighten the bureaucratic and disciplinary framework of the work colonies. In terms of the new act, idlers could be compulsorily sent to the work colonies. Its definition of idleness included white men over twenty-one who were habitual beggars, who did not provide food and clothing for their families, and significantly, when menial work was being created for whites through "civilized labor" policies, who declined offers of work. The presumption that hard work could restore an individual to industry, health, and respectability was emphasized by the fact that no one could be sent to a work colony if he was not physically capable of hard labor.[38] Under the 1927 act, several new work colonies for the white idle were established: Die Nuwebergse Dwaarsleereserwe Werkkolonie in the Caledon district of the Cape in June 1929; Swartfontein near Nelspruit in the eastern Transvaal in December 1938; and Eersterivier in 1940, where the government took over the forest reserve with the intention of housing not only detainees but also their families. None of these work colonies were very successful. Nuweberg, for instance, only accepted fourteen detainees and was closed down after five months. Pieterse believed that the major reason for their failure was the "unsuitability" of inmates, with convicted criminals still being detained alongside the drunk and the idle; also, many assigned to the work colonies were physically unsuited to the "corrective purpose" of the work colonies, with their emphasis on hard labor.[39] In practice, state work colonies during these years remained institutions where a motley collection of criminal, idle, and chronically drunk white men were imprisoned, rather ineffectively.

Despite their lack of success, the work colonies provided a precedent for the ways that the government of the day would seek to reform idle and delinquent whites through a regime of forced institutionalization and hard labor. Their history revealed particular class and gender inclinations in the ways that the authorities identified delinquency and other social ills. Men and later women from the ranks of the white working classes and unemployed were far more likely to come to the attention of those empowered to make decisions about delinquency than other, more affluent and educated whites. The idea represented by the work colonies in the 1910s to 1930s would be resurrected and expanded under apartheid after 1948.

Afrikaner nationalists who dominated the new Pact government after 1924 were more acutely sensitive to the plight of the urban white poor than their predecessors in the SAP. Not only did they represent a potential threat to South Africa's racial hierarchy, but they also evoked fears that they might find common cause with the poor of other races. Part of the Pact administration's bid to rescue the white poor included extending racial segregation in the workplace.

By the early 1920s, a color bar was well entrenched in the South African mines and industry. Between 1907 and 1922, there were a series of clashes between white gold miners in favor of a color bar and mine owners who "did not see 'white men and black men'; they saw only 'grades of labour.'"[40] According to contemporary botanist, historian, trade union organizer, and sometime communist Eddie Roux, strikes on the Witwatersrand gold fields around the color bar matched in bitterness any workplace conflict or labor skirmish to be found elsewhere in the world at the time. There were major strikes in 1907, 1913, and 1914, but 1922 saw the apogee of hostility between capital and white labor. One infamous slogan captured the revolutionary-yet-racist spirit of the 1922 strike: "Workers of the world, unite and fight for a white South Africa." The strike developed into a full-blown revolt and on March 10, 1922, an estimated 10,000 white mine workers attacked Black workers, police stations, mines, and railway lines in Johannesburg. Prime Minister Jan Smuts declared martial law and called in the army, including air support and artillery. After five days of fighting, during which 214 people were killed, the revolt was crushed, and 4 strike leaders were sent to the gallows.[41] This ongoing industrial warfare prompted even the SAP government—with a pinch of reluctance—to pass color bar legislation, the most significant of which was the Industrial Conciliation Act (1924), which afforded white workers a preferential position to Blacks within the system of industrial bargaining.[42]

While the extension of job color bars gave immense advantage to skilled and semiskilled whites, it did not immediately benefit all whites, even all white men. According to a 1922 Unemployment Commission, 120,000 of an economically active population of 540,000 white men were out of work. The Pact government—or more precisely, the Afrikaner nationalist component of it—wished to place these men in jobs where they could maintain "the standard generally accepted as tolerable from a European standpoint."[43] This was the essence of the Pact's "civilized labor" policy, and it was driven largely from within the state sector, although other employers were also expected to pay "civilized wages" to whites. As far as possible, Black workers were replaced by whites. New industries, including Iscor (the Iron and Steel Corporation) and Eskom (the electricity supply corporation), were established in the late 1920s and early 1930s with all-white labor corps.

Under the Pact, the Department of Labour was created, and one of its major tasks was to oversee the implementation of "civilized labor" policies. This included placing unskilled whites in laborers' positions and casual employment with city and government departments. The railway was by far the biggest employer of unskilled "European labor": by 1926 it employed 10,919 (a figure that increased each year until 1939), along with around 5,000 who were employed on a casual basis.[44] In something of a commentary on the limited purchase of compulsory schooling, no educational qualification was required of these men, although those with the "necessary education and qualifications" could be promoted into graded positions.

Placing these men in jobs was never separate from ongoing concerns about the welfare of whites. Just like the supply of public housing, "civilized labor" opportunities were interventions designed to monitor and, if need be, improve the family lives of white laborers employed in railway gangs. Noting the "under-developed physical, cultural, and moral existence inherent in the circle from which many staff are recruited," government social workers expressed concern that these deficits would be exacerbated by the isolated nature of work on a railway gang. They urged that gangs should be based near "centres where schooling and other social amenities are readily available." "Lady welfare officers" were assigned to undertake "prophylactic work amongst families on the basis that 'prevention is better than cure.'"[45] The extent to which prospective "European laborers" demonstrated a decline in the physical condition of white men provided railway authorities with cause for concern—a concern they shared with officials from the work colonies. Due to the nature of the work, railway gangs needed to be "composed of servants who are physically fit and in all respects suitable for the important duties assigned to them."[46] Yet at a time of mass unemployment there was, paradoxically, difficulty in recruiting suitable white applicants for employment as rail workers, since far too many fell short of the physical requirements of the job. To this end, authorities actively promoted physical education classes. They also funded the establishment of fifty recreation clubs across the Union that provided [white] "railway servants and their families access to various forms of sport."[47] Alas, the sale of subsidized liquor at these clubs rather undermined their purpose of healthy physical activity and friendly sporting competition.

This is the world that the adult Karel negotiated, one simultaneously raising him up from poverty and wary of the dangers he represented to the *volk* and the still fragile social order. He was a beneficiary of civilized labor and was appointed to a gang of laborers who terraced the gardens of the Union Buildings in Pretoria.[48] This work was not dissimilar to his toil as a *togt* laborer—a spade man—but at least it brought a more reliable and steady income. By 1928 or 1929, his work at the Union Buildings came to an end, and he was a recipient of another civilized labor job, this time as a toilet attendant in Durban. He and his little family were given third-class tickets to Durban, purposefully one-way, because it was widely believed that poor whites would leave stable appointments and return to the familiarity of their squalor in cities like Pretoria.

Becoming an Englishman

Durban remains to this day, along with Pietermaritzburg, that most emphatically un-Afrikaans-speaking of South African cities, and this description was even more apt in the 1920s. Realizing that speaking English would be necessary to slot into white working-class society there, Karel made a series of pragmatic decisions that would set him at odds with the hopes and ideals of contemporary Afrikaner nationalism. These decisions also meant that he represented much of what Afrikaner nationalism's cultural brokers feared about the dissolution of the *volk*. He became an Englishman. Anglicizing his name from Karel to Charles, he left the NGK, moved to the Presbyterians (theologically not too distant from the NGK), and insisted that his family speak English. His wife, my Grandmother Roos, was never able to make the transition, becoming increasingly insular. My memory of her in the late 1960s is of an old lady unable to communicate with me or share her language with her young grandson, who had virtually no Afrikaans.

For nearly thirty years, Charles's civilized labor job in Durban was to maintain, attend, and guard a fairly elaborate Art Deco public toilet in Smith Street in Durban's city center.[49] We are unsure of the exact nature of his work beyond his "being" there; and in the context of segregated South Africa in the 1920s and 1930s, as well as the longer *durée* of Charles's life, this probably meant ensuring that no Black people attempted access to the public facility and, possibly, assaulting "poofters," male homosexuals who sometimes met in toilets such as the one Charles attended. Charles remained a supporter of Smuts, who was sometimes in power and sometimes on the opposition benches from the 1920s until Smuts's death in 1950. Charles's support for Smuts was deeply visceral. During the Second World War, and into the late 1940s and early 1950s, political contests between UP supporters, Smuts men, and Afrikaner nationalists often turned violent, and Charles showed himself to be a true *bloedsap*. In 1952, a by-election was called in the Wakkerstroom constituency of the eastern Transvaal. Once a safe UP seat, it had been won by the NP in 1948 and the by-election was thus of major importance not only for the NP as it tried to consolidate its small parliamentary majority but also for the UP, reeling after its surprise loss.

In the often-violent political battles between Smuts supporters, those who supported SA's participation in the World War, and, on the other hand, Afrikaner nationalists, Charles was a loyal and enthusiastic foot soldier. My family's oral tradition has it that Charles, a large man, was not above participating in the disruption of meetings, street fights with party political opponents, and the roving fights between Afrikaner nationalists and United Party supporters in the 1952 Wakkerstroom by-election.[50] The by-election campaign in the rural Wakkerstroom constituency was bitter, with regular evening fights between militant Afrikaner nationalists and members of the War Veterans' Torch Commando, a movement of white Second World War veterans who supported the UP candidate.[51] These fights, which usually took place over who would occupy the chair at town hall political meetings across the far-flung constituency, were often vicious. Bicycle chains, baseball bats, and beer bottles supplemented fists and boots. Charles was a physically imposing man, even in late middle age, and these same oral histories have him encamped at Wakkerstroom as part of the Torch Commando detachment. It also has him in the thick of violent confrontations between the Torchmen and nationalists.

Charles was not a heroic figure, nor for that matter did he represent any progressive currents in South African history or historiography. He acted rather with expedience and adaptability, and while his decisions set him at odds with Afrikaner nationalism, a close reading of his everyday life renders these decisions easy to comprehend. He represents the ultimate subaltern figure. His consciousness and everyday life were defined in relation to the state bureaucracy as it directed him to the routines of regular wage labor, vigorously tried to improve his family circumstances, and held over him the threat of discipline should he step out of line. The specter of the work colony, while seldom mentioned publicly, was never far away. Yet as his spiky history demonstrates, just as he was dominated, he was seldom subordinate. And as we shall see, language became a terrain over which tensions of domination and subordination were played out even further within the confines of his home.

I know virtually nothing about Grandmother Roos. Indeed, one of the ironies of this family history is that while changing his name represented a watershed in Karel/Charles's life, I don't even know what Grandmother Roos's name was. Reading, once again, slivers of evidence and suggestion handed down through the generations, I gather that she had little choice in the moves that took her as a young bride from the Cape veld to a Pretoria slum and then to a working-class neighborhood in Durban, or the even longer journey away from her language and culture. She kept her language and, in another irony, just as Charles shook his fist at Afrikaner nationalism, she became the ultimate *volksmoeder* ("mother of the nation").[52] She stayed at home and kept her family together. And whether by inclination or by her inability to master English, she kept the *taal*, the language, understood by Afrikaner nationalist intellectuals as one of the key constituents to Afrikaner identity and survival.

Acculturation, Middle Class Respectability, and *Insluipers*

Grandfather and Grandmother Roos had three children: two sons and a daughter. With South Africa's entry into the Second World War on the side of the Allies in 1939, all three siblings signed up. My father, Dick, like his father before him, became a child soldier, signing up in 1939 as a sixteen-year-old; his younger brother and sister followed his example a few years later. Like many white South African volunteers, they joined not out of any innate sense of patriotism or belonging to Empire, but out of pragmatism. There were few other choices available to children of poor whites of limited education. Charles tried to sign up alongside his son, but was promptly turned away because of his age.

My father was an infantryman and served across the North African theater of war where the South African armies were involved in battles first against the Italians and then against Rommel's desert corps. The North African phase of the Second World War saw intense battles interspersed with long rest periods where soldiers waited.[53] Clearly, the young Private Roos had special bonds of affection toward his mother, for he sent her special gifts in the form of china tea sets, from Cairo, Tripoli, and Alexandria: beautiful, delicate tea sets that became family heirlooms. While he was poorly schooled, he clearly had a keen sense of respectability, what it meant to his mother, and the ways in which she might have dreamed about a world different from that of a poor white. This world involved beautiful things like tea sets, which would never be used.

Dick and his siblings returned home after the Second World War and, like many returning veterans, they struggled to readjust to civilian life. Their sister soon married, but Dick and his brother Vic drifted from job to job. They drank heavily and lacked the sort of ambition that was becoming associated

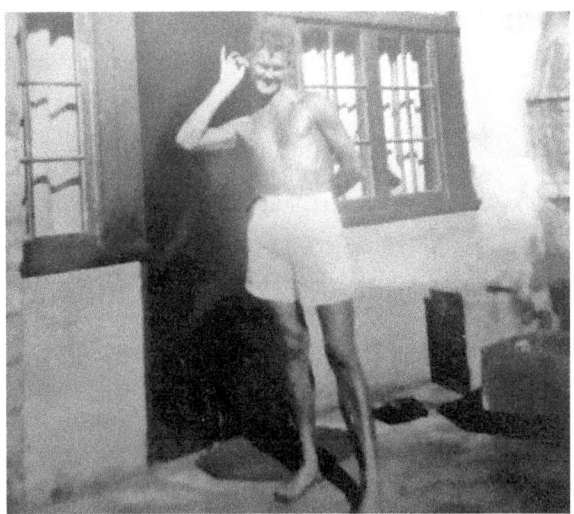

Figure 3.1, Figure 3.2, and Figure 3.3 Dick Roos, in wartime (*top left*, North Africa) and in peacetime (*top right*, Durban, South Africa). He was sometimes called "Tarzan" for his inclination to go shirtless, a habit he probably developed during his time as a young soldier in North Africa. In the third image (fig. 3.3) he is dressed, in his work clothes. Author's personal collection.

with what was considered respectable white male identity in the apartheid years. In 1950, these two men were assigned to the work colony; in just five years the caring boy soldier, who sent things of beauty to his mother, had been defined by the new apartheid government as a problem, a miscreant, and someone to be incarcerated.

These apartheid-era work colonies were very much the brainchild of Geoffrey Cronjé, an Afrikaner nationalist sociologist who saw his star rise after the nationalists took power in 1948. As we shall see in the next chapter, Cronjé was deeply concerned about the coherence, survival, and moral integrity of the Afrikaner *volk*. People like Dick, Vic, and especially Charles, offended Cronjé's nationalist sensibilities. All three were deculturated, they had lost the Afrikaans language, they had no real jobs or aspirations toward the middle class, they were poorly educated, they had all taken the red oath and gone to war, and they were certainly not Afrikaner nationalists. For Cronjé, people like these men were *"insluipers"* (intruders), a loose term he applied to whites he considered traitorous, untrustworthy, and a threat to the health of the Afrikaner *volk* as a whole. On the other hand, Grandfather L, with his veneer of middle-class respectability and his Englishness, escaped the close attention of both Afrikaner nationalists with an interest in whites and the state that these nationalists occupied after 1948. Cronjé and those nationalists who shared his ideas about the coherence and health of the Afrikaner *volk* relentlessly directed not only state policy but also welfare organizations and social workers toward people like Charles, Dick, and Vic. Detached as they were from Afrikaner nationalism and even the Afrikaner *volk*, they remained Afrikaners by blood. Through the 1950s, Afrikaner nationalists in various positions of authority and influence sought to erase the legacies of poor whiteism. It was people like these, men and women deemed to be on the economic, social, and cultural frontiers of Afrikanerdom, who would provide the focus and the rationale for these elites' determination to surveil, police, and restructure white society.

4

INSLUIPERS, GEOFFREY CRONJÉ, AND SOCIAL POLICY

Geoffrey Cronjé and the White Lower Classes

Geoffrey Cronjé (1907–1992) was an obsessive man. In the early apartheid years, he was one of a new breed of intellectuals who could comfortably straddle the halls of the academy and the machinery of state. Between the 1930s and the 1960s, he was an important Afrikaner nationalist professor, and like all of his generation of Afrikaner nationalist intellectuals who came of age during the Great Depression, he was centrally concerned about the fate of the Afrikaner people. He wrote and taught extensively about poor whites. According to his analysis, whites were endangered by cataclysms of racial impurity, which meant that he never spoke exclusively about white Afrikaners. This set Cronjé apart from most of his contemporaries. For him, whites like Dick, Vic, and Charles, who not only remained on the lower margins of white working-class society but also demonstrated few bonds of kinship to their historical "people" (the Afrikaner *volk*), represented a threat to the very survival of the white race. Within the broader ambit of Afrikaner nationalism, Cronjé was part of a sub-tradition of explicitly racist thought, and his horror of racial dissolution fueled a career-long quest to identify ways in which the white race might be betrayed.[1] He also sought to develop strategies to contain and reform those who undermined (or potentially undermined) the coherence and integrity of white society. This represented the foundation of his obsession. J. M. Coetzee, who would go on to win a Nobel prize for literature, attributed a kind of "madness" to Cronjé in his relentless pursuit of this obsession.[2]

Social policy toward whites in the early apartheid years was premised on substantial intellectual work. Whether or not he was tainted by madness, Cronjé was immensely energetic. His industry and capacity to move fluidly between the university and the policy-making domains of the state gave him significant power to shape government social policy toward whites for a few years from the late 1940s until the late 1950s. In understanding the ways in which whites were policed, managed, and subject to reform in the early apartheid years, Cronjé's career thus represents an important entry point, albeit with one caveat. Scholars like Coetzee who have shown an interest in Cronjé have tended to concentrate on his published work.[3] However, Cronjé is perhaps better understood as a historical rather than a literary figure. To comprehend his role in engineering "the nation," we of course need to understand his writing and its genealogies. But these are just a starting point; we also need to inquire ethnographically how his ideas were advanced, transformed, contested, and instantiated in the ideologies, routines, and disciplines of white everyday life. This approach to Cronjé's career should go some way toward illuminating the interaction between ideology, (social) science, and techniques of discipline, regulation, and management in the social history of whites in early apartheid society. It will also demonstrate some of the ways that ideology was made real for ordinary whites, and how Cronjé's variant of "apartheid thinking" resonated with more popular strands.

Secular Intellectual and European Legacies—of a Sort

Cronjé was born on December 30, 1907 on a farm called Brandrivier in the Barrydale district of the southern Cape. He was the last of fourteen children and, like many rural whites, began his education at a farm school.[4] Young Geoffrey's farm school education did not exceed the infant grades, as his father died and the family moved to the town of Riversdal. He was then sent as a boarder to Paarl Boys' High School, where he remained until he matriculated.[5] He must have been a good student, for he won a scholarship to the Stellenbosch University where he took a bachelor's degree and then a master's degree in the classics.[6]

Cronjé then secured another scholarship, this time to study abroad, and in 1930 traveled to the Netherlands. Making a significant shift from his earlier training, he registered for a doctoral degree in sociology at the University of Amsterdam. Cronjé's move to sociology and choice of the self-consciously secular University of Amsterdam marked a departure from the trend common among young Stellenbosch graduates who tended to prefer that great seat of reformed Calvinist scholarship, the Vrije Universiteit Amsterdam. This shift presaged later changes in the kind of disciplinary influences that shaped Afrikaner nationalism: under apartheid, secular scientific knowledge from disciplines like anthropology and sociology became more important for the organization of society than it had been under any former South African regime. Cronjé was more interested in social work and criminology than in classical sociology, and he graduated in 1933 with a thesis on divorce and the dissolution of families, becoming the first South African to earn a doctoral degree in sociology.[7]

We have few traces of Cronjé's time in the Netherlands, especially personal ones, but his career points to two major impacts, one on his thinking and the other on his standing in Afrikaner intellectual circles. First, while Cronjé's scholarly (and later, commissioned) research always concentrated on South African questions, it also suggests that during his stay in Amsterdam he developed connections to some sophisticated intellectual circuits, and in particular was influenced by ideologies of corporativism that gained currency in the wake of social dislocation caused by the First World War. Broadly, the tenets of secular corporativism encouraged national cohesion and elevated collectivist corporate bodies (like business organizations and labor) to become cornerstones of political and economic life, while deemphasizing the value of individual liberty.[8] Corporativist ideas were used by numerous conservative, radical right, and fascist parties to organize and rationalize their regimes, but in the first decades of the twentieth century, they also represented an alternative to both liberal democracy and socialism and were particularly appealing to technical elites (like Cronjé) as a "third way."[9] As corporativism took root politically and bureaucratically in several authoritarian, nationalist, and fascist states in Europe and Latin America in the 1920s and 1930s, it was characterized by strong central planning and attempts to infiltrate and control every aspect of social life.[10] As such, the foundations of corporativism were not dissimilar to the variants of authoritarian Afrikaner nationalism being elaborated from the 1930s onward, particularly in the Transvaal.[11] Although there was not much unity among Afrikaner nationalists, they generally shared the core ideas of the *volkseie*, the assertion that a people should control its own destiny, and *volksgebondenheid*, which referred to the unity of the Afrikaner *volk*, or nation. The pillars of the *volkseie* and *volksgebondenheid* were accompanied by the assumption that an individual could exist only through the nation.[12] These ideas fed into a kind of hypernationalism that Afrikaner nationalism shared with other 1930s-vintage corporativist and authoritarian ideologies. But in addition to more philosophical claims about the ideal form of the state and the relationship between the individual and the state, European social scientists with an inclination to corporativism were beginning to champion social engineering as a methodology to manage society. Social engineering, an emerging trend in applied social science, held that society might be changed or managed ("engineered") if one had adequate "scientific" data and appropriate policy, regulatory, and administrative tools to carry out the engineering. Cronjé would later become one of the most ardent South African disciples of social engineering. It is likely that his time spent immersed in the secular European intellectual culture he found at Amsterdam influenced his particular interpretation of it. Thus, failures of Afrikaner nationalism were manifest in the conduct of men like Dick, Vic, and Charles, and these failures could be remedied through careful sociological research, gathering of data, and appropriate interventions. Second, Cronjé became part of a group of influential Afrikaner scholars known as "Hollanders," men who had studied in the Netherlands and who gravitated to the very heart of Afrikaner intellectual culture, although they never organized themselves as a separate rump. He carried this status until the end of his professional life at the University of Pretoria in the late 1960s.[13]

The University of Pretoria and Cronjé's Prolific Years

Shortly after his return from the Netherlands, Cronjé received a telegram from the University of Pretoria (UP) with an offer of a post as senior lecturer and head of the Department of Sociology and Social Work.[14] At the time the university was in a state of transition to becoming an important Afrikaner institution. In 1931, some 65 percent of the student body were Afrikaans speaking, yet 68 percent of its classes were taught in English. In 1932, the University Council decided that Afrikaans would be the only medium of instruction. This decision, however, was not reflected in the composition of the academic faculty, and curricula hardly reflected Afrikaner-nationalist interests or indeed even more moderately stated Afrikaner ones. The Department of Social Work represented one of the first attempts by Afrikaner nationalists to establish a beachhead at UP. It was established in 1929 with the support of a grant of £8,000 from the nationalist Suid-Afrikaanse Vrouefederasie (SAVF) to fund a child guidance clinic, employ a lecturer to teach social work,[15] and offer extension lectures in social work to members of the SAVF.[16] Dr. Maria te Water, who had trained initially as a medical doctor, was appointed to this position. However, the Great Depression took its toll on the SAVF's resources, and her five-year term was not extended. Te Water's short stay at UP nonetheless set in place some important intellectual trajectories for the development of social work and sociology at UP. During her residence as a medical student in Britain, she had undertaken extensive welfare work in slums, assisting with medical inspections of school children. She then proceeded to America on a Rockefeller fellowship for the study of "subnormal and difficult" children.[17] Her approach, which combined social work and medicine, proved remarkably resilient for over fifty years at UP. In some instances the focus was on physical health, in others the health of the community, and in others yet, it was difficult to disentangle the two.

Anticipating the end of SAVF funding, the university convened a committee—known as the Roos Committee—to assess the future of both the clinic and the Department of Social Work. The committee acknowledged the community value of the clinic and the importance of social work as a field of study, but it pointed out that the Department of Social Work needed to be reorganized. It advised further that a lecturer be appointed to guide social work and its adjacent discipline, sociology, in a new department, Sociology and Social Work.[18] These recommendations pointed to another feature of sociology at Pretoria: that it would be closer on the spectrum to social work than to the more theoretical reaches of the discipline. Ultimately, the people who would be the subjects of his research for at least the next forty years would be white.

In 1937, Cronjé was promoted to the rank of professor.[19] He was young, enthusiastic, and full of new ideas, and he turned his attention to curriculum reform. Working with W. A. Willemse, a psychologist with an interest in criminal psychology and youth crime, he began by revising the sociology curriculum in ways that stand as testament to contemporary Afrikaner nationalist concerns about whites and that explicitly positioned the curriculum as "Christian"—one of the new courses was "Christian social work."[20] Characteristically, Cronjé took on all of the undergraduate lectures as well as lectures in educational sociology at Normaal Kollege Pretoria, a teachers' training college founded in 1902 to train Afrikaans teachers and an early rallying point for the development of Afrikaner nationalism after the Anglo-Boer War.[21] There were courses on labor and unemployment, poverty and community development in South Africa, rural dispossession, urbanization, and children and poverty. These themes reflected prevailing elite analyses of the causes and consequences of white poverty, and the case studies used as the major teaching methodology were all drawn from the history and experience of poor whiteism in nineteenth- and twentieth-century South Africa. There were also courses on order and disorder, the latter emphasizing alcoholism and juvenile delinquency. This orientation might have reflected Willemse's influence and was not particularly novel for a sociology program. What did feature as a particularly Afrikaner nationalist stamp, however, was the way in which the family was positioned in every instance as a counter to "disorder." This favorite refrain in Afrikaner nationalism situated the family, rather than the individual, as the core social unit of the *volk*. To this end, identifying challenges to the family and then engineering interventions, using the capacity of the state where possible, became a distinguishing theme in Cronjé's work as an intellectual and a bureaucrat for the next thirty-five-odd years. In 1948, following Willemse's death, criminology was added to the departmental roster.[22] By 1959, it was the biggest department at the University of Pretoria, with 1,200 students, demonstrating the importance that university authorities as well as prospective students from the Afrikaans-speaking sections of the white population attached to social work and its adjacent disciplines. It also offered night classes for practicing social workers.[23]

The years of the Second World War represented a phase of ideological ferment and potential in South Africa: for Blacks opposed to segregation, for the liberal whites and, also, for those of a more authoritarian inclination. The years during and immediately after the war also saw Cronjé at his most prolific, producing several major books—the texts analyzed by J. M. Coetzee. In 1943 he wrote *'n Tuiste vir die Nageslag* (A permanent home), the first book-length study propagating apartheid. This was followed in 1945 by *Afrika sonder die Asiaat: Die Blywende Oplossing van Suid-Afrika se Asiatevraagstuk* (Africa without the Asian: A lasting solution to South Africa's Asian question) where he advocated the repatriation to India of the descendants of Indian immigrants. The book that cemented his status as a leading apartheid intellectual, and arguably his magnum opus, was *Regverdige Rasse-Apartheid* (Just racial apartheid), published in 1947. In 1948, he wrote *Voogdyskap en Apartheid* (Guardianship and apartheid), which set out to mark the social horizons for the Afrikaner community, namely separation from Blacks, accompanied by "complete control of its weaker and more deviant-prone elements."[24]

Cronjé's published texts formed part of a Transvaal canon of radical Afrikaner nationalist republicanism. This canon flourished in the heady period of the early 1940s, at a juncture in European history when it seemed possible that states organized on corporativist-style ideologies offered a prospect of order and coherence, seen as a viable alternative to the spectacle of weak and apparently chaotic liberal western democracies. Cronjé's writing demonstrated a strand of authoritarianism woven around political philosophies that he would have encountered as a student in Amsterdam in the 1930s and nurtured in the promising political climate of the early war years. This was before Germany began to suffer military setbacks, arguably from the Battle of Stalingrad which took place between August 1942 and February 1943. German military defeat and the almost universal discrediting of Nazism did not provide Cronjé with a moment for intellectual pause or disrupt his arguments for authoritarian—"Christian"—styles of government and social organization. Rather, events on the global stage, notably the advance of communism in Eastern Europe and the rise of anti-colonial movements in Africa, Asia, the Caribbean, and Latin America, infused his work with a new resolve to find solutions to the challenges of order (in his terms, mainly dissolution of the races or racial mingling) and to protect the identity and safeguard the future of Afrikaners in South Africa. Dating back to at least the early 1920s and struggles on the Rand for the allegiance of Afrikaner workers—men and women—"communism" was considered by the adherents of Afrikaner nationalism as the antithesis of everything they stood for.

Coetzee points out that, in his books, Cronjé demonstrated a surprisingly rudimentary understanding of political society. For his model of authority, he took the family as it existed among rural Afrikaans speakers before the twentieth century: the patriarch whose authority extended over his progeny and the Black families feudally beholden to him. The patriarch laid down the law. Without any other theory of the state, his was thus a totally authoritarian view of politics.[25] With the exception of Cronjé's harangue against "Asians" and his arguments that these "immigrants" be repatriated to India—the irony of which apparently escaped him—white Afrikaners were the major focus of the books that he wrote during the mid-1940s. He reserved his most impassioned arguments for obsessive ranting about the dangers of "blood mixing"—*bloedvermenging*.[26] Associated with the horrors of *bloedvermenging*—mingling of white and non-white blood—was the question of desire. Cronjé was deeply concerned about the treacherous *insluiper* (a creature who intrudes or "slips in"). Sometimes the *insluiper* has been cast as a drunken and contaminating bogeyman, invoked by campaigning NP politicians, but Coetzee suggests that, for Cronjé, the *insluiper* was something more, an insidious sliding into indifference (Charles's and his sons' indifference to Afrikaner nationalism and the *volk*?). The insluiper was emblematic of a system of (obsessive) order based on keeping things apart, and Cronjé was deeply concerned that there were among whites treacherous "blood mixers" who would admit the *insluiper*. According to Coetzee, Cronjé's apartheid thinking thus developed as a counterattack on desire and blood mixing rather than a specific appeal for spatial segregation—although the latter was necessary to insure against the former.[27] Coetzee assumed that the *bloedvermenging* that so appalled Cronjé was race mixing—of white and non-white blood—and that apartheid was thus designed to counter the *insluiper*'s more base desires. It is plausible though that the danger of *bloedvermenging* to which Cronjé alluded was not only of the kind encouraged between racial groups by the *insluiper* who cared little for the order of the races, according to the values of Afrikaner nationalism. The danger might have been closer to home, another type of indifference, roiled in problems of blood and blood mixing: incest.

From the middle of the nineteenth century, in the wake of domestic dislocation wrought by industrialization, urbanization, and proletarianization, the family became increasingly significant in the minds of west

European and American social reformers. As the importance of the nuclear family for social stability under conditions of industrial capitalism became more widely acknowledged, incest laws correspondingly received new moral and legal impetus. Until then, criminal codes contained few specific sanctions against "sexual relations between closely related family members," although in Britain, at least, incest was the subject of canon law's regulation of marriage.[28]

In South Africa, court records indicate a growing number of whites being prosecuted for incest during this period—precisely when the social structures of white (and Black) society were under siege from the multiple pressures of capitalist development. These incest cases were concentrated in the last decade of the nineteenth and first two decades of the twentieth century. They were far more common in the Cape than the Transvaal, with very few cases among whites reported in Natal and only one recorded in the Orange Free State.[29] In 1906, for example, under the prompting of her husband, a Mrs. Smit from Germiston made an affidavit to the police. She had married on September 10, 1906 and gave birth to a son on October 25 of that year, "never [having] had connection with my husband." The child, she swore, was her father's, who twice "had connection" with her, "against my will."[30] In the same year, twelve-year-old Susanna van Vuuren from Heidelberg made a similar affidavit against her father who "inserted his person into my person which hurt very much"—since the "alleged assaults" took place before the girl's twelfth birthday, the secretary for the Law Department advised the public prosecutor to charge her father with rape.[31]

Given the immersion that Cronjé shared with other Afrikaner nationalists of the day in the diverse problems associated with white poverty, as well as his particular interest in social work, it is likely that he would have been aware of incest cases like these. If this proposition holds true, then it might account for Cronjé's intense, almost paranoid, suspicion of working-class, unemployed whites, and those considered "miscreant." The *insluiper* posed a threat not only to the survival of the *volk* and the race, but to the family as well. This hypothesis does not challenge Coetzee's assertion that apartheid represented an attack on desire, but it does emphasize the extent to which apartheid incorporated strategies not only for the separation of races, but also for the management of whites, not least in their homes. The potential for illicit desire existed not only between people of different races, but also within the confines of white families and households. This hypothesis also helps to explain Cronjé's determination, especially in the late 1940s and the 1950s when he was able to wield considerable political and bureaucratic clout, to subject these whites to monitoring by social workers, and, if necessary, to assign them to the case list of a social worker, send them to an alcoholic retreat or work colony, or remove their children to foster care or a reformatory.

As a body of thought, Cronjé's ideas became fashionable in Afrikaner nationalist circles for a time. He gained considerable traction among scholars in the Afrikaans universities, and some of his students—the most notable of whom was his protégé, Jannie Pieterse, who later succeeded Cronjé as the chair of sociology at Pretoria—advanced to senior and influential positions within the Afrikaner intellectual establishment. In 1963, he won the Stals prize, awarded by the Suid-Afrikaanse Akademie vir Wetenskap en Kuns (South African Science and Art Academy), as its highest honor for "a series of outstanding publications" in the humanities. He also received honorary doctorates from the Universities of South Africa (1977), Pretoria (1979), and the Orange Free State (1983), as well as the State President's Award for Distinguished Service in 1987.[32] By any measure, Cronjé's writing stands as a significant body of Afrikaner nationalist thought, and it offers opportunities for engagement not only by intellectual historians and literary scholars but also by social historians who ask different questions of the "life" of his books, essays, reports, and other voluminous writing.

Until his retirement Cronjé never relinquished his roles in the formal affairs of the university; in fact, his responsibilities increased over time. In 1948, for instance, he became dean of the Faculty of Arts and Philosophy, a post he held for six years. However, the period toward the end of the Second World War, when he wrote so prolifically, marked the first of two major transitions in Cronjé's professional life away from teaching and research, the more conventional pursuits of a scholar. In the first transition, manifest in the publication of his major books, he contributed to generating new "discursive horizons" for Afrikaner nationalism (racial biology) as well as symbols for Afrikaner civil religion (the *insluiper; bloedvermenging*).[33] The second transition, where he gravitated towards work as a public intellectual, a policy maker, an expert, and a bureaucrat, arguably represented Cronjé's greatest impact on white everyday life.

Sociologist, Social Worker, and Bureaucrat

Cronjé's first excursion into the realm of social policy came in 1944, when he was appointed to the Instituut vir Volkswelsyn (Institute for Public Welfare), which was a permanent commission of experts organized by the Federasie van Afrikaanse Kultuurverenigings (FAK), a powerful umbrella group for Afrikaner nationalist movements with a broadly cultural mandate.[34] Cronjé was already respected as a university scholar; this appointment signaled his growing stature within the broader Afrikaner nationalist movement.

However, it was the dynamics in and around the NP at the time that it swept to power in 1948 that opened fresh political and ideological space for Cronjé's influence to grow. Although the NP quickly passed some significant pieces of racial legislation (including the 1949 ban on interracial sex), the systemic implementation of apartheid was slow. Ironically, in its first years in office, the NP devoted considerable energy to white people, particularly Afrikaans speakers. This concentration must be read in the context of some of the NP's abiding concerns.

The NP understood itself as the *volksparty* (people's party) for Afrikaners. Shortly after assuming office, Prime Minister Dr. D. F. Malan announced that "today South Africa belongs to us once more. South Africa is our own for the first time since Union and may God grant that it will remain our own."[35] Yet behind the façade of shared purpose, the NP was fractious and unstable. During the war years, bitter *broedertwis* (internecine struggle) had emerged between northern and southern factions of Afrikaner nationalism. In particular, Malan's Cape allies in the Herenigde NP engaged in a bitter struggle with the paramilitary Ossewa Brandwag and other, smaller, extra-parliamentary republican groups. Malan and J. G. Strijdom, Transvaal head of the NP, loathed each other, and Transvaal nationalists were unconvinced of the republican convictions of the Cape party.[36] While the NP's factions and the ideologies that each promoted were never homogenous, the party was, in a general sense, committed to shepherding the poorest of Afrikaans speakers into the middle class; and Dan O'Meara believes that the "presumed relative economic deprivation of all Afrikaners, from the chairman of Sanlam to the poorest of 'poor whites'" lay at the core of Afrikaner nationalism in the 1930s and 1940s.[37]

Nevertheless, some, like Cronjé, considered that more should be done than simply uplifting the *volk* economically, and that progress of the *volk* as a whole demanded cultivation of "respectability" and certain moral dispositions among those who were beneficiaries of state-sponsored economic and social advancement. His was not a lone voice and it is noteworthy that the 1947 (before the NP took office) Volkskongres (People's Congress) was directed toward the cultural, moral, and religious challenges faced by Afrikaans speakers in the cities. In his presentation to the Kongres, Cronjé expressed his apprehension about threats posed by alcohol to the Afrikaner *volk*—to its public morality, Afrikaners' ability to climb the economic ladder, and the coherence and stability of Afrikaner families. Principally, he believed that alcohol, abused by whites in the impoverished and alienating conditions of the city, could lead to a specific kind of deviancy—*rasvermenging* (miscegenation).[38] Despite his secular leaning, he shared with Calvinist fundamentalists an utter contempt for and revulsion to drinkers, whom he associated with depravity and disorder.[39]

Like most Afrikaner nationalists of the day, Geoffrey Cronjé understood the family as the core social unit of the *volk* and held that men were the rightful supporters and heads of families. He believed that alcohol was the major reason for conflict and the breakup of the family unit. It was to this aspect of behavior he deemed antisocial that Cronjé would turn in the favorable political climate after 1948. Demonstrating his faith in ideas of central management, the planned state, and social engineering, he believed that alcoholism was a variable that could be manipulated to reduce antisocial behavior, that social welfare should be pursued primarily by the state rather than be left to the churches and charitable foundations, and that rehabilitation needed to be a conscious process of correction as opposed to one of moral suasion.

In 1947, Cronjé was appointed to the Work Colonies Advisory Board and elevated to chairman a year later. No doubt he lobbied on the board's behalf within influential Afrikaner nationalist circles, and in its first full parliamentary session after occupying power, the NP passed the Work Colonies Act of 1949. The national grid of work colonies as para-penal institutions for white men expanded under Cronjé's watch, and Cronjé's role in the development of these colonies is discussed later in this volume. For now, it will suffice to note that during the 1950s, the work colonies provided Geoffrey Cronjé with a laboratory for social engineering, but that his experiments were unsuccessful. This failure is significant, not only for navigating the directions of Cronjé's career, but also for developing a more nuanced understanding of the evolving ways that whites, especially working-class whites, the unemployed, and those who, at various times, were considered misfits, featured in the imagination of the apartheid state.

The work colonies consumed substantial human and financial resources, yet the number of those men formally committed was never more than about 0.07 percent of the white population. Cronjé's marked lack of success in rehabilitating men detained in the work colonies as well as grumbles from the Treasury about the cost prompted him to invest more energy in other approaches to fighting the fiends of indifference and moral lapse in white society. His deep involvement in the expensive but ineffective work colony administration may have cost him credibility and political capital in sections of the party and state elite. Or perhaps he realized that a lighter hand could yield better results. But as the work colony project began to fray—as we shall see, long before the colonies were formally abolished—Cronjé had begun to orientate himself away from the hands-on business of directing large and cumbersome institutions of state, tasks he had assumed in his capacity as the heavily-involved chairman of the Work Colonies' Advisory Board. He now took on roles that drew more explicitly on his expert scientific knowledge. In other words, he repositioned himself away from the pace, tedium, and frustration of bureaucratic work to becoming an expert. This work was wholly suited to his scholarly temperament. Cronjé also shifted his attention to larger swaths of society, and henceforth concentrated on whites more generally. He was no longer as concerned with the challenges of rehabilitating individual deviants, but with the signs of deviance among whites more generally. In a sense this shift represented a return to the claims he had made in his earlier writing about rooting out indifference and exposing the *insluiper*.

While the failure of the work colonies likely influenced Cronjé's approach, his growing preference for welfare and medical approaches over punitive ones was also no doubt spurred by changes to the class structure of white society, particularly among Afrikaans speakers. For much of the century, poor whites were considered a problem and seen as deserving of punishment when they failed to respond favorably to coercive types of so-called improvement imposed upon them. By the 1950s, however, destitution among whites was a thing of the past. As O'Meara, Davies, and others have shown, the state had aggressively advanced the interests of white workers, with Afrikaans-speaking males the major beneficiaries of expansion in the public service and parastatals, and job regrading in both.[40] Penal confinement of the sort represented by work colonies was no longer a suitable technique for the management of a society that was becoming more widely middle-class. A more appropriate approach included methods that would not disrupt the fiction of "respectability" nor the still tenuous trajectory of upward social mobility. This approach required a basic legal fence against race mixing, which was provided by one of the cornerstones of the nascent policy framework for apartheid, the 1949 Mixed Marriages Act, a piece of legislation which disallowed marriages between white people and people of other race groups. The 1950 Immorality Amendment Act, which extended the provisions of the 1927 Act to prohibit not only sexual intercourse but "immoral or indecent acts" between whites and anyone not white, was also significant in this respect. Moreover, the threat of penal sanction never entirely disappeared, and this continued threat represented a nascent style of governance for the management of whites that spread to other domains of their lives.

During the 1950s, Cronjé was involved in several state commissions. Adam Ashforth has written on ways that commissions of inquiry produced legitimating ideologies for the apartheid state, and Cronjé's career sheds additional light on the workings of such commissions in apartheid society, including the ways that they shaped the everyday worlds of whites.[41] Cronjé was a strong and domineering character, he had the status of being European-trained, and he was professor of sociology (and later dean of the Faculty of Humanities) at the University of Pretoria. As the decade progressed, he operated not so much as a university-bound scholar or even a bureaucrat, but as the quintessential gray eminence. This type of protagonist emerged in the intellectual climate of Afrikaner nationalism under apartheid, as social scientific data and analyses took on greater impact in policymaking. Others included Piet Cillié, who became editor of the influential Cape Nationalist mouthpiece, *Die Burger,* in 1954; W. M. M. "Max" Eiselen, a former professor of anthropology at the University of Pretoria who was appointed secretary of Bantu administration in 1951; and Piet Meyer, who assumed chairmanship of the board of the South African Broadcasting Commission (SABC) in 1959.

Cronjé was able to generate concern across bureaucracies and among powerful political brokers around a range of social welfare issues in white society, including drinking. These anxieties were manifest in a cascading series of commissions and committees that collectively generated a degree of consensus around what constituted "problems" among whites, as well as new approaches to questions of welfare, moral discipline, and rehabilitation. A few examples that highlight Cronjé's areas of interest and his style of operation will suffice. In August 1951, on the urging of the Nasionale Raad van Welsynsorganisasies (National Council of Welfare Organizations), the Federale Vroueraad (Federal Women's Council), the Federale Armesorgraad (Federal Council for Indigent Relief), and the four Dutch Reformed Churches, the minister of health and social welfare, Karl Bremer, convened a commission of inquiry into white family life.[42] Cronjé was appointed chair, and the commission was run from the Letteregebou, the humanities building at the University of Pretoria. R. McLachlan, the commission's full-time secretary, was a former student of Cronjé's with an interest in indigent white families and sheltered employment.[43] Cronjé was included specifically for his scientific expertise, and presumably it was his background and reputation as a sociologist that positioned him to play a substantial role in identifying themes for investigation by the commission.[44] A memorandum explaining the commission's purpose began by linking the importance of white family life in South Africa to the values and traditions of "western civilization." It then identified a catalog of threats to white family life—not surprisingly, alcohol featured prominently. At once patriarchal and particularly representative of Afrikaner nationalist concerns, the list developed by Cronjé also included women's work, divorce, unmarried mothers, juvenile delinquency, children in institutions, and prostitution, with an accent on how these were rooted in alcoholism and a lack of religious observance.[45]

Cronjé also chaired a National Committee on Alcoholism convened in 1951, as well as a Committee into the Funding of Voluntary Welfare Organisations, which sat between 1951 and 1953.[46] In one of those rare unguarded insights so useful to the historian, perhaps emphasized by Cronjé himself, or maybe recorded by an overzealous secretary, Cronjé bequeathed to the archive an insight into his modus operandi. Speaking first at a meeting of the committee in February 1952, he insisted that the minister should be "persuaded," and that he, Cronjé, was the right person to convey a summarized version of the meeting's deliberations and recommendations to the minister.[47] Evidently, he was confident in his role as a broker of behind-the-scenes influence.

During the 1950s and beyond, Cronjé acquired a measure of infamy among opponents of apartheid, ranging from genteel liberals to banned communists and African nationalists, as the most influential architect of South Africa's censorship regime. Censorship was not in itself a product of the apartheid state, as it had been a feature in twentieth-century South Africa since the early years of Union, when the 1913 Customs Management Act prohibited the importation of "articles which are indecent, obscene or objectionable." It empowered the minister of the interior as the final arbiter. In 1931, the Entertainment (Censorship) Act enabled the establishment of the first board of state censors in the Union, which concentrated initially on film and pictures, but expanded in 1934 to include books and periodicals.[48]

Since the 1930s, the Dutch Reformed churches had been concerned about the circulation of pornography among Afrikaners. This concern boiled over with a 1953 court case relating to several articles on prostitution that appeared in Afrikaans magazines and aggravated concerns about licentiousness among whites, particularly Afrikaners.[49] Prime Minister Malan was sympathetic to the clerics' concerns, and this episode provided a spur for him to act. He appointed the formidable Geoffrey Cronjé to convene and chair an investigation, known formally as the Commission of Inquiry into Undesirable Publications (or more informally as the Cronjé Commission), into the most effective ways of combatting the evils of indecent, offensive, or harmful literature. The Cronjé Commission sat between 1954 and 1959, and as Cronjé developed its terms, these included the book trade, reading in schools and the family, the promotion of good literature, and reading matter for the newly and semi-literate.[50] The commission made sweeping recommendations to tighten existing censorship regulations, including a system of prepublication censorship, formal licensing of all publishers, printers, booksellers, and periodicals, and the establishment of a national enforcement agency (known later as the Publications Control Board) to review all local and imported books, magazines, and periodicals.[51] Archie Dick points out that the ways that the Cronjé Commission, and subsequently the Publications Control Board, decided what—besides pornography—was "objectionable" or "undesirable" was not based on sophisticated moral reasoning but rather on pragmatic political considerations.

Macdonald argues that the new system of censorship, inaugurated by the Cronjé Commission, was part of a broader state initiative to seize control of the public space. It was designed to curtail flows of information, to prevent so-called degeneration among whites, and, on the other side, to manage "Bantu" perceptions of "European" culture and block the circulation of politically subversive material. This system coincided with an inquiry into the press that ran for thirteen years from 1950, while also following a battery of legislation used to silence political challenges to apartheid, most notoriously the 1950 Suppression of Communism Act.[52]

In 1959, more than 250 titles had been listed as "undesirable" in the Government Gazette. Censors' reports are generally elusive; in most cases, we are obliged to rely on databases generated by individuals and institutions with an interest in censorship.[53] The list of "undesirable" books included seemingly innocuous western novels like Nelson Nye's *A Bullet for Billy the Kid*, banned on "moral grounds." More understandable additions to the list were Julian Strange's *Adventures in Nakedness* and Lila van Saher's *Adam and Two Eves*, both also banned on "moral grounds." Occasionally, censor reports are available, and these reveal some of the political and moral threats that perturbed the censorship bureaucracy. *A World of Strangers*, written by Nadine Gordimer, a South African author who would go on to become a Nobel laureate in 1991, was banned in 1958. The key protagonists in the novel were Toby Hood, a young Englishman who lived in apartheid-era Johannesburg, and his friend Stephen Sithole, a Black man. The censors acknowledged that the novel avoided "deliberate protest and propaganda" and that it contained no "objectionable sex" (helpfully defined on the official form which they were required to fill in as "intimate descriptions of women's bodies, passionate lovemaking, sexual relations and loose morals"). However, its account of "intermingling" and a "suggestion of mixed sexual relations" painted a "picture of an irrationality in racial isolation." The censors considered the book as "likely to arouse feelings of hatred between the black and white races," and on these grounds, it was banned.[54]

For our case, the significance of the Cronjé Commission goes beyond its role as yet another sentinel for apartheid. It bore the imprint of Cronjé's career as a sociologist vexed by the problems of poor whiteism and the challenges poor whites posed to the Afrikaner *volk* and whites in general, his belief in social engineering, and ultimately his anxieties—what Coetzee calls his "madness." Cronjé's university and bureaucratic career revolved around whites—poor whites, working-class whites, the unemployed, juvenile delinquents, and the criminally inclined. These whites, along with Jews, sailors, and "mentally retarded" whites, were all potential *insluipers*, "low grade people" who had "degenerated" in "morality, self-respect and racial pride."[55] His role in elaborating a draconian framework for censorship provided Cronjé with a bureaucratic and political platform from which to propose centralized statutory censorship as a safeguard against the dangerous "desire" he had identified earlier.

In a sense, the inner logic of Cronjé's apartheid thinking described by Coetzee—that whiff of hysteria, paranoia, and panic—lay at the heart of those apartheid-era projects bearing Cronjé's stamp. Certainly, the regime of censorship that Cronjé designed did block the flow of information and reduced the reading commons available to all South Africans.

This regime of censorship also had implications for our arguments about accommodation among whites in apartheid society. As the columns of *Vrou en Moeder*, the periodical of the nationalist Suid-Afrikaanse Vrouefederasie (SAVF), would testify, Cronjé's censoring was embraced eagerly by sections of the Afrikaner nationalist establishment who had long bemoaned how books, magazines, and newspapers brought both permissiveness and political danger. As Archie Dick tells us, public librarians in Johannesburg, Cape Town, and Durban—none of these cities Afrikaner nationalist strongholds—destroyed books that they feared might run afoul of the censors. In Johannesburg and Cape Town, librarians, some of them "liberals," oversaw the burning of books, and in Durban, books were torn up and routinely pulped. This preemptive censorship was surely one of the many low points in the history of whites in apartheid society, and we shall return to this point more substantially in the conclusion.

Dramatology and a Return to the Academy

In the early 1960s, currents that Cronjé had identified in the course of his work as a public intellectual, while undertaking commissioned, applied research, prompted a final realignment in his career. In a sense, this shift witnessed a series of returns to places that had long held Cronjé's passions, namely, the theater and the university. From the mid-1960s, he committed much of his professional life to establishing "Dramatology" as a new academic department at the University of Pretoria, applying his customary single-mindedness and showing a willingness to exploit the influence and connections available to him.

White society, especially the Afrikaans-speaking section of it, became more affluent during the 1950s, not least because of the massive expansion of public service employment, the growth of parastatals, and attacks on African wages. The upward social mobility of whites, and the ways that they connected with the fast-paced world of western popular culture, brought tensions to the Afrikaner nationalist hopes for Afrikaner cultural revival. The more that Afrikaners, notably the young, were exposed to the influences of rock and roll, western youth fashion, and the moods of western youth rebellion that were manifested locally in the upsurge of ducktailism in parts of urban South Africa, the less inclined they were to the idea of the *volk* and its sacred mission enunciated by Cronjé and other ideologues of the Afrikaner civil religion.

In May 1964, Cronjé and Jannie Pieterse, who by that stage was also a professor in the sociology department at Pretoria, were approached by the Nasionale Jeugraad (National Youth Council) of the FAK to convene a commission into the "problems of white youth in South Africa"—known more informally as the Jeugondersoek Kommissie (Commission of Inquiry into the Youth).[56] Around this time, Cronjé started marshaling arguments and allies for the establishment of a drama department at his university. Since his youth, Cronjé had maintained an interest in drama—his master's thesis in classics at Stellenbosch examined the use of dramatic techniques in Greek tragedy. He had spent many years since his return to South Africa in 1934 actively involved in promoting and administering Afrikaans drama and was eventually made an honorary life member of the Pretoria Kunsvereniging (Pretoria Association for the Arts, another FAK affiliate).[57] While it would be tempting to correlate the alarm with which he and Pieterse viewed white youth and his energies to institute a drama department at UP, the archival record is seldom that explicit or convenient. But we can speculate.

Attempts to establish a drama department at UP were not new. As early as 1949, a Transvaal Provincial Commission of Enquiry—chaired, unsurprisingly, by Cronjé—put out feelers to the university. Tasked to investigate the future of the Pretoria Kunssentrum (Art Center), the commission recommended that its activities be broadened from performances and productions to include training and that it should be incorporated as part of the university. The Transvaal Provincial Administration, it baldly stated, had no money to maintain or expand the Kunssentrum.[58] Not much came of this recommendation, and in 1954 there was another proposal, put this time by the Nasionale Toneelorganisasie (NTO)—Cronjé was a member of its executive committee.[59] The NTO proposed that UP take on responsibility for education and training in the dramatic arts, while the NTO would manage professional Afrikaans theater in Pretoria. Again, the university did not seriously entertain this proposition. Around the same time that Cronjé began his work on the Jeugondersoek Kommissie, the Transvaalse Raad vir Uitvoerende Kunste (TRUK), which was the successor to the NTO and predictably included Cronjé on its executive committee, again approached the University of Pretoria with a request that it establish a drama department.[60] Once more the rector declined, pointing out that the university would not be able to claim state subsidy for a drama department. Indicative of the priority that TRUK gave to the establishment of a drama department, and suggestive too of Cronjé's influence and the hopes he assigned to the inauguration of drama in the stable environment of the university, the TRUK board then offered to subsidize the creation of a drama department by paying the salaries of a professor and a senior lecturer.[61]

In 1964, Cronjé prepared a submission on the structure, orientation, and operation of the new department, which was accepted by the university council. It also approved the acceptance of students, to commence from January 1965.[62] In his proposal, Cronjé argued that the name of the department should be "dramatology," a European subfield of drama studies that was populated at that time by historians, sociologists, and theorists.[63] From this intellectual foundation, he wrote that the new department would prioritize "theoretical" training, while an Institute for Speech and Drama would present more practical courses and stage productions. He managed to get Anna Neethling-Pohl, the doyenne of Afrikaans radio drama and theater, appointed to a post that was upgraded from senior lecturer to professor.[64]

Cronjé maintained an evolving interest in managing populations, and he was alarmed at the ill winds of defiant youth culture blowing into apartheid South Africa from western Europe and North America. These sociological and political concerns, as well as the structure of the department, with its foundation in "theoretical" training and its proposed emphasis on radio drama, invite us to hypothesize that Cronjé would be responsible for teaching history and theory; that the program would produce a pipeline of graduates immersed in the ideologies and intellectual orientation of Afrikaner nationalism; and that they would be equipped with the technical skills to participate in radio drama. In the absence of television and the rising importance of sound cultures over reading, radio was potentially a potent medium to communicate with and educate whites. Cronjé's second inaugural lecture, delivered in September 1967, points to his pedagogical hopes for the department: "Drama as a view of life."[65] Clearly, he was invested in the idea that drama could provide a kind of cultural and ideological template for white everyday life.

The dramatology department opened in January 1965 with Cronjé as head, a post he took on in addition to retaining the chair of the sociology department. At the end of 1966, he relinquished his position in sociology and moved full-time to the new department.[66] Initially he hoped that the department would attract a group of about twenty students, and he must have been delighted when a cohort of forty-five registered in 1965.[67] However, if he did indeed harbor long-term plans for the department as a place to nurture Afrikaner nationalist actors and producers under his ideological tutelage and Anna Neethling-Pohl's practical guidance, these aspirations soon withered. He and Neethling-Pohl had a falling-out, and with her experience and stature in the field of radio drama, it was she, rather than Cronjé, who became the driving force behind the department. For the first time in more than thirty years at the University of Pretoria, Cronjé was forced into a lesser—and largely symbolic—role. He assumed increasingly eccentric behavior, cultivating a dramatic, Sartre-like look, with a beret and a cigarette holder, appropriating the appearance of a hip, beatnik, sixties intellectual.[68] During these years, he was still viewed with awe at the University of Pretoria, especially by younger faculty who saw him even in the late 1960s as the formidable, aloof "Hollander." Cronjé was a creature of the Verwoerd technocratic ascendancy in Afrikaner nationalist circles, but by the late 1960s, his star had waned. After Verwoerd's assassination in 1966, the NP, now headed by "the real hard man" in the government, former Minister of Justice and Police John Vorster, was subject to new securocratic moods. Cronjé's thinking had become outmoded.

Cronjé and Social Histories of Whites

Considering the career of an individual like Geoffrey Cronjé adds ethnographic texture to the ways that intellectuals like him engineered whiteness, the global currents as well as the local ideological traditions they drew on, and the pathways of power and influence they trod. It also gives insight into the ways that ideology acquired a scientific respectability and became real for white people living in early apartheid society: kernels of a subaltern biography. Although Cronjé was not representative of all—or even the majority of—apartheid intellectuals or bureaucrats, his history does reveal something of the operation of a state under circumstances of big government. His history also testifies to the role of the intellectual—and the expert—during specific phases of apartheid. His emphasis on classification through the methods of sociology helped him to define those beyond the pale of the "normal"—the *insluiper*, the miscreant, the neglectful father, the youth who had forsaken their *volk*. Of course, his definitions and the ways that he targeted sectors of white society were shaped not only by sociological data, however dubious, but also by something more personal: his apparent dislike for and distrust of whites from the working classes, the unemployed, those who survived on apartheid social subsidies. Not only were they potential blood traitors, but they were also perpetual moral transgressors, and they could be found not only among Afrikaners, but among all whites. Moving commandingly between the university, the Afrikaans-speaking private sector, *volk* organizations, and the state, he used these ideologies to transform and organize the everyday world of white people, by describing multiple conditions of deviance and thus what it meant to be "normal," "respectable," and "decent." Cronjé's belief in social engineering, his very vigor, and the fields of influence available to him during the first decade of apartheid history, created the conditions for state intervention in the ways that whites conducted their everyday lives. This involved not only disciplining individuals—like those sent to the work colonies—but also gathering data to manage populations and preempting "dangers" like the rise of popular cultures that respected neither the *volk,* nor its borders, nor its historic mission.

Cronjé combined fairly ill-informed, inchoate ideologies about the state and the nation, moral codes about the family, and schemes of knowledge from sociology, social work, and eugenics with elements of "insanity"—or perhaps more charitably, great zeal and ambition. From this starting point he was also able to introduce methods of reform, most notably the new, apartheid-era work colonies. Just as he concentrated on abnormal behavior, *insluipers,* and their potential to erode the moral and biological foundations of white society, other whites, who could hardly be characterized as "deviant," were also subject to systems of regulation and discipline. These systems extended to their workplaces, their homes, and the places where they took their leisure, all of which locked them into the logics and ideologies of the apartheid state. As we shall see in the next two chapters, Cronjé's misgivings about the stability and reliability of working whites found an echo among managers of the public service. Some of his ideologies and methods percolated through to how the public service was organized, how public servants were managed, and how gender relations among whites were regulated in the public service.

WORK AND IDEOLOGY IN THE APARTHEID PUBLIC SERVICE

5

Big Government in the 1930s and 1940s

From the 1930s, well before the advent of apartheid, ideology within the ruling United Party (UP) aligned itself with a global trend toward a large and interventionist central state, but the concomitant expansion of the bureaucracy for an "administrative" state lagged.[1] This situation was exacerbated during the Second World War as many public servants took leave from their posts or resigned to volunteer in the Union Defence Force. The public service emerged from the war years in some disarray. Not only were staff stretched thin, but morale was low. Salaries paid to top officials were increased substantially in 1942, yet for those outside of the service's senior ranks, salaries, cost of living allowances, and benefits stagnated due to the prioritization of the war effort.[2] Dissatisfaction with conditions of service rose and was combined with a sense of marginalization felt by those mainly Afrikaans speakers who had opposed South Africa's participation in the war. Testifying before a commission, some of these individuals described how they had suffered frequent denigration that not only took on an ethnic hue, but also questioned their status as whites and thus deserving of privileged status in segregated society. At work, these "Dutch bastards," as they were often called, were ordered to "speak white" (in other words, not Afrikaans).[3] By mid-1946 there were signs of discontent, and disgruntled public servants were reportedly meeting in towns and cities across the Union. In Pretoria, for instance, "thousands" crowded the City Hall where they resolved "with deep regret" to embark on a go-slow, or work slowdown.[4] Interdepartmental differences in conditions of service added to a general and widespread dissatisfaction among public servants, particularly those in the non-managerial echelons.[5]

In response to the crises of morale in the public service, Minister of the Interior C. F. Clarkson announced in May 1946 a salary increase of half an increment for all public servants, along with certain "special allowances."[6]

Clarkson's concession generated little enthusiasm, and during that year, an estimated 250 to 300 white public servants resigned each month.[7] General Secretary of the Public Servants' Association J. H. Basson noted caustically that few except the lowest-graded officers qualified for Clarkson's "special allowances" and that "the allowance . . . is purely and simply a recruiting measure to make the public service more attractive to new entrants."[8] Resignations continued unabated into the next year, and Basson took to print to explain that salaries were not the only reason for staff losses. Other causes included the absence of medical benefits and housing schemes, which added to the burdens of a high cost of living, especially on the Witwatersrand, and the restriction on holiday travel concessions.[9] Salaries in other parts of the region were higher than those in the Union, and Southern Rhodesia in particular became a popular destination for teachers, nurses, and those with technical skills like agricultural scientists.[10]

After the NP's poll victory in 1948, representatives of its various ideological groups ranging from theologically inclined Afrikaner nationalists to secular corporativists like Cronjé shared the UP's preference for big government. But despite tendencies in the NP toward a more expansive public service—albeit of a different hue than that which developed under the UP government—the rate at which the public service establishment expanded slowed in the year after the NP occupied office. In 1948, the number of whites employed in the public service (excluding the military and the police) grew by only 6,652 to 105,051, compared to a growth of 9,566 the previous year.[11]

Managing White Public Servants

Histories of whites in the government service, the *staatsdiens* (public service), highlight ironies and tensions unleashed by the NP's very success in providing steady and well-paid work for whites.[12] In the *staatsdiens*, whites, especially men, occupied a privileged position. This was the case across the economy, but I have focused on the *staatsdiens* for several reasons. First, the early years of apartheid witnessed a considerable expansion of the public service, as well as of the military and the police. This growth in the bureaucracy and the extension of the state's repressive capacity was necessary for the implementation of apartheid. It also increased the number of jobs available to whites: between 1946 and 1961, the number of white public servants, the majority of whom were Afrikaners, increased by a staggering 98.5 percent. By the late 1950s, the public service employed around 30 percent of all working whites, making it the largest single employer of this group; as it expanded through the late 1940s and 1950s, it was rapidly Afrikanerized. Second, under the NP, the public service was one of the major institutions whereby whites participated in the production of apartheid society. Consideration of the racialized and gendered public service labor processes, the ideologies, regulations, and routines that shaped it, and the ways that white public servants responded, sheds light on the core questions around accommodation that shape this book.

In understanding the development of the *staatsdiens*, it is important to emphasize the role of the Public Service Commission (PSC), a permanent commission whose major formal responsibility lay in recommending public service appointments and promotions. In his work on the NP during its decades in power, Dan O'Meara writes that the *staatsdiens* under apartheid broke with the Westminster-derived culture of public service neutrality, and the "mythology of the state-as-arbiter." The NP, O'Meara asserts, pushed a new ethos on the public service based on its understanding of the state as an instrument to serve the *volk*, which was itself embodied in the *volksfront* of the NP.[13] His claim will be assessed in the course of this chapter, especially the ways in which the *staatsdiens* as a whole departed from British public service traditions. In opening up employment for whites, the *staatsdiens* drifted away from the Westminster style of public administration in other ways, too, as it evolved from an institution built on a relatively small corps of professional civil servants (the archetype was the native commissioner—a category of work eliminated under apartheid) to one notable for its large number of fairly junior employees. The expansion of the public service, the ideal that it should be close to the government of the day—even if this was initially an aspiration rather than reality, and one that was contested from some quarters of the service—and new expectations of loyalty imposed on public servants all raise other issues. These issues relate to broader historical questions of social discipline and attempts by states to minimize dissonance.[14] Notably, they oblige us to ask whether, and in what ways, the public service hemmed whites into the apartheid state and apartheid society, and to what extent public service created a favorable environment to "educate" whites (mainly but not exclusively Afrikaners) in particular styles and moral regimes of whiteness.

We must, however, be aware of the ways that history, especially social history, counters too literal a rendering of the formulation that the public service bound and socialized white public servants in particular ways. Elucidating some of the terms of these *beamptes*' (officials') incorporation into both the *staatsdiens* and apartheid society acknowledges the contingent nature and messiness of this historical process. As we shall see, white public servants were seldom as docile, obedient, or loyal as their supervisors would have liked. For instance, much like employees in any large organization, they defied regulations. They made up their own work rules, skipped work, and concocted schemes for personal enrichment. Sometimes they challenged the very ideological precepts of both the public service and apartheid society. These officials did enjoy various forms of agency, though of course there were limits. Occasions when public servants stepped out of the roles assigned to them by ideology and bureaucratic structure, when they disrupted familiar ideas, are moments when *radical* history is possible. As Geoff Eley writes: "Depending on how the story is told the past provides potential sites for opposition. It allows us to say 'it didn't have to happen like this. And in future it could be different.'"[15]

Appreciating the complexity that reigns between the Public Service Commission's (PSC's) intent and white public servants' agency is important. This complexity presents an antidote to the PSC's image of its own accomplishment, as evident in its annual reports. But it does something more, demonstrating, on the one hand, the limits of the PSC and the public service labor process in molding whites, and on the other, white public servants' capacity for agency. In so doing it eliminates any historical or moral assertion that whites—in this case, white public servants—were somehow little more than ciphers for ideologies imposed from above, or that they knew nothing of the discrimination, exclusion, and repression at the heart of apartheid. This complexity does moreover invite us to explore how these working white people went about negotiating and stating what it meant to be a white person in early apartheid society.

Political Transition and the Public Service

Initially, at least, the institution of a new government was not matched by wholesale changes to the upper ranks of the bureaucracy: during the NP's first year in office, only three new heads of department were appointed.[16] Nor was there much sign yet of the new party-partisan ethos for the public service described by O'Meara. Perhaps the most obvious manifestation in the public service of the new political climate was the alacrity with which the government responded to complaints from public servants who claimed to have suffered prejudice during the war as a result of their political opposition to the war effort. In August 1948, A. E. Gerhart, a Pretoria architect and public servant, appealed to Dr. T. E. Donges, the minister of the interior, for approval to perform private work in addition to his official duties. During the war he had been dismissed from the public service and then interned as a Nazi supporter. Gerhart insisted that regular salary progression could not compensate for his loss of income, and he thus begged for permission (also on behalf of other ex-internees and, disingenuously, ex-servicemen) to "attend to other business for remuneration provided that such business does not collide with, or involve any government time." He ended his letter with a well-aimed dart at a government whose route to power was via a minority vote, reminding Donges that "such permission would evoke a deep gratitude in many thousands towards our Government."[17] Donges and his ministerial peers must have received other similar appeals, because on August 15, 1948, he convened a small committee with wide powers to investigate issues of wartime discrimination around appointments, promotions, and dismissals among staff in the Department of Posts and Telegraphs. More particularly, the committee was to consider whether such discrimination was based on political considerations—"the assumption that civil servants were not in agreement with the war policy, or their unwillingness to enlist, or participate actively in the war effort."[18]

After investigating 102 cases over a period of a year, the committee confirmed only twenty-eight instances of "discrimination." While many had received insults and slurs for their opposition to the war, the real problem, the committee discovered, was not so much wartime discrimination as the challenge of reincorporating returned war veterans and "plac[ing] each man on the list for which he would probably have reached had he not gone on active service."[19] Although the evidence for discrimination was tenuous, the minister of posts and telegraphs nevertheless assured the postmaster general in 1950 that he would introduce legislation to address the situation of ex-internees.[20] But the findings of the committee seemed to have dampened the government's appetite to expend political capital on behalf of ex-detainees and other public servants who had opposed the war, for, despite the minister's promise, legislation favoring them was never introduced. Further, beyond the short-lived interest in the injustices that anti-war public servants claimed to have suffered, there was little sign of any systematic party political intervention in appointments or promotions, especially in the lower ranks.

Beyond the installation of a new guard in the Union Buildings, the key to understanding the apartheid-era modernization and expansion of the public service is the role of the five-man PSC (Public Service Commission). This was a five-man permanent commission whose major responsibility lay in recommending public service appointments and promotions. The PSC predated the advent of the NP government, but during the Union's earlier decades, where department heads were immensely powerful and traditionally resisted any interference in the affairs of their department under the Westminster style of civil service described by O'Meara, its influence was limited. As the public service expanded in the ideological climate of Afrikaner nationalism, which favored *volkseenheid* (national unity) and new types of loyalty and institutional cohesion, the PSC evolved into a kind of supra-bureaucracy.

In the immediate aftermath of the political transition in 1948 that swept the NP to power, there emerged some strain between the executive and the PSC focusing on the role of the bureaucracy and its relationship to the government. Much as O'Meara claims, the former envisaged a public service that would support its political ambitions and its hope to entrench Afrikaner nationalism as the dominant ethos for (white) public life in South Africa. PSC commissioners, all veterans of the service and schooled in the tradition of public service "neutrality," favored a public service corps that was less susceptible to executive influence. In its second year of office, the government tried to make a raft of new senior appointments, recommending seven new heads of department, up from three the previous year. The government did have the prerogative of identifying its preferred candidates for posts as department heads, but by custom was expected to work closely with the PSC to ensure that the new appointments did not curtail the career prospects of senior officials already in the service. But the large number of appointments in 1949 suggests that they were not in the usual order of retirements, promotions, or departmental transfers, and that Ministers were trying to use their discretionary powers liberally to bring the public service closer to the government. The PSC did not favor overt party political meddling in public service appointments and promotions, and it was lukewarm to these candidates. In particular, it raised its institutional eyebrows at the appointment of Werner Eiselen (an anthropologist and, like Cronjé, an epitome of the apartheid intellectual/bureaucrat) as secretary for native affairs. The PSC's opposition was not on ideological grounds, but procedural: Eiselen was appointed from outside of the public service. In what developed as something of a turf battle, the PSC asked archly whether the post could not be "satisfactorily filled by the transfer or promotion thereto of an officer already in the Public Service," and refused to endorse the minister's recommendation.[21] In this instance the responsible minister, E. G. Jansen, approached the governor general, who overrode the PSC's objection.[22] The PSC's difference with the minister over Werner Eiselen does however reveal its relationship with the executive, how it resisted strong-arm political pressure, and how it insisted upon working within regulations and established procedure. The well-publicized sidelining of Major-General Evered Poole, next in line to become chief of the general staff, and the resignation of W. Marshall Clark as general manager of the South African Railways in 1949, generated myth among non-nationalist whites, especially English speakers, that the NP purged its political opponents from the public service. However, there is little evidence that the PSC choreographed a systematic eviction of non-nationalists from the senior ranks of the public service.[23]

Besides the heads of department, one notable exception to the general rule of executive non-interference came with the appointment in 1950 of a new secretary to the PSC. Described by the PSC as "one of the most important key positions in the Public Service," this post became vacant after the transfer of the incumbent.[24] The minister of the interior recommended one D. J. C. Steyn, at that time employed in the Department of Justice. However, the commission, ever wary of executive intervention, rejected his nomination. The new secretary of the PSC, the commissioners insisted, needed to command the kind of knowledge and experience that could only be acquired through years of "close contact with all departments and administrations," implying that Steyn lacked such gravitas.[25] As in the case of Werner Eiselen, the minister appealed successfully to the governor general.[26] While it is difficult to determine whether Steyn's "political" appointment, albeit from within the body of the public service, brought the PSC manifestly closer to the executive of government, it did chip away at the Westminster-style tenet that had hitherto governed the relationship between the executive and its administration. If the executive generally acknowledged the role of the PSC and accepted the principle of no—or at least, limited—party political interference in appointments, this was not always the case among members of Parliament (MPs). Through the 1950s, the archive is scattered with examples of parliamentarians who, dependent on the goodwill of local NP committees for reelection, wrote to Ministers begging favors for their constituents. In most cases, their requests were turned down.[27]

Afrikanerizing the Public Service

Recruiting for the *staatsdiens* as a whole fell to the PSC. Histories of recruitment during the early apartheid years expose some of the ongoing tensions generated between ideological and political pressures from the government and the PSC's more bureaucratic obligations to manage staff and stretch staffing budgets by accelerating the drive for "efficiency." They also yield some insight into the gradual Afrikanerization of the service. Posts for whites in the public service, those sectors of the public service responsible for the daily exercise of government, were characterized by a distinction between policy-making and policy-implementation jobs. The latter were associated with procedural and routine administrative tasks. This structure, which owed its origins to the imperial connection and had been refined in the Indian Civil Service during the early twentieth century, permitted a high degree of centralization.[28] In the apartheid-era *staatsdiens*, this structure was manifest in four basic divisions of work: administrative, or managerial; specialist or technical; clerical (whose staff performed skilled white-collar work with few decision-making responsibilities); and a large general division where workers were assigned to a range of low-level manual, administrative, technical, and, sometimes, supervisory tasks.[29]

Anticipating that the heaviest demand for public service labor would be in the general bands, in 1949 the PSC initiated "special measures"—circulars and brochures sent to all magistrates and school principals—to solicit applications for these posts. While the PSC persistently distanced itself from cruder forms of intervention and politicization, the focus of recruiting drives for white general staff shifted to the *platteland*, which was the heartland of the NP's support. Although figures for the previous year are not available, the PSC report for 1948 found it noteworthy that of 2,004 applications for entry positions, 73 percent were from smaller centers and country districts.[30] Moreover, the report revealed the possibility of more subtle forms of patronage when it declared that the recruiting drive received the best results when local officials made personal contact with "youths and girls in their final year at school," along with their parents and teachers.[31]

Overall, however, the results were disappointing, especially with respect to male applicants.[32] In its attempts to increase the pool of recruits into the general division, the PSC was forced to tamper with existing age limits for entry into the service. Under the 1923 Public Service Act, male candidates appointed to the clerical division had to be between the ages of sixteen and twenty-five, while females between eighteen and twenty-five were eligible for consideration.[33] The PSC and the minister of the interior agreed to a suspension of the regulations to allow temporary appointments to the general division of men under fifty years of age. Notably though, these regulations were not altered for women—testament to the gendered ways that both the PSC and the minister imagined the public service. The concessions that the PSC was forced to make do moreover testify to an element of desperation.

During the first years of the NP administration, the PSC also tried to recruit staff into the more prestigious and well-paid clerical bands. Reflecting numerous European and colonial legacies, the most common route to entry into the clerical grades of the public service was via the Public Service Competitive Examination (although candidates were also admitted under a system of local selection, and some, like ex-military officers and those holding university degrees, were exempted).[34] In 1949, 1,864 men and women passed the exam, but to the consternation of the Commission, 1,495 candidates failed to reply to letters informing them of their appointments.[35] Responding in much the same way as the Indian Civil Service did when it was faced with a shortage of prospective candidates for the upper divisions of the service, the PSC decided in 1950 to do away altogether with the exam.[36] Instead it would concentrate on recruiting a bigger pool of white school-leavers for entry into the general division, and from this group it would identify candidates for future promotion into the clerical bands. It contacted 5,000 candidates, emphasizing the gross salary they would earn on appointment.[37] These efforts, however, met with little success. More saliently, the PSC's vacillation about where precisely to target its recruiting efforts might also have reflected some uncertainty about the expansion of the public service from a smaller entity, dependent upon a layer of self-consciously professional public servants, to a larger entity structured on centralized authority, hierarchical order, and ultimately the labor of large numbers of relatively junior staff.

Under apartheid, the PSC incorporated women into the *staatsdiens* more comprehensively than before, in both permanent and temporary capacities. This theme will be discussed in greater detail in the next chapter. It is however germane that just as the PSC institutionalized and expanded the permanent employment of women, and made provision for their training and advancement, it envisaged that this influx would occur within the lowest grades of the service—typists and junior clerks in the general division.[38] Revealing the myth among the PSC and the heads of public service departments that women represented short-term and expedient help in the *staatsdiens*, the number of women on the permanent roster remained consistently lower than those deemed "temporary." Nevertheless, the trend toward the permanent employment of women was a cause of concern to the PSC, as by 1958 it insisted that departments not only report on the number of women on their respective establishments, but also explain the reason for any increases.[39]

Complaints about the paucity and quality of white applicants was a recurring theme in the PSC's annual reports for much of the decade as it repeatedly noted that the number of applications for employment fell far short of requirements.[40] In its own analysis, the PSC attributed the critical shortfall of applicants to "competition for the services of a work seeker."[41] The conditions of competition noticed by the PSC were rooted in rapid growth of the national economy after the Second World War. After the War, new goldfields were opened up in the Orange Free State, as well as to the east and west of the original Witwatersrand goldfields. Wartime import substitution had provided a spur to manufacturing, and there was substantial expansion in the metals, engineering, textiles, and chemical industries. With slight setbacks in 1948, 1952, and 1958, net national income was on an upward trend.[42] In an economy with a racially segregated labor force, this growth spread the available pool of white recruits thin across the whole economy. Given the buoyant labor market for whites, the public service was poorly positioned to attract those who were able to access more lucrative private sector employment. The class and social stratification of South African society, and respective patterns of class formation among Afrikaans- and English-speaking whites, meant that while English speakers were generally better positioned to enter the private sector, the bulk of the new white public servants were Afrikaners.[43] These structural and cultural factors, more than the operation of Tammany Hall-type interventions designed to overcome the stain of exclusion and marginalization inherent in insults like "Dutch bastards," contributed to the Afrikanerization of the public service. The particular histories of recruitment into the public service, overseen by the PSC, coincide with Posel's observation that public servants under apartheid developed into a disrespected stratum of white society. Starting in the 1950s, she reminds us that Van der Merwe jokes became all the rage in white English-speaking society. "Van" was cast as a stupid, boorish, and incompetent public servant; I remember how, in the early 1970s, telling these jokes served to remind other white working-class folk like my family and neighbors that they were better than "them"—public servants and the stereotyped "Van."[44] As noted previously, as a child I was not allowed to play with the "railway children," meaning Afrikaans children. Expansion of the public service during the first decade of apartheid also brought into the fold a greater number of people, including the military and the police. They were already exposed at the town hall and the pulpit to certain ideologies about progress, the *volk, godsdienstigheid* (religious observance), and the races. As discussed below, the structured world of the *staatsdiens* added layers of regulation and methods of discipline to these ideologies, and sometimes modified them.

In the late 1940s and early 1950s, the PSC's recruiting measures were based on posters spelling out the salaries and terms of employment in the public service, as ineffectual as they were unimaginative. The PSC blamed the failure of successive recruiting campaigns on "a great deal of ignorance about the Public Service at universities and schools as well as among members of the general public," yet it persisted with this approach until 1953.[45] In that year it engaged the services of an advertising agency to produce publicity material, extracting from an ever-parsimonious Treasury a sum of £23,500.[46] These posters and other recruiting materials are useful in the ways that it offers a tableau of how the PSC imagined the world of work in the public service.

In 1955, for instance, the PSC published a brochure titled *Successful Careers in Service of Your Country*.[47] Inviting young whites to apply for careers in the public service, the brochure began by elucidating the civic and personal dimensions of work in the service. It was a golden age to serve South Africa, and the public service represented a significant opportunity to serve the country and its people. The service presented young people with the prospect of personal development and "gaining insight into all realms of *die volkslewe*"—the life of the *volk*. In a particularly telling comment about the self-delusion generated from within apartheid society, the brochure asserted that "the public service knows no difference of race, religion, language or political affiliation." In an appeal rather off the mark given the ways the public servants were in fact seen by the white public at large, it declared that the public service was well suited to those who cared for their community and were "willing to accept the status of leadership within the community."[48] The brochure emphasized that hard work could take one to the top of the service. Contesting a popular myth that work in the public service was boring, it admitted that some work *was* indeed routine, just as it was in the private sector. These tasks were however stepping stones on the way to "service of the nation, work that could not possibly be uninteresting"—an observation that demonstrated the author's proximity, ideologically and discursively, to Afrikaner nationalism. The brochure went on to point out that there were wide career choices, educational opportunities, and clear channels for promotion in the public service. Touching on the ideal of stability central to middle-class whiteness that was emerging in the 1950s, it pointed out to potential candidates that their position and future were protected by law, that they could expect regular salary increases, and that they would enjoy assistance with insurance and the purchase of a house. This brochure, which was distributed to all high schools, elicited an "encouraging" number of applications.[49] During the next year the PSC commissioned a film called *John Citizen and the State*, which was shown in cinemas before the main feature film.[50] A year later, it reported that the film had an "excellent reception."[51] Picking up a theme developed in the brochure, the film reminded viewers that the purpose of the state was to provide services, welfare, and management of public affairs for its citizens, while at the same time the citizenry owed loyalty and duty to the state; a neat if rather bland enunciation of Afrikaner nationalist citizenship doctrine. The point that it made was that the public servant was at the center of this relationship. Another glossy brochure distributed by the PSC in 1958 reflected the gathering importance of management in the public service, both as an organizing principle and as a category of work. It also tapped into the surge of upward social mobility of Afrikaners by the late 1950s (a theme to be taken up in chapter 6). Titled *Do you want to become a Manager?*, it sought to demonstrate to applicants that they could work their way from a start in the lower clerical bands through

Figure 5.1 *The Public Servant,* January 1950, published by the Public Servants' Association. It regularly ran features encouraging young whites to pursue careers in the *staatsdiens,* as well as a high volume of advertisements that helped to shape consumption, taste, and aspiration among its readers. Image courtesy of Public Servants Association of South Africa.

the administrative ranks and into management, with the concomitant lure of salaries and status.[52]

Any discussion of recruiting into the apartheid public service and its Afrikanerization, particularly during the first years of the apartheid state, would be incomplete without a discussion of language testing. A belief emerged in white non-nationalist circles that language testing was used as a barrier to preclude non-nationalists (actually, white English speakers) from the public service, the military, and the police. This belief was a companion to the rumor that those lukewarm to the nationalist agenda were purged from senior public service positions. While language had been a thorny issue in public life since at least 1912, with the formation of the original NP, it surfaced in the apartheid public service in about 1949, ironically with the realization that very few of the new clerical recruits drawn from the *platteland*, particularly males, were able to understand English—only 28.3 percent were proficient in the use of both official languages, Afrikaans and English.[53] By the next year the situation had deteriorated further, and only 21.8 percent were "reasonably bilingual."[54] In the way of bureaucracies, a committee was convened to "determine in a standardized manner the standard of bilingualism of public servants."[55] Sitting intermittently from late 1952, the committee finally reported in 1954, announcing that it was ready to introduce language tests, developed on a scientific basis at the University of Pretoria.[56] Further details of the tests and their scientific development have proven elusive in the archive. Records do however indicate that in 1955 and 1956, around 9,000 public servants were tested each year, mainly those coming up for promotion.[57] The PSC report for 1957 commented that of the 8,561 officers tested, 536 failed the English component while 1,210 failed Afrikaans, a difference that might represent greater levels of Afrikaans/English bilingualism among Afrikaans speakers.[58] By 1958, the numbers of those passing the English and Afrikaans sections of the test were more or less even, and by 1959, the number of candidates sitting for the tests had declined, largely due to the fact that most of those obliged by regulation to undertake language testing had by then done so.[59] Interestingly, but not surprisingly given the apartheid project of racial administration, there was another feature of language testing that received little attention at the time. This component, introduced in 1959, entailed the payment of an additional allowance to public servants who learned a "Bantu" language (Northern and Southern Sotho, isiZulu, isiXhosa or SeTswana). The uptake was however limited, and the language examination rigorous: of 280 officials tested in that year, only 109 passed their final assessment.[60]

Language testing was undoubtedly one of the factors that contributed to the Afrikanerization of the public service—along with the perceived political bias of the services, the PSC's recruiting practices, emigration to colonial destinations like Southern Rhodesia, and a general expansion of work opportunities in other sectors of the economy. At a time of new Afrikaner nationalist assertiveness, it is quite easy to see how the idea took root in some white circles that language testing was part of a "smelling out" to cleanse the public service of English speakers.[61] But to understand how the ideologies of Afrikaner nationalism and the cultural knowledge and dispositions of apartheid society were inscribed upon public servants, we must look beyond the contemporary hysteria of non-nationalist whites, agitated by fears of purges in the service and language testing.

The expansion of the public service effectively ended poor whiteism and erased most of the material traces of the Great Depression from white society; gone were the shanties and long lines of men waiting for the meager chance of a day wage from this section of the population. In a sense, the state was the creator of a large clerical white working class. But as we have seen, this growth stimulated other contradictions that emerged periodically in white society, in times of both growth and of war: a shortage of white labor. The PSC was thus obliged to rely substantially on "temporary units," usually pensioners or married women. In 1958, for instance, the public service engaged 2,109 men along with 2,567 temporary male employees; 942 women were taken on permanently, as against 916 temporary appointments.[62] Ironically, just as the PSC's recruiting practices and promotions policies sought to consolidate Afrikaner nationalism's gendered hierarchies, the growth of the public service to meet the needs of the apartheid state obliged it to rely increasingly on the labor of white women.

Scientific Management

In addition to recruiting, the PSC's most significant work during the first decade of apartheid was to reform the organizational sociology of the public service. These changes brought centralization that positioned the public service as the bureaucratic counterpart to ideologies of Afrikaner nationalism and corporativism. In the early twentieth century, American engineer Frederick Taylor's principles of scientific management, with their siren song of efficiency, were implemented in much of the industrial world, including South Africa.[63] By the end of the Second World War the novelty of scientific management had worn off globally, but it received a boost following the success of the quality control movement, pioneered in Japanese industry by W. Edwards Deering. South African industrialists like Albert Wessels, founder of the local affiliate of the Toyota Motor Corporation, were greatly impressed by the possibilities of quality control, and no doubt discussed its merits among peers back home.[64] Internationally, the production benefits of quality control helped to revive the manufacturing sector's interests in scientific management. It was however something of an innovation for the management of bureaucracies that the PSC applied some of the principles of quality control to the reorganization of the *staatsdiens*.

Scientific management was imported to the public service piecemeal, and in rather unconventional ways, beginning not with the usual organizational chart and description of positions, but with the introduction of new techniques for reporting on staff performance and systems for merit assessment. This approach might have reflected not only the current popularity of quality control but also contrary demands on the PSC: just as its commissioners and technocrats were developing strategies to implement scientific management, they were also expected by government to absorb into the public service workforce large numbers of comparatively unskilled whites. Working from an organizational chart, analyzing the positions, and measuring the work outputs ascribed to it would surely have exposed these contradictions, whereas the implementation of more comprehensive methods of individual merit assessment and quality control allowed officers to be evaluated and for some sort of rank order for advancement to be established. As the PSC later explained, this would "eliminate the whispering campaigns so prevalent in the Service today": presumably the "smelling out" rumors and the belief that those close to the NP received preferential treatment.[65]

For much of the twentieth century, white South African elites emphasized the European genealogies and connections of white South African society, part of an ongoing project to invoke Europe's intellectual legacy and so lay claim to European versions of modernity.[66] Thus, as the PSC announced a new "standard staff report form," it was keen to report that this was developed after intensive investigations of workplace practice in Europe and North America.[67] The aim of the new reporting form was to arrive at a "score" of each public servant's performance. Yet, just as the new system sought to silence "whispering campaigns" animated by allegations of favoritism, it created a bureaucratic framework for surveillance and other versions of favoritism. Although it was seldom enunciated explicitly, public servants were expected to be familiar with a cultural curriculum primarily made up of knowledge about race, but also gender, and sometimes class. As the racial and gendered struts of apartheid society were firmed up, the racial and gendered knowledge required of its servants receded to the background of the archive, evidence of the taken-for-granted presence of these hierarchies in white South African society. At times, however, the official archive does reveal quite clearly the demand for such knowledge. "What is your knowledge of coloureds?" asked a 1951 memorandum setting out the questions for merit assessment.[68] And behind the illusion of fairness and objectivity, the reporting form asked probing and intimate questions about the use of intoxicants and narcotics, dress, personal demeanor, personality, physical appearance, and "special qualities."[69] In addition to these substantial written reports, the new system of merit assessment also required that each staff member be given an interview to "place before the Committee such facts as may have a bearing on their merit assessment."[70]

In December 1952 it emerged, however, that the Department of Inland Revenue had refused to implement the new system. The senior echelons of this department were heavily populated by professional auditors and accountants whose appointment and, in many cases, seniority preceded the advent of the NP government. Familiar with different kinds of public service loyalty, it is plausible that these officials resented the centralization suggested by the PSC's directives on staff reporting. They received short shrift. Noting the department's refusal to carry out a "full scale personal inspection," the secretary of the PSC prepared a report insisting that it carry out "full scale merit assessment" and warned that further defiance would warrant cabinet censure with serious consequences for the senior officers of the department.[71] As part of the scaffolding for scientific management, merit assessment sought primarily to standardize procedures for management of individuals in the public service. But it went beyond measuring individuals' work, as it also created an objective criterion to monitor and regulate those departments who resisted the tendencies toward centralized control implicit in merit assessment and scientific management more generally.

In August 1954, a conference of all heads of department to discuss merit assessment was held under the chairmanship of Donges, the minister of the interior.[72] Although the subject was merit assessment, this gathering represented a significant event in the public service's history of centralization: heads of department had not previously been successfully summoned together, and the PSC's capacity to convene the meeting also sent a strong message about its role at the pinnacle of the bureaucracy. By that year, "good progress" had been made in extending and properly implementing merit assessment, and in its report to the heads of department, the PSC pointed out that the "difficult periods" in the introduction of the system, which it hinted darkly were inspired by party political allegiance to the old UP government (in the Department of Inland Revenue), had ended.[73]

In 1957, the PSC reported that 8,561 officers were assessed, and that the system had been further extended to those who did not normally qualify for merit assessment.[74] Numbers continued to grow: 9,059 in 1958, 8,904 in 1959, and 10,549 in 1960.[75] The PSC attributed the steady increase in the number of officials who were assessed to a shortened qualifying period of service, and this in turn might have represented a drive by the PSC to advance the upward social mobility of public servants, an initiative that coincided with the broader Afrikaner national imperative to advance the interests of the *volk*.

Merit was the first dimension of the PSC's reform of the operation and management of the public service around principles of scientific management, and it gave early momentum to discourses within the service about efficiency. As the PSC later observed, merit allowed it to identify and then discipline, demote, or in some cases, dismiss those who performed poorly.[76]

In its early days, heads of department were reluctant to connect the new assessment system to sanctioning officers for inefficiency, and the PSC noted that instead of leaving this task to the discretion of departments, it would have to develop the means to prosecute inefficiency under the 1923 Public Service Act. However, the existing act, legislated long before the drive to efficiency, was cumbersome, and by 1953, the PSC had managed to get an amendment passed by the House of Assembly. In that year, it reported that one female officer had been reduced in rank and her salary reduced by twenty pounds per annum, while a male officer was dismissed.[77] It boasted later that those subject to merit assessment showed a marked improvement in the quality of their work, although there may have been an element of self-justification in this claim, given the energy and resources allocated to developing its procedures and application.[78]

The demand for bigger government grew as apartheid's imprint on South African society became larger and more complex. Along with a government decision to suspend increases in the public service establishment, the government pushed the PSC to engage more deeply with scientific management.[79] Moving from monitoring of the individual, it began to pay increasing attention to "methods and systems of work," that is, greater efficiency.[80] By 1954, the PSC had deployed management experts at the State Sawmills in Pretoria, and with great delight, it reported that this experiment, on a very small scale, had yielded "remarkable efficiencies": production increased by 14 percent, productivity of "European" and "native" staff rose by 218 and 201 percent respectively, and savings of £54,741 were achieved that year.[81] In what became a model for the training of public service *"werkstudie"* (work-study, or efficiency) officers, eighteen were trained at the Pretoria Sawmill site in the methods of analyzing and improving workplace efficiency.[82] More ambitious after its early successes, the PSC proposed that Organization and Methods Study (O & M) sections be established in every state department.[83] During 1954, it had already designated one hundred staff members as O & M officers.[84] By the following year, it had in place a series of three-week training courses that covered the fundamentals of scientific management such as techniques of work measurement, analysis and improvement of organization, calculation of staff requirements, and office mechanization.[85] The PSC's enthusiasm for scientific management was unwavering, and by 1961 it had trained 169 O & M officers, and it had decided to send several O & M inspectors to Canada and the United States to study the latest innovations in the field.[86]

Reflecting the growing international interest in human resource management, the PSC in the late 1950s added this feature to its repertoire of management instruments. Its particular interest was "occupational adjustment problems," and between 1959 (when a pilot scheme was introduced) and 1961, vocational psychologists investigated 442 public servants. The reporting categories used by the PSC were vague: persons misplaced (158); persons who needed psychological therapy and occupational guidance (179); and persons with other problems (105).[87] However, given the extent to which merit assessment roamed into the reaches of the personal as well as the overarching ideological framework of the bureaucracy, it is not implausible to presume that in addition to more conventional cases of people being in the wrong jobs, or suffering more universal psychological disorders, there were included in this number officials who were "misplaced" or "problematic" in terms of the cultural strictures of apartheid society. In a novel study, Will Jackson draws on some of Frantz Fanon's key claims to demonstrate how conditions of colonialism created certain psychopathologies among whites in colonial Kenya.[88] Quite possibly, similar dynamics were at play within the occupational adjustment scheme. Moreover, the merit assessment system became another tool for discipline, regulation, and the production of ideological and cultural uniformity among public servants.

The drive for efficiency across the *staatsdiens* was not without its contradictions, and it often clashed with the Afrikaner nationalist ideal—and apartheid policy—of "civilized labor" for whites, and of providing livelihoods for otherwise unemployable whites. Referring to staff outside of the administrative sections, Minister of Labour Ben Schoeman announced in 1951 that "we should not create a permanent stratum of unskilled European labour. We should . . . take out those unskilled Europeans who are adaptable, who have the necessary aptitude . . . [and] give them training. That is how we will get the movement from the unskilled, right up to the skilled."[89] His declaration effectively relocated the color bar to a higher level, and nowhere were the principles of civilized labor applied with greater vigor than in those divisions of the *staatsdiens* where manual labor predominated. Between 1948 and 1959, for instance, whites working in the railways were steadily reassigned from laboring to supervisory positions. During that decade, the number of white "railworkers" (laborers) fell from 17,407, or 17.7 percent of the total number of white employees, to 12,131, or 10.7 percent.[90] The tasks that the men performed hardly changed, yet their wages were significantly improved. Native Representative in the House of Assembly Margaret Ballinger tartly noted that "non-Europeans" were being engaged at a pay rate of two shillings and sixpence to three shillings and sixpence a day, while "Europeans" doing the same work were paid at supervisors' rates and taken on at eight shillings and sixpence to fourteen shillings and sixpence per day. "This is going to mean a very considerable increase in the burden of the Public Service," she concluded.[91]

Since at least the advent of Union in 1910, whites had found the state a source of sheltered employment. After the NP took office, however, it tried to expand this type of protection to cater specifically to disabled and poorly educated whites, with the Ministry of Health and Welfare its greatest champion. Numerically these whites were not a significant source of electoral support for the NP, but culturally, they struck a chord with Afrikaner elites who held a deep dread of whites being reduced to pecuniary, to beggary, and to the socio-economic status of South Africa's subject races. Plans during the early apartheid years to provide sheltered work took two forms. First, the ministry proposed the idea of establishing factories and workshops to employ physically and mentally handicapped whites, especially the blind and "the type who won't find work easily," and to this end, in August 1949, the minister convened a Commission of Enquiry into Protected Work. However, the PSC's submission to the commission revealed differences between it and the government on the role of the state in supporting these whites. Presenting as case studies two state-run factories for the disabled, one at Pietersburg and the other at Potchefstroom, the PSC showed how each was running way below capacity. In addition, while the Potchefstroom factory cost the Treasury £9,546 in 1948–49, the provision of pensions for the entire complement in sheltered work at the factory would cost only £4,000 per annum. Faced with these wretched statistics, the commission recommended that it was neither sensible nor economic to implement a system of workshops and factories for the white disabled, and if the government wished to pursue the idea, it should do so in collaboration with private business.[92] The PSC won this round, as the minister quietly dropped his proposal.

Second, the minister prevailed upon his colleagues in other departments to employ another category of whites that "wouldn't find work easily." These men and women were not physically disabled, but they were described in the brutish language that Afrikanerdom's elite sometimes used toward its subalterns as *halfgeskooldes*—half-educated people. Those who were employed were incorporated into the public service, and in the sanitized "bureaucratese" of PSC reports, their jobs were listed as "non-prescribed posts," that is, jobs that lacked formal job descriptions. This was an anomaly in an increasingly regulated public service, and in 1949 these posts numbered 1,122; 1,748 in 1952; 1,510 in 1955; and by 1961, 1,361.[93] These workers were used as bag-carriers in the post office, porters in hospitals and railway stations, and as sub-wardens in work colonies and psychiatric facilities. In the work colonies, it was *halfgeskooldes* who marshaled the grinding routines that constituted "rehabilitation," and they were also responsible for punishing detainees. In short, the *halfgeskoolde* public servants, although few in number, stood at some of the apartheid state's punitive edges, a site where the state was "made real" for South Africans, both Black and white.

Just as the incorporation of *halfgeskooldes* into the public service provided these men and women with livelihoods and located them in a position where they could be monitored, it opened up other tensions and spawned resistance from the public service's management ranks. As a Mr. Buys, chief staff clerk for the post office, complained in 1957, the post office had for many years operated as a welfare service for *halfgeskooldes*. While he understood the importance of absorbing these individuals, he emphasized that they required close attention from welfare officers. If welfare officers were not seconded from the Department of Social Welfare, it placed additional and intolerable burdens on the post office's staffing budget.[94] Buys's comments were roundly supported by his peers from other departments that also employed *halfgeskooldes*—although no resolution was made to increase the number of welfare officers, or even to fill vacant posts as a matter of urgency.

If the organization of the labor process, the mechanisms for monitoring, and correction offered by scientific management and seldom-specified cultural imperatives were not adequate to shape the dispositions and everyday world of white public servants, they were also subject to induction. In 1956, the PSC reported that it was ready to implement an induction training program that aimed to "orientate the young public servant for his career and broaden his Public Service background."[95] A year later, it reported that it had laid on fourteen part-time induction courses, each lasting three weeks.[96] It gave details of the courses:

i. The constitution, organization and functions of the State;
ii. How the State operates;
iii. The place and role of the public servant in the scheme of the State's activities;
iv. The public servant and his conditions of service;
v. The public servant and his work;
vi. The public servant and the citizens of South Africa.[97]

In addition to its explanation of public service work, the emphasis that induction training placed on the state, and the public servants' duty to the state and "his" role in connecting citizens (white ones) to the state, tied in neatly with the concerns of Afrikaner nationalism. By the following year the PSC could report that clerical assistants on probation, as well as the majority of clerical assistants appointed over the previous two years, had undergone induction training.[98] Clearly, younger and more junior entrants were targeted for training. The Afrikaner establishment had harbored anxieties about the white poor for more than half a century. The way that public service induction training was conceived and implemented suggests that this anxiety was spreading to the young as the PSC management began to doubt their steadfastness, their sense of purpose, and their commitment to the *volk*. Through the rest of the decade, and up to the late 1980s—maybe beyond—this anxiety gathered momentum across elite echelons of white society, particularly the Afrikaans-speaking sections of it.

Scientific management in the public service is important for our argument. It changed substantially the structure of work in the *staatsdiens*, and it created a framework for the introduction of new and expansive disciplinary interventions. These measures effectively provided some of the structural conditions to mark out the fields of agency available to public servants. Through its efforts to standardize work procedures, the PSC organized the labor process in ways that were not crassly nor explicitly "political," but that brought to it centralization and an emphasis on hierarchy that served well the interests of a corporativist-type state. And the PSC's reforms made efficiency the language of the *staatsdiens*. The archival record gives few examples of reference by public servants to apartheid's projects, grand or small, but it is replete with anxious references to "efficiency." This suggests that public servants—with the obvious exception of those more senior officials responsible for policymaking—were not compelled to directly and actively enter the difficult political, ideological, and moral terrain of apartheid, but needed instead to make regular and consistent choices about "efficiency." At the same time, capacity to act with indifference to the implications of their work, particularly among those working in departments most closely involved in the administration of the state, does point to an acceptance among white public servants of the nascent ideological and developmental project of apartheid.

Social Discipline, Public Service Work, and Doubt

In a party political climate where the NP's claims to the state were grounded not only in its electoral majority, but included theological elements and the idea of sacred history, the public service during the first decade of NP rule became a formidable "steel frame" not only for the administration of apartheid society, but also for the management of *beamptes* (officials).[99] The "steel frame" was centralized, well organized, and hierarchical, with sophisticated management tools to administer apartheid society and advance the interests of Afrikaner capital—a closeness between the state and capital that was nowhere more obviously apparent than in Albert Wessels's influence on the organizational sociology of the public service. Internally, it developed mechanisms to advance, or retard, individual public servants' progress.

At its most literal, the archive is dense with evidence of the twists and turns of institutional development and state-building activities. Yet it sometimes opens up to reveal instances of uncertainty and doubt on the part of the PSC and public service managers, usually evident in tone, prose style, word choice, and the repetition of particular phrases and refrains, about their ability to manage both departments and individuals.[100] These strains were exposed as the PSC belatedly stepped into a simmering dispute between the Public Servants' Association (PSA), the representative body for white public servants, and the senior officials in the Department of Finance over a matter that was, on the face of it, quite mundane: dress codes. This dispute began in March 1952 when the PSA wrote to the Department of Finance requesting permission for men to wear summer dress appropriate for the harsh climatic conditions in the inland provinces.[101] J. L. Jooste, secretary of the treasury, wrote back curtly, pointing out that dress codes were in fact not determined by regulation but by custom.[102] The matter must have dragged intermittently on, for in 1956, Jooste took the trouble to draft a substantial treatise on dress codes. While sticking to his earlier claims about the weight of custom, he seemed to relent on his earlier opposition to more informal styles of dress. Insisting that tradition is one of a *volk*'s finest characteristics, he pointed out that it should not be slavishly followed. Although "our ancestors" came from cold northern climes, deference to tradition meant that "we continued to dress similarly to them." He described how men, especially, were prickly, restless, and sleepy at work, precisely the opposite of the demeanor required of the "modern public servant"—not because they were bored or uninterested, but because they were physically uncomfortable. Reiterating that nowhere did dress codes feature in any regulations, other than to specify that a person be neat and tidy, he proposed that safari suits, worn with knee-length socks, be encouraged among men as an alternative to suits, jackets, and ties,[103] at which point the PSC intervened, with the secretary of the PSC writing thunderously that the PSC was now faced with a "revolutionary situation."[104] Whether it was the fact of one department negotiating an arrangement with the PSA or the proposed new dress codes that were "revolutionary" is unclear. Nonetheless, the timbre of the PSC's comment and strange use of the word "revolutionary" suggest that there was more at stake than one department usurping the PSA's authority to bargain, or a concession in favor of more relaxed dress codes. These hints of uncertainty, while uncommon, were not isolated incidents, and they were also on display lower down the public service hierarchy. For instance, correspondence between work colony superintendents in 1950 shows that they agreed that at a forthcoming meeting, they should pass a resolution that their subordinates address them as "sir."[105] Clearly the superintendents were of the opinion that proper respect for their status had been hitherto absent.

Furthermore, there were attempts by the PSC to exercise control over white public servants not only in the workplace, but also during their leisure time. In just one example, we find the PSC trying to regulate the sort of establishments where public servants spent their free time. In the early 1950s it vainly issued a series of regional directives prohibiting public servants from visiting places it considered insalubrious. These included hotels, usually in working-class neighborhoods (in Pretoria, the Western; in Durban, the Rossburgh); nightclubs, especially those in docklands (like the notorious Smuggler's Inn in Durban's Point Road); and amusement arcades (like Newton's bingo on the Durban beachfront). To all account these proscriptions were completely ignored.[106]

Race in the Everyday Life of the Public Service

Seeking signs of class-based consciousness and organization among white public servants, Deborah Posel looks to the PSA and finds it wanting. Despite dissatisfaction with their conditions of service, she writes, public servants were not able to "resist" due to the weakness of the PSA and its unwillingness to robustly challenge the government.[107] However, a turn to social history indicates that, while the PSA might have been chronically timid in its dealings with state authorities, it would be wrong to assume that officials lower down the public service hierarchy were passive recipients of the ideologies, moral codes, and social regulations imposed from above by the public service labor process. *Beamptes* laid claim to considerable agency, sometimes by way of collective workplace organization and, at other times, more individually. These excursions to social history show *beamptes* organizing and defying the conditions under which they labored. Equally importantly, they show officials iteratively developing their own understandings of racial hierarchies. They point to officials acting "compassionately" in a system otherwise premised on the impersonal and immutable banalities of bureaucratic regulations rather than on any measure of empathy or humaneness. In addition, they expose an underbelly of popular racist violence that even the apartheid state, itself built on many layers of violence, would repudiate. Collectively, these examples highlight some of the ways in which white public servants crafted their accommodation with the public service, and with apartheid society more generally.

In 1952, for example, it was reported in the House of Assembly that there had been a spate of spontaneous go-slow strikes across the public service, including the railways. These strikes went on for at least a year, and according to statements made by opposition members of Parliament, they represented a groundswell of popular dissatisfaction with the merit system, especially the way it "restricted" promotion.[108] Some railways workers from Natal found additional cause to protest as they revealed their suspicion of the government's seriousness about maintaining the color bar. Organized not in the PSA but by a body called the Artisan Staff Association, the workers "demanded answers from the Railways Administration" after the circulation of rumors that it was contemplating the employment of Indian artisans in that province.[109]

Public servants, as discussed, were subject to an induction program, although it is unclear precisely how far induction extended beyond the administrative divisions of the service. Testimony from an informant who joined the service in 1958, where he was employed as a general worker at a workshop in the Orange Free State provincial roads department, suggests that in the workplace, other kinds of regulations and ethics could prevail.[110] For his first two weeks, the informant recalls, he was assigned no work and did little but sit around and read comics. Then, one afternoon he was summoned to a storeroom where he was roughed up, pushed around, punched, kicked, and sworn at by more senior colleagues, including the workshop foreman. Following this assault, which came with no explanation, he was made to stand up tall, salute, and sing "Die Stem," the national anthem. He was then taken outside, told to sit down, and offered a cup of tea while being given a sort of induction—very different to the formal one given by the PSC. He was told that he was expected to clock everyone's attendance card at seven o'clock in the morning, even if they had not yet arrived at work; and again at four o'clock, even if they had already left. He was also told to respect his seniors, including those Black workers who "were older than him," and that "nothing went beyond the workshop." After about two years, he was taken with an artisan to work on a private motor vehicle and paid a small allowance. Even though he had no formal training in motor mechanics, he, his senior, and sometimes a Black worker did these jobs quite regularly. They used government tools and parts and, on occasion, brought cars to the government workshop—but this necessitated giving the security guard "lunch money." In this vignette we see white public servants establishing their own workplace rules, along with a kind of "induction" to ensure that the workers who would be bound by these rules understood them. They bore little relation to the values that the PSC sought to develop and, in fact, the kinds of systematic corruption that they sometimes entailed ran directly counter to the PSC's commitment to efficiency and state-building. There was also a suggestion of collusion across the color line that would not have found much enthusiasm in the official hierarchies of the public service—despite the fact that this was around corruption. My informant remembers that while Black workers participated in his workshop's racket, they were however not given the kind of brutal "induction" he experienced.[111]

On another occasion, we are witness to an escalating disagreement between two bureaucrats, both white men, that had one of the antagonists issuing something of a monologue on race relations, social class, and the kind of etiquette necessary to mediate interactions between people of different race and social origins. The incident began with a water dispute between the state entomologist and the medical superintendent of Tower Hospital in Fort Beaufort, and it boiled over into an angry complaint of how a Mr. Yorke, head male nurse at the hospital, addressed the entomologist. In the hospital dining room, Yorke "hectored and brow-beat" the entomologist in front of junior staff. This "high-handed action and attitude" to a superior was unacceptable, wrote the entomologist; moreover, Yorke's demeanor and tone were more suitable for "addressing a non-European labourer."[112] The entomologist's outrage seemed most piqued at Yorke's disregard for the multiple hierarchies of apartheid society (although he was silent on gender), and it suggests that he had a clear vision of the social order that was beginning to coalesce under apartheid. His understanding was cast in a grain markedly finer than the broad racial categories that informed apartheid administration at the time.

Then, the strange case of the "Mauritians." This is a case of greater historiographic significance than political, for it challenges the idea of the state as all-powerful as well as the laws and regulations that were its proxy. This case also offers an instance where officials were able to resist and overturn not just the letter of the law but its very intent. One of the foundations of apartheid legislation was the 1950 Population Registration Act, which obliged each inhabitant of South Africa to register according to racial characteristics as white, African, "colored," or Asian. For state officials, the logic of bureaucratic work meant that they followed regulations and could not tamper with these racial categories. There is evidence, however, that at least some of them acted with what amounted to compassion. In Durban (the South African city most connected with the Indian ocean world), they did so by making use of the subcategory "Mauritian." "Mauritian" was a designation devoid of any particular or unique racial characteristics. No one knew what a "Mauritian" should look like, at least according to the grammar of apartheid bureaucracy. "Mauritians" were a subcategory of the white racial group, and there were examples where officials subverted the act by reclassifying families, usually coloreds or Asians, as "Mauritian." This measure enabled these families to become "white" and so to claim access to better wages, education, healthcare, and subsidized housing. Examples like this are few and far between, and they hardly soften the relentless inhumanity of apartheid. But they do offer a counter against the totalizing assumption of the *staatsdiens* as a wholly effective cipher for apartheid ideologies, an institution that completely stripped from its officials any possibility of agency, defiance, or human solidarity.

Apartheid society was premised not only on white privilege, but also on violence. It was important for the sort of "order" imagined under apartheid that violence was bureaucratic and regulated, sometimes juridical, and always the prerogative of the state. Lynching-type violence, exercised by individuals, was not tolerated. A pertinent example of how the state responded to random, individual violence emerged from the late 1950s. In 1957, one G. O. Opperman, a clerk in the Department of Labour, was riding his bicycle inside the corridor of an office, "when his progress was impeded by [a] native who was walking through the doorway at the time." It appears that this annoyed Opperman, who "there-upon assaulted the native." The archive yields no pronouncements or regulations on violence, although it does show swift punishment for those white public servants who arbitrarily assumed the right to punish presumed infractions, slights, and insults. In this case, Opperman found himself discharged from the public service and charged by the police.[113] Of the assaulted African, nothing is mentioned after his brief and painful vignette as the object of Opperman's unacceptable assault. That this episode attracted detailed correspondence suggests that violence of the sort demonstrated by Opperman was probably quite uncommon, a tremor that unsettled the style of race and social relations, the form of white supremacy, that underlay apartheid.

Conclusion

It is evident that the experience of work in the *staatsdiens* was important in shaping the behavior and dispositions of white public servants. Given the long history of elite Afrikaner anxiety about the cultural and political reliability of working-class and poor whites, it is hardly surprising that whatever else they achieved, reforms of the public service gave so much attention to surveilling, policing, and, where necessary, reforming whites in the lower ranks of the service: those occupying policy-implementation posts in the administrative divisions or performing non-skilled work in the service more broadly. Yet, as we have seen, these intentions were the subject of contestation from lower-level *beamptes*. It is another irony that the very whites who caused Afrikaner politicians, bureaucrats, and intellectuals such distress, the kind of public servants who became the butt of "Van" jokes and *halfgeskooldes,* were sometimes relatively unaffected by the battery of public service regulations, because possibilities for upward mobility offered by the merit system were simply beyond them.

Although the PSC resisted clumsy political interference in appointments, it did oversee recruiting practices that shifted the public service closer to the demographic and ideological heartland of Afrikaner nationalism. The progressive introduction of scientific management standardized work across departments and reduced the possibility of departments or individuals acting in renegade ways. It provided systems to monitor public servants and measure them on aspects of their work that related to the technical requirements of the job as well as to the new elite's frames of ideological and cultural reference. These matrices furthermore provided the basis for advancement, for the identification of those with "occupational adjustment problems," and also for punitive action. Collectively, the role of the public service labor process in managing whites suggests that just as the development of the apartheid state was a haphazard and contradictory process, there was in fact evidence of the kernel of a project to reimagine society in ways beyond the older pragmatics of white supremacy. However, even as the new state was founded on the vision of Afrikaner nationalism, there is evidence that in the PSC's concern to avoid overt signs of favoritism or discrimination ("smelling out"), this project tentatively included not only Afrikaners but also other whites. While the full horrors of apartheid state planning and its efforts to manage populations through social engineering would be visited upon Blacks from the 1960s, this kind of state-making vision was manifest earlier in endeavors to manage whites, at least those employed by the state and thus at easy reach.

The expansion of the public service was responsible for the emergence of a new, increasingly Afrikanerized class of whites employed in clerical jobs. We shall see in the next chapter that it confirmed and modernized gender relations among whites, primarily in the workplace but in ways that also shaped white domestic life. Although public servants were seldom obliged to act in specifically racist ways, or to demonstrate any signs of political allegiance, it could however be argued that in the ideological climate of a racial state, diligent work along with the ways that public servants were regulated and disciplined, and the types of knowledge they were expected to demonstrate, helped sustain the thoughtlessness, lack of empathy, and, ultimately, the self-deception that they were part of a "normal" society.

White public servants demonstrated significant agency in the ways in which they staked their place in apartheid society, and the kind of identities, behavior, and racial rules they assumed. Even in the workplace, the planes and affective currents of the archive suggest that they were often far from docile, and as the case studies suggest, they were occasionally defiant. The *beamptes*' assertion of some autonomy and their transgression is significant—and it is not. It should not for a moment descend to the kind of cynical revisionism that seeks to put a human face on apartheid's beneficiaries or to move these whites into a column headed "opposition." At every turn these *beamptes*' history reminds us how they too participated in race-making, that race was made not only from the top, by the state, but also from the bottom, by citizens. This examination does however challenge some of the moral and historiographic certainties about apartheid history: about the coherence of the apartheid project, about the stability of racial categories, and about the existence of riposte and challenge from within white society—and its limits. Furthermore, the shards of humanity that they sometimes showed are a counter against essentialized whiteness, a tool in unmaking the history of whites as one exclusively of racial domination, self-interest and deception, accommodation and complicity. Yet the examples represented in these case studies also remind us that just as these public servants occasionally acted compassionately or crossed the color line, they did not repudiate apartheid. The Durban officials, for instance, used the very language and categories of apartheid to help a few families "cross"—testament, perhaps, to the observation that while there were many currents of racial supremacy in apartheid South Africa, and that some of these jarred, few whites were either immune or hostile to racist ideologies. This ambiguities of not-belonging-yet-belonging, of defying-yet-not-defying, are key to understanding processes of accommodation made between white public servants and the *staatsdiens* of which they were part.

WOMEN, THE LABOR MARKET, AND THE DOMESTIC ECONOMY

6

Sheila's Work

My mother was the main source of income in our family. Yet for most of her working life, Sheila kept a tenuous balance between providing for her little family and holding up the façade of my father as the provider and head of the household. She invariably took pains to ensure that the jobs she took as a legal secretary, always "temporary," often "half day," never visibly placed her at a loftier social level of white society than that occupied by my father.

Despite her lowly position in the hierarchy of white labor, Sheila maintained an active civic life. In addition to her political interests, she served on the local school board and was district secretary for the Boy Scouts. Yet she could never open a bank account or sign a rental lease. I discovered this as a student when we moved from our council-owned flat to a small house. My father and I, a graduate student at the time, were acceptable signatories for house leases or small bank loans—but not Sheila, the only one with a stable income. On those occasions that called for the authority of a (male) head of the household, like visits to the bank, the city housing authority, or the insurance office, she would literally pilot my father through the door, stand behind him, and do all the talking. He would then sign whatever needed to be signed and leave the details to my mother.

The sensitivities that Sheila navigated with deftness and (mostly) forbearance were certainly whims of our family circumstance, but they were also more than that. These scenarios were also indicative of concerns among elements within Afrikaner nationalism during the 1950s about white women in the workplace and the fate of the family, and ultimately the fate of the white race in South Africa. Apprehensions about white women in the evolving political economy of South Africa, stated in terms that Geoffrey Cronjé would be familiar with, and with no less conviction than his prose, found expression in the writings of Dr. Maria Prinsloo.

A Treatise on White Working Women

In 1957, Maria Prinsloo, a South African, completed her doctoral thesis in sociology at the University of Gröningen in the Netherlands.[1] She worked under the supervision of P. J. Bouman, a sociologist best known for his interest in the connection between "social forms and social psychology." The topic of her thesis was "White Women's Work in the Union of South Africa." Later that year her thesis was published in South Africa as a monograph.[2]

Although focused on the world of work, Prinsloo's book was much more than a dry catalog of white women's growing significance in the labor market of apartheid South Africa. It ascended into a polemic that identified the rise of white female wage labor as a threat to white civilization. Noting how the number of women in wage labor had accelerated, she developed an alarmist claim that this trend, if left unchecked and unregulated, could "influence social disintegration." As Afrikaner nationalist intellectuals of the day were inclined to do, she moored her arguments about whites to the development of Western civilization—whites in South Africa were, after all, "Europeans." In Western culture, Prinsloo stated, a woman's role was historically as wife and mother, and her critique revolved around ways that wage labor undermined this natural and "civilized" order of things.

Elaborating on the social and cultural implications of work, Prinsloo began her account with a discussion of "matrimony, paternity and fertility," noting with consternation that "European" birth rates in South Africa were substantially lower than those of "non-Europeans." Although she referred to "whites," and sometimes "Europeans," she actually meant Afrikaners. She tracked this demographic threat to the survival of the *volk* all the way back to the ravages of the Anglo-Boer War (1899–1902), since it had impoverished Afrikaners, dispossessed them of their land, and driven them to the cities. As a matter of survival, women—widows, wives, and daughters—were forced to seek work. Yet the effects of women's work extended well beyond the demographic dangers of a declining birth rate. Over time, Prinsloo argued, economic necessity had been overtaken by "social and psychological conditioning" as women came to prefer their "occupational life" to more "natural" roles as housewife and mother. This shift coincided with the "spirit of individualism" that was on the rise in most western countries. Prinsloo noted, quite correctly, that women seldom obtained well-paid or high-status jobs, and from this observation she challenged the economic argument for women's work, which held that in order to make ends meet, modern families needed the supplement of an additional wage. Moreover, as women paid less attention to household chores, the family inevitably accrued "extra household expenses"—an oblique reference to the growing phenomenon of Black women performing domestic work in white households.

Prinsloo demonstrated Bouman's intellectual influence in the ways that she drew a correlation between the emergence of new social arrangements and the psyche of the *volk* as she connected white women's wage labor not only to a drop in Afrikaner birth rates, but to divorce, juvenile delinquency, neglect of the child, and the threat of moral dissipation in the family. Like Geoffrey Cronjé, she saw the family as fundamental to the social cohesion of the *volk*. The root of the problem, Prinsloo insisted, lay with modern ideas of freedom, which was measured according to "monetary remuneration through occupational behavior and the social status acquired through an occupational life." Among her conclusions, she recommended that the state take the lead in regulating and managing the entry of white women into the labor market through the establishment of a Bureau of Female Labour in the Department of Labour. She also urged that social studies be given greater prominence in the school curriculum (for whites, of course). This would counter the dissolution of values becoming apparent in western societies, and give learners—boys and girls—"sound attitudes" toward marriage, home economics, child raising, and labor.

Prinsloo's text was quite remarkable in that it pegged the rise of white women's labor as antithetical to so many of Afrikaner nationalism's key ideological assumptions about the organization of white society, the political philosophy that underpinned these, and the role of the state. Perhaps these troubling resonances accounted for the book's traction, suggested by its rapid progress from thesis to published monograph. An underlying concern threaded through Prinsloo's book was the question of what could happen when people—in this case, women—slipped the boundaries of "proper" conduct. Periods of crisis and anxiety triggered responses from the state and its allies (usually, but not always, Afrikaner nationalists), and these complex social histories had implications for the ways that white people were bound into apartheid society.

As we saw in the previous chapter, the growth of the apartheid-era *staatsdiens* went some way toward meeting the key objectives of Afrikaner nationalism by providing employment for large numbers of whites who were the bedrock of the NP's electoral support. Work in the public service also became a kind of "steel frame" for elites in the Public Service Commission (PSC) and the upper ranks of the public service to monitor white public servants—to whatever extent such ambitions were realized or frustrated. Yet as Prinsloo's strident claims testify, the growth of the *staatsdiens* energized other challenges to the ideals of Afrikaner nationalism. The *staatsdiens* was host to the most substantial expansion of jobs in the administrative divisions, almost exclusively office work, for white women during the first decade of apartheid.

The idea of the *volksmoeder* is central to any understanding of Afrikaner national gender ideology and of white, particularly Afrikaner, femininity under apartheid. Further, employment for white women was institutionalized and structured as the *staatsdiens* burgeoned during the 1950s. The growth of the *staatsdiens* provided new opportunities for women, but women were not universally welcome in the service. Their entry spawned both glaring ironies and workplace struggle, and the PSC sought to manage this new generation of working women who became increasingly indispensable for the functioning of apartheid's bureaucracies. As in the public service more generally, women who secured employment during apartheid's first decade were mostly Afrikaners. The journey into the ranks of the *staatsdiens* introduced significant change into these women's everyday lives. The new circumstances had cultural and ideological implications for women's roles in the family and society more generally, and these were negotiated by Afrikaner nationalist women's movements and by working women themselves. The phenomenon of working, "respectable" Afrikaans women loosened and sometimes disrupted the gendered bonds of Afrikaner society and, perhaps, of white society in general. The unease that stemmed from the rapid growth of office work among white women helped to generate new strategies to deal with women's changing circumstances, and these circumstances eventually led to the development of new ideologies about white femininity among Afrikaner nationalist women's groups. They also gave rise to new sets of cultural codes, new standards by which white women (especially Afrikaner women) were expected to behave, and by which they were judged, largely by women in the Afrikaner nationalist women's movement. This advice represented a nascent common sense of what it meant to be a respectable, white (Afrikaans) women in 1950s South Africa.[3]

The *Volksmoeder* and Afrikaner Femininity

During the late nineteenth and early twentieth centuries, the concept of the *volksmoeder* developed as one of the more significant cultural influences on the shape of white Afrikaner femininity. For most of these years and beyond, the *volksmoeder* offered an image of idealized womanhood but, as Elsabé Brink observed in what remains the most comprehensive essay on the subject, the foundations of the *volksmoeder* varied over time, and the concept as a whole was seldom defined with much precision.[4]

Privations wrought upon Afrikaners, especially those in the former Zuid-Afrikaansche (South African) and Orange Free State republics during the Anglo-Boer War, provided the material and ideological context for the emergence of the *volksmoeder* trope. Urbanization, widespread unemployment, and the squalid living conditions of many newly urbanized Afrikaners, in rented accommodation and squatter settlements, fanned concerns among middle class Afrikaners that poverty could be the harbinger of degeneracy among the *volk*. Brink observes that these concerns were not dissimilar to Victorian-era British alarm about the social ills that were presumed to fester in an impoverished working class.[5] In Johannesburg and Pretoria, the situation was exacerbated by the presence of large numbers of unsupervised and unattached men and women in cities, which gave those in the state, the church, and welfare organizations additional cause for apprehension. In this context Afrikaner women became important in reasserting the stabilizing influence of the family and developing a historical telling of Afrikaner nationalism that had as its foundation women's steadfastness and struggle in the face of deep social crisis.

On December 16, 1913, the Vrouemonument (Women's Memorial) was inaugurated in Bloemfontein to commemorate Afrikaner women and children who had died in British concentration camps during the South African War. This event was a significant marker in the development of the *volksmoeder* mythology and, shortly afterward, the poet Totius (J. D. du Toit) and his brother-in-law Willem Postma both wrote pieces that specifically linked Afrikaner nationalism to the strength of the *volksmoeder*.[6] Postma's 1918 book, *Die Boervrou: Moeder van Haar Volk* (The Boer Woman: Mother of Her Nation), became the "orthodoxy." He was quite clear that just as women's work was in the home, women had no role in the party political arena.[7]

In the years between the two world wars, a number of studies undertaken, significantly, by women challenged the mythology of the *volksmoeder*. The pioneering study was written by Totius's sister, Marie du Toit, and was published in 1921. Titled *Vrou en Feminis—Of Iets oor die Vroue-Vraagstuk* (Women and Feminist—Or Something on the Women's Question), it objected to the conventional gender roles that were central to the *volksmoeder* ideology: "Continually we hear only of lesser, of lower value.... A beast-of-burden position of honour," she wrote wryly. In addition to Marie du Toit's exposure of the unfairness and hypocrisy of the patriarchal society of which she was part, and the position of disadvantage that the *volksmoeder* ideology imposed upon Afrikaner women, there appeared in the interwar years three studies, all of which were critical of the idealized ways in which advocates of the *volksmoeder* idea (often men) portrayed women.

The first of these studies was written by M. E. Rothmann, the only female member of the Carnegie Commission of Investigation on the Poor White Question in South Africa (1930–1932). As part of her work for the commission, Rothmann undertook an investigation into the problems of mothers and daughters in poor white families. While accepting Postma's notion that women's major responsibility was nurturing the family, she approached her subjects with care and empathy as she depicted the plight of impoverished women in the towns and countryside. Her emphasis on the grit, desperation, and compromises that textured these ordinary women's lives questioned the *volksmoeder*'s heroic nationalist brushstrokes. The second was written by Hansi Pollack for her 1932 master's thesis, in which she investigated working conditions among white women on the Witwatersrand during the early 1930s Great Depression. Like Rothmann, Pollack demonstrated deep compassion for her subjects, most of whom worked in the manufacturing sector, as they struggled to manage the burdens of factory and home. The third study was conducted by Erika Theron, who was supervised by Hendrik Verwoerd—the future prime minister—at Stellenbosch University. Theron undertook a study similar to Pollack's into the lives of white and colored factory workers in Cape Town.[8]

All of these investigations, deeply ethnographic in their methodology, highlighted the vicissitudes of poor women's lives and were in stark contrast to Postma's idealized images of Afrikaner women that lay at the heart of the *volksmoeder* mythology. However, they had little impact in Afrikaner nationalist circles, no doubt partly due to the fact that their conclusions were awkward to reconcile with the romantic image of the *volksmoeder*.

In addition to these intellectual rebuttals of the *volksmoeder* as a simple and expedient prop for Afrikaner nationalism, particular currents in working-class politics also exerted pressure on the middle-class moorings of *volksmoeder* orthodoxy developed by Postma. During the late 1920s and early 1930s, working-class women in the Garment Workers' Union (GWU) allied themselves more closely with militant class-conscious trade unionism rather than with Afrikaner nationalism. Yet this progressive orientation was tenuous. As Louise Vincent has shown, women's association with class-based union politics under the leadership of general secretary Solly Sachs (a member of the Communist Party of South Africa's Central Committee until his expulsion in 1930), and with office-bearers who were all Afrikaner women (Anna Scheepers, president; Johanna Cornelius, national organizer; and Dulcie Hartwell, assistant secretary) never cast them adrift from ethnic identification as Afrikaners. Particularly for recent arrivals in the city whose social standing was uncertain, the principles of steadfastness and stability represented by the *volksmoeder*, as well as her connection to family and the *volk*, were very appealing. Sensitive to this deep emotional and cultural attachment to the *volk*, women leaders in the GWU did their best to emphasize that the need for workplace solidarity and the cultural values of the *volksmoeder* were not incompatible—that in fact the ideal of the *volksmoeder* had particular resonance for the lives of factory women. For instance, Johanna Cornelius declared herself a "better Afrikaner" than those of the middle class who were distressed, sometimes scandalized, by working-class life but did nothing to ameliorate its harshness.[9]

This alternate, working-class (and class-conscious) appropriation of the *volksmoeder* was however short-lived. As Jonathan Hyslop writes, the rise of D. F. Malan's brand of Afrikaner nationalism from the mid-1930s represented a populist departure from the relatively elitist style of J. B. M. Hertzog. Malan could only succeed by organizing a revolt against Hertzog's alliance of wealthy Afrikaner farmers and notables. This effort involved something of a tightrope act for Malan as he had to bring working-class Afrikaner women—electorally important since their enfranchisement in 1930—into his alliance, while simultaneously reestablishing gender hierarchies where men asserted social, political, and economic control over women.[10] A growing sense of unease among the Afrikaner middle classes during the 1930s that working-class women were socially and sexually out of control contributed to Malan's cause as the Malanites capitalized on the ruling United Party's reluctance to pass legislation banning "mixed" marriages (marriages across the color line).[11] By portraying white women as sexually threatened by Black men, the Malanites not only attacked the United Party (UP) but also tapped into anxieties, common in racially segregated societies, that these women were potentially "traitors at the heart of whiteness" and allowed Afrikaner men to claim their role as "protectors" and thus reassert their patriarchy.[12]

These claims enabled Malan's nationalists to successfully confront the ways that Sachs and other left-wing unionists sought to link the *volksmoeder* to class-based organization. Sachs's ties to the Communist Party and the GWU's socialist orientation left the Union vulnerable to Afrikaner nationalist tactics that regularly connected trade unionism ("communism" in the crude argot of the nationalists) and racial integration.[13] This association was made again and again, and in 1938 events leading up to the centenary celebrations of the Great Trek, a northward migration of Dutch-speaking settlers to the interior of what would become South Africa, proved to be a key moment in bringing working-class Afrikaner women into the fold of Afrikaner nationalism. The time leading up to the Trek centenary was a period of massive ethnic mobilization, and Vincent writes that only by claiming their rightful place within the *volk*—and disassociating with left-wing unionism—could working-class women silence those critics who remained suspicious of their morality and respectability, portraying them as little better than prostitutes or "maids" or dismissing them as "Free State girls come to Johannesburg to dance with kaffirs."[14] To enable their participation in the celebrations, special units called *kappie kommandos* (bonnet brigades) were established under the leadership of Johanna and Hester Cornelius, who were themselves veterans of the GWU.[15] By 1938, the battle to instill class consciousness among working women in the GWU was effectively lost. More than anything, it was their marginal status and hopes for respectability that caused these women to reinterpret their social and workplace struggles within the racial and gendered framework of Afrikaner nationalism.

While struggles for the heart and soul of working-class Afrikaner women saw them turn from the GWU's version of class solidarity to ethnic mobilization, they also repudiated more fundamentalist interpretations of the *volksmoeder* that were gaining favor in some Afrikaner nationalist circles: namely, the idea that wage labor was no place for women.[16] The acknowledgment that necessity obliged some women to seek employment was an important condition for incorporating working-class women into the Afrikaner nationalist alliance during the 1930s and 1940s, and it made the ideal of the *volksmoeder* somewhat more inclusive. The outcome of these cultural struggles during the late 1930s, however, meant that by the end of the decade, the feisty radicalism of working-class women was gone. These struggles also meant that the *volksmoeder* could be claimed solely as a symbol of Afrikaner nationalism, articulated by middle-class Afrikaners, albeit in slightly modified form.

Developments in the labor market during the Second World War provided some white women, factory workers who were employed for the duration of the conflict, with an opportunity to upset prevailing ideologies about the *volksmoeder*, her relationship to wage labor, and her position within the gender and racial hierarchies of South African society. This they did through everyday, pragmatic workplace decisions. South Africa's entry into the war initiated great pressure to expand the Union's engineering and manufacturing capacity as the Union government agreed to contribute munitions to the Allied war effort. New factory techniques of mass production were needed in order to meet this commitment. Mass production in turn required new types of labor: semiskilled operatives. The growing demand for semiskilled operatives represented a new division of labor in South Africa, and identifying a significant source of semiskilled workers proved to be a dilemma for both the government and employers. On the one hand, neither government nor employers wanted to promote labor instability by encroaching on the status quo that kept skilled work for white men; on the other, both wanted to keep African men classified as unskilled laborers and thus prohibited under labor regulations from joining unions.[17] As Nancy Clark writes, white female labor presented both the government and employers with a means to "dilute" skilled jobs in the interests of mass production for the war effort without disturbing the sensitive racial and skill balances of the segregated labor market.[18]

In 1940, the government negotiated an agreement with employers and unions to permit the employment of "emergency workers," who would not normally be considered qualified for such jobs, who would be paid 85 percent of the going rate. Initially, the government tried to directly recruit white men, but the results of this initiative were dismal. There were millions of Africans available, but all stakeholders were afraid that their introduction into semiskilled work would provoke antagonism from white artisans. White women thus provided the obvious source for "diluted" labor. These women came in great numbers to seek employment as "emergency" workers: they were drawn from those sectors of society identified by the Carnegie Commission as "paupers" and they were mainly Afrikaners. As Clark writes, most were rural, young, and single Afrikaans women responsible for the upkeep of impoverished families. Others had been on the Rand for several years and had already been driven into factory work, poorly paid jobs in shops, or domestic labor. Yet others were elderly women, sometimes widowed or abandoned.[19]

These women were never guaranteed long-term employment after the war, and conditions were very poor for female wartime workers. Not only were they paid substantially less than men, but they were excluded from the benefits of a sick fund. The South African mint was the most notorious employer of female labor, and at its munitions plants in Pretoria, Johannesburg, and Kimberley, women were housed in grim hostels where they were subject to curfews, controls, and punishment, including salary deductions for breaking strict housekeeping rules. The Afrikaner national trade union movement did little for these Afrikaner wartime factory workers beyond appealing to them not to travel to work on buses driven by Africans and warning them of the dangers of "godless communists."[20]

The women did try to mobilize in order to improve their conditions of work, but without much success. Initially, the South African Trades and Labor Council (SATLC), recognizing the presence of women in the engineering industry, organized a separate section for women war workers, but it subsequently betrayed them when it excluded women from industry-wide negotiations. Frustrated, women then began to seek cooperation with African male workers in the munitions factories. Before this alliance could be developed and put to the test, though, it was overtaken by certain events. By early 1945, with the end of the war in sight, the government began to shut down armament factories. Worried that women would remain in the cities to seek similar jobs, the government offered them a one-way rail pass (a tactic officials had employed with poor whites like Karel/Charles twenty years before) to go "home." Clark points out that these policies returned them to precisely the poverty they had tried to escape.[21] Their willingness to collaborate with male African workers hints that they might have turned away from the ethnic solidarity that lay at the heart of both Afrikaner nationalism and the *volksmoeder* idea, or at least combined this with other kinds of alliances in the workplace.

One place where the racial, ethnic, and gendered ideals of the *volksmoeder* were reiterated, reaffirmed, and partially modified during the war years was in the Ossewa Brandwag (OB), a paramilitary mass movement of Afrikaners that emerged from the euphoria of the 1938 Great Trek celebrations. The OB was virulently anti-British, and at the outbreak of the Second World War, it sided with Nazi Germany and initiated a campaign of sabotage against the war effort in South Africa. While its paramilitary activities are fairly well known, there is only one account of the role of women in the OB, written by Charl Blignaut.[22] Blignaut shows how the *volksmoeder* ideology shaped women's understanding of their role in the OB, and how their activities, in turn, added substance and content to some of the stylized ideals of the *volksmoeder*. Thus, women were given their own "special place" in the OB Women's Division and their major area of responsibility was *"volksorg"* (taking care of the *volk*). They were required to learn about rudimentary budget administration, hygiene, educational issues, home caregiving, nutrition, and first aid—activities that, after the war, formed the rump of the Afrikaner nationalist *Suid-Afrikaanse Vrouefederasie*'s (SAVF) program of engagement with working-class Afrikaner women. OB women were also expected to undertake basic social welfare assessments. When men were interned on suspicion of subversion or sabotage, it was members of the Women's Division who were detailed to investigate whether the family qualified for support from the OB's Emergency Fund.[23]

After the war, women from the OB drifted into mainstream Afrikaner nationalist women's movements like the SAVF. Experience during the war, when they had taken on a range of practical responsibilities, shaped the ways in which they understood the ideal of the *volksmoeder* after the advent of the NP government in 1948. These years were prosperous, but they also brought new challenges for the *volk*. While the OB women hardly shifted the middle-class identity of the women's movements, they nonetheless joined up (while still retaining their prior class allegiances), and they brought to these movements a certain practical, "muscular" quality to the ways in which they undertook their role as *volksmoeders*. This broadening had significance for the ways that these movements responded to circumstances that took white women into the new world of clerical work in the *staatsdiens*.

The Rise of Women's Work in the *Staatsdiens*, 1948–1961

The machinery of the South African state expanded substantially under apartheid, requiring a growing public service labor force, a process that continued more or less unchecked until the late 1980s.[24] A bigger state required more labor, especially white labor. This occasioned an influx of women into the *staatsdiens* that in turn meant that the bulk of white women's jobs in the economy generally shifted from their prewar concentration in manufacturing to semiskilled clerical work: by the end of the 1950s, there were about 537,926 white women with a grade ten education, making them eligible for employment in the *staatsdiens*, and of these, 152,174 were public servants.[25]

The demand for women in the *staatsdiens* was directly related to the growth of the apartheid state. However, this demand also affected some of the ways that apartheid-era whiteness was framed within Afrikaner nationalism, most particularly the role of women within the family, that fundamental building block of *volk*, and within a highly patriarchal society more generally. As Prinsloo's book shows, discomfort on the part of elite men and women about new signs of assertiveness made possible to poorer women as they entered wage labor were often expressed in the idiom of "danger" to the family. These concerns prompted a battery of ideological, bureaucratic, and welfare responses from both the state and Afrikaner nationalist women's movements.

Since at least the beginning of the First World War in 1914, women had found employment in the *staatsdiens*, although in very junior positions, doing "women's work" (like typing), and occupying nonpermanent positions—although some held their jobs for decades. Their positions and status rendered them virtually invisible and helped to sustain the fiction that the business of state was "men's work." As the *staatsdiens* grew under apartheid, senior figures in the NP and the PSC would have preferred the new posts to be occupied by white men, with some exceptions made during the Second World War when so many men were away on military service. This preference was not that different to any previous South African administration.

For much of apartheid's first decade, as we have seen, the PSC was dogged by an inadequate number of white applicants to public service posts. This shortage had a gendered dimension, and one of the PSC's earliest staffing challenges came from the quarter of the service that was historically feminine: the typing pool. Already in 1948, the PSC reported that there was a severe scarcity, across the service, of suitably qualified shorthand typists.[26] In a gesture that highlighted the importance of these women's work, it complained that the shortage of typists was severely undermining the administrative efficiency of the entire service.

While there was no particular enthusiasm in the PSC for employing women, the simple arithmetic of the public service's labor needs, and the gendered structure of work within it, meant that as the service grew it had to recruit more women. In its early efforts to incorporate more women, the PSC took care not to greatly upset the gendered structure of work where women were assigned particular jobs and not placed in positions where they supervised men. "A woman typist is better than a woman clerk," according to the minutes of a 1951 meeting of chief departmental staff clerks.[27] These departmental sentiments underscored the PSC's approach to increasing the staff complement of women in the service: their place was in the junior, administrative ranks, with one notable exception: social workers.[28]

The PSC was very particular during the early apartheid years about the places in the public service hierarchy best suited to women, and the relentless demand for public service labor as the state bureaucracy expanded meant that it was also far more systematic than previous administrations in institutionalizing the work undertaken by women. It had in place strategies to recruit women. Moreover, it established schemes to train women for the type of work they could be expected to do, and by 1950 the PSC had opened training schools for typists (*tikskole*) in Pretoria, Cape Town, Durban, and Bloemfontein.[29] The ten-week courses offered by the *tikskole* proved, however, to be not only costly, but also unpopular among women.[30] "We stayed in a hostel near the railway workers. It was freezing. All we did every day, we signed in, had prayers and practiced typing. I didn't learn anything. I already had a typing certificate," said one woman who attended "tikskool" in Bloemfontein during the early 1950s.[31] But just as the PSC formalized women's work in some sectors of the service, it formalized their exclusion from others, particularly those parts of it considered to be more masculine. Acting on the recommendation of the permanent Public Service Commission of Enquiry, which included representatives of the churches, women's groups, and the Public Servants' Association (PSA), the PSC announced that women would not be considered for work in the diplomatic or consular service, nor would they be eligible for the police service.[32]

The growing numbers of women employed in the *staatsdiens*, and its increasing dependence on their labor, provided these women with some leverage for collective action to address their positions of inferiority in the workplace. The number of posts authorized for women rose steadily: 35 percent of all new posts in 1946 went to women, a figure that increased to 37 percent in 1949, 38 percent in 1950, 40 percent in 1951, 41 percent in 1954, 42 percent in 1955, and 44 percent by 1957.[33] Furthermore, the ongoing "labor shortage" meant that the PSC was forced to employ "an excess of females" against posts reserved for men.[34] Although they were scattered among departments and working in offices throughout the country, these women were, like nearly all white public servants, members of the PSA. Deborah Posel has described the PSA as "deferential in the extreme and wedded to a notion of service that precluded any assertiveness."[35] Certainly, the broader history of its engagement with the PSC confirms Posel's opinion of the PSA, but in the contexts of a growing bureaucracy and labor shortage in the 1950s, the PSA Women's Section was able to extract a number of concessions that brought more women into the *staatsdiens*, improved their conditions of work, and secured limited advancement for women in the service hierarchy.

In 1948 and 1949, the Public Service Commission of Enquiry investigated whether women should be promoted to supervisory or managerial positions—in the PSC's lexicon, the clerical band. Having interviewed only men, it unsurprisingly discovered that men were opposed to being placed under the authority of women, and it "could recommend no material departure from established policy."[36] During these years, the PSC was still publicly confident that its recruiting drive would pay off and that it would be able to fill more senior decision-making posts, those in the clerical division, with men. Behind its confidence there was however a glimpse of worry, as it was obliged to send an "urgent memorandum" to regional offices asking that they identify and solicit male candidates for clerical posts who were above the prescribed maximum age of twenty-five years.[37]

By the next year, the PSC had adjusted its position. In its own words, this was due partly to "representations" from the PSA Women's Section, although its newfound pragmatism was probably also driven by the sheer pressure to fill posts. Thus, in early 1950, it overrode the advice of the Public Service Commission of Enquiry and ruled that women could in fact progress to senior clerical or administrative posts; in other words, women could enter the management bands.[38] The proviso, which kept patriarchy in the public service intact, was that "staff controlled by the [female] incumbent should be predominantly women."[39]

Persisting with the assumption that a woman's real place was in the home, successive Union governments since 1910 had held to the policy that female employment in state departments was a temporary, stopgap measure and refused therefore to sanction permanent female appointments.[40] In the early apartheid years, the PSC generally endorsed this position, although in 1948 it introduced a minor reform to retain more experienced women. To that date the *staatsdiens* had only employed unmarried women, and if a woman chose to marry, she was expected to resign. In 1948 the PSC announced that women who resigned to marry, and did not go through with their marriage plans, could be reinstated without any loss of seniority. "Very few women" sought readmission via this concession.[41]

The PSA Women's Section persistently raised the issue of permanent appointments for women with the PSC. Its regular, polite appeals were unsuccessful until 1953 when, in the wake of five years of bleak returns from its recruitment drives, and facing competition from a buoyant private sector, the PSC announced that it would in future allow women to apply for permanent posts.[42] The early 1950s also saw the PSC change its position on the employment of married women, although they were still classed as "non-permanent." By the time the PSC published its 1952 report, it was including statistics on married women, suggesting some concern about the projected numbers of married women who would be employed: in that year they tallied 3,395 of a complement of 8,190 temporary employees.[43] Collectively these developments not only abolished the myth that women were temporary help in the *staatsdiens*, but also emphasized that wage labor was not restricted to the not-yet-married or those disinclined to marry, and that in these modern times, the working wife and working mother was not a coarse factory *"meid"* but a respectable woman performing white-collar work in a government department. By way of a double layer of discrimination, women earned considerably less than men in the *staatsdiens*, reflecting both the abiding assumption—which sometimes lagged behind other institutional developments in the public service—that women were "temporary" workers in the service and also the gendered one that men ought to be the major providers of household income. Women generally occupied lower-paid posts than men, and moreover there were "male" and "female" salary scales for the same work. It was another crisis in the troublesome typing pool that prompted some improvement to women's salaries, if not to the structural sources that kept their salaries low. The recruitment of typists, especially those with shorthand skills, into the *staatsdiens* continued to be sluggish, and between 1951 and 1954 there developed once more a dire shortage. While the PSC resolved in 1951 to review public service salary scales, it began with those in the higher bands, assigning little priority to typists' pay.[44] Although typists were offered on-the-job training (the unpopular *tikskole*), their salaries were on the lowest possible grade. Consequently, the number of applications for typing posts fell far short of the PSC's expectations, and the PSC was twice obliged to introduce "emergency" measures that raised the entry-level salaries for typists, in 1952 and again in 1954. There were no male typists, so while this salary adjustment did have implications for the treasury and the typists, it had little significance for the imbalance between "male" and "female" salaries.

Attempts later in the decade by the PSC to streamline salaries by incorporating into them a range of allowances served to publicly highlight the differences between "male" and "female" scales. Under the circumstances of a chronic shortage of public service labor, this provided an issue around which the PSA Women's Section could lobby. In 1959, the PSC recommended that cost of living and other allowances be included in salaries.[45] Only those on the permanent roster received these allowances, which meant that while nearly all men effectively received a substantial salary increase, only those women who were permanently employed qualified. The PSC's attempts to modernize its salary structures therefore effectively widened the gap between men and women's salaries. Objections against what they described as "discrimination" from the PSA Women's Sections and other organizations including, significantly, the biggest Afrikaner nationalist women's movement, the SAVF, "prompted the PSC," in its prosaic bureaucratese, "to investigate."[46] Although "the principle of absolute parity could not be adopted," the PSC agreed, after consultation with the treasury, to appoint women on the same salary scales as men; in other words, to abolish the separate "male" and "female" scales. This was a significant gain for women, but it did not by any means indicate real salary parity between men and women in the *staatsdiens*: women would follow a "less favorable" rate of progression and those without permanent appointment would not enjoy the benefit of the now-incorporated cost of living allowance.[47]

While women achieved a measure of gradual advancement in the public service during the 1950s, this did little to challenge the service's institutional culture, especially its gendered power structures and hierarchies. Despite the PSC's growing dependence on women's labor, and the concessions for women that were wrested from the PSC, women hardly registered on the service's collective institutional consciousness. As late as 1957, induction training (the formal kind, run by the PSC) was limited to those with permanent appointments, therefore excluding a significant percentage of the female labor force.[48] A Commission of Inquiry into the Structure of the Public Service (different from the standing commission referred to earlier) sat from 1952 to 1956. Its investigations were summarized in the annual PSC reports, and nowhere is there any reference to women public servants; what is noteworthy in these reports is the absence of any reference to female members of the public service, rather than their presence.

Women's impact on the collective psyche of the *staatsdiens* might have been limited—except, in the negative sense, when there were labor shortages. But the implications of their entry into the labor market were felt elsewhere. The history of white women's work in the public service during the 1950s raises several points of significance for this chapter around the ways that early apartheid-era whiteness was imagined, and what happened when the growing presence of women in the workplace meant that powerful Afrikaner nationalist ideas about women and motherhood came under siege. By 1959, some 59 percent of all white adult males were in employment, compared with 22 percent of all women, many of the latter in the public service.[49] Women were out of the home, and they were earning wages—sometimes more than their husbands. They were drifting away from the moorings of the *volksmoeder*, whose historical role was to tend the hearth of family and *volk*. Although neither Afrikaans-speaking nor a public servant, my mother Sheila once again typified this trend. Unlike her mother-in-law, Grandmother Roos, Sheila was far removed from the idea of the *volksmoeder*, not by any particular determination to be contrarian but out of the sheer necessity to provide for her family. As age took its toll on my father, diminishing his capacity to secure the semiskilled jobs as barman and storeman that had always been his lot, his meager war pension proved inadequate for his and Sheila's needs. Sheila finally took a better job as a senior bookkeeper at a major Durban law firm, one of the many ironies of her life, given her time-honored suspicion of lawyers. She worked there until five days before her death from cancer in 1991. And to this day the china tea set that she inherited from her mother-on-law, that generational heirloom that iterated a woman's role in a stable and respectable family, remains unopened in its box.

Developments around the growth of white women's wage labor kindled a range of responses from Afrikaner nationalist women's movements like the SAVF. Responses from organizations like the SAVF coincided with some of the anxieties articulated by Prinsloo, but they also revealed moments of misgiving around the place of women—and also men—in 1950s white society, and the nature of intimate relationships in the home between Black and white. Sometimes these tensions remained just that, upwellings of anxiety; sometimes they involved more complex rationalization of particular circumstances; and at other times they activated concrete and systematic ideological, political, or welfare interventions.

Work, Anxiety, and the Suid-Afrikaanse Vrouefederasie

In the late 1940s and into the 1950s, the Afrikaner nationalist women's movements attached a dizzying array of ideological, cultural, and domestic consequences to women entering the labor force. Concerned not so much with the conditions under which the new public servants worked, nor with the gender discrimination they experienced in the *staatsdiens*, women in organizations like the SAVF were more troubled that work took women out of the home and disrupted the ideals of femininity clustered under the *volksmoeder* ideology.

As the Afrikaner nationalist women's movements incorporated women from the clothing industry in the late 1930s, and as women in the OB added social work to the principles of the *volksmoeder*, the idea of the *volksmoeder* began to assume more pragmatic, everyday dimensions. During the second half of the 1940s and the 1950s, the *volksmoeder* concept lost some of the earlier intellectualism that had seen it develop as an archetype, grounded in particular interpretations of Afrikaner history. Despite including working-class women and expanding their range of activities, these movements did not shed their earlier class character, and their leadership, their orientation, and their style remained middle-class and (fairly) elite.

As thousands of white women (mainly Afrikaners) took on employment in the *staatsdiens*, the women's movements were roused to both ideological angst and practical action. In their practical work, the women's movements acted as part moral guardians, part social workers, an approach marked by a certain mistrust and sense of suspicion that the new public servants somehow represented an imminent threat to the *volk*. These dispositions were common to middle-class Afrikaner nationalist elites across society and not that different to ones that characterized relations between an earlier generation of church officials, social workers, moral reformers, and newly urbanized poor whites in the 1920s and early 1930s.

There was of course considerable continuity before and after the inauguration of the apartheid state in the work undertaken by the women's movements. In the years immediately after the war, they focused on the Christian family, motherhood, and the household. For instance, in 1946, the SAVF journal, *Vrou en Moeder*, advised women through a series of articles on "health for the family."[50] The tone of these guidelines suggested that they were aimed at those who were not particularly familiar with "good" housekeeping practices expected of Afrikaner women: there was advice on proper nutrition, food storage, hygiene in the kitchen, the importance of uncluttered bedrooms with neat and simple curtains, and maintaining a garden. In collaboration with the Transvaal Provincial Council and the Pretoria City Council, the SAVF sponsored an organization called the Bond van Afrikaanse Moeders (League of Afrikaner Mothers).[51] During these years, the SAVF began to express deep concern about the decline of the Afrikaner family, pointing to rising divorce rates during the war that undermined the family, that cornerstone of the *volk*.[52] These themes would receive regular attention during the next decade and beyond, but it is noteworthy that in the early postwar years there was no acknowledgment that just as they were expected to meet ideals of family propriety and management, the "new" women also had to negotiate wage labor.

As the number of women entering the public service increased, the women's movements could not help but acknowledge their presence as respectable women and working mothers, quite different to the *"meide"* epithet of earlier decades—not that the SAVF or its provincial affiliates became strong advocates for these new state employees. On the contrary, they occupied the more conservative side of a debate that had moved through most western societies from the 1920s, which held that the work of wives was dangerous for both economic and moral reasons.[53] Acting more as ciphers for the broader concerns of Afrikaner nationalism than as champions for women's issues, the women's movements revealed some of the anxieties about women's work and the position of the *volksmoeder* at the heart (and hearth) of the *volk*.

Foreshadowing some of the themes manifest a few years later in Prinsloo's book, a 1954 edition of *Vrou en Moeder* published a long opinion piece on women in society where it argued that the family was a gift from God and the "living cornerstone" from which a *volk* is built.[54] The essay then developed a variant of the argument against women's work that raised the specter of "race suicide." These assertions echoed arguments developed earlier in the century by American eugenicists like Paul Popenoe. Writing in the 1920s, Popenoe's pseudoscientific hypotheses tried to demonstrate that working white women were having fewer children than new Eastern European immigrants and African American women, thus contributing to a fall in the "quality" of the American population and making these women guilty of a "crime against the race."[55] Noting that white Afrikaner birth rates were dropping, the *Vrou en Moeder* article exclaimed luridly that the only place that the Afrikaner might be saved was in the womb.[56] Wage labor lay at the core of this demographic crisis, and the article insisted that there was something profoundly wrong with a society that expected women to seek paid employment, or worse, where the cost of living was so high that they were duty-bound to work.[57] It was, however, not always cruel market forces that drove women into wage labor. Introducing a theme that would, as we shall see in the next chapter, become more dominant over the next decade in elite Afrikaner nationalist circles, the article noted that financial need was quite subjective and speculated that Afrikaner families were succumbing to Mammon. The idea of unseemly greed was a recurring theme: in 1958, for instance, a Mrs. A. Verster wrote an article for *Vrou en Moeder* in which she railed against the "materialist spirit" that had taken working women into its grip, and which meant that they neglected their chores, their children, and their *volk*.[58]

In 1956, Minister of Labour Jan de Klerk opened the SAVF's annual conference. Whether or not he based his speech on what he presumed the women wanted to hear, or whether he reflected the party line or his own ideological belief, he reiterated the idea of imminent racial danger. Pointing out that the economy was growing at an unprecedented rate, he warned that growth was outstripping the available supply of white labor. Taking for granted the women's role as *volksmoeders*, he told them that their most important task was to ensure that their sons' career choices would make the white man "the master of his trade"—and to have bigger families. He made no reference to daughters, to the fact that women themselves were increasingly important for the state labor force, or to the conditions under which women worked.[59]

The language used to describe dangers to the race, and the logic of large families, emerged as growing numbers of women took to work, and it was eloquent testimony to the SAVF's understanding of the role of women in the *volk* and its attitude to waged work. In 1944, the SAVF had called for birth control to be made available to poor women, arguing that many children, born close together, was a major cause of white poverty.[60] Yet a little more than a decade later, small families, associated with the rise of wage labor among women, were considered a danger to white civilization. In her article in April 1958, the ubiquitous Mrs. Verster proposed that, as an alternative to "the materialist spirit," technical colleges provide courses for married women on "profitable home industry."[61]

Just as the SAVF expressed ideological disapproval of women's work, it sought to shore up those kinds of knowledge that were most fundamental to the *volksmoeder* style of femininity. This entailed support for *werkklubs* (work clubs) established under the auspices of SAVF branches, where women could practice and compete against each other in "traditional" skills like spinning and weaving, hat-making, knitting, and quilting.[62] More ambitiously, these efforts also involved the development of a formal curriculum for *moederkunde* (mothercraft). Reflecting back on the development of the subject, an article in the July 1957 edition of *Vrou en Moeder* pointed out that the health of a nation could be seen in the way that it treated children, especially babies. In earlier generations, a girl would have learned from her mother, but under new economic circumstances, she tended to start work much younger. Thus, the article rationalized, there was very little opportunity for her to learn the "crafts of motherhood" outside of school, which made *moederkunde* such an important addition to high school curricula. Introduced first in the Orange

Free State, where the curriculum was developed at the elite Christelike Nasionale Meisieskool Oranje in Bloemfontein, it taught junior high girls the basics of physiology, anatomy, and first aid. Those who chose to do so could continue with the subject for the remaining three years of high school, where they were exposed to an intensive program of baby care.[63] At Oranje this extended to a practical component of care for a baby. The school took a child from a local orphanage, usually the baby of a poor and unmarried mother, and the child would live at the school until the age of two, when it would be given up for adoption. Under the guidance of the *moederkunde* teacher, girls would undergo seven-week cycles of "baby duty" where they would live with the infant in a building on the school premises and play with, feed, and attend to it during the night. According to a former teacher, *moederkunde* never attracted the most academically talented learners or those most ambitious to succeed in the world of formal employment.[64] As opportunities for women in the *staatsdiens*, commerce, and the professions expanded during the 1960s, interest in *moederkunde* declined, and the subject was discontinued and phased out between 1971 and 1974.

Collectively, these efforts represented an attempt to reproduce the cultural knowledge and habits of an earlier generation of the idealized *volksmoeder*. But the Afrikaner nationalist women's movements did more than articulate ideological antagonism to the idea of the working mother, hearkening back nostalgically to a time when women demonstrated virtues more appropriate to the development of the *volk*. They also responded in more practical ways to the new social world of whites, Afrikaners in particular, that was evolving as respectable women joined the labor force. Reiterating and reinvigorating wartime traditions of amateur social work, the SAVF urged its branches to undertake *huisbesoek* (home visits). Whereas earlier, visits were intended to identify and address the depredations of poverty, they now began to expressly include an element of surveillance. Maintaining a family had become increasingly difficult, especially with women "leaving" home for work. Once, communities had been blighted by the number of families who suffered the indignities of poverty, but now, just as Afrikaners' material circumstances had begun to improve, the number of those whom the SAVF considered "culturally underprivileged" was on the rise, especially in new working-class communities.[65] Demonstrating the SAVF's own sense of guardianship over white working class communities, it declared with rather condescending benevolence that through visits by its members, it "brought the aims and concerns of the SAVF to the less-privileged." One of the major characteristics of these "less privileged" individuals was that they were not adequately "*Afrikaans-bewus*" (Afrikaans-aware), and by implication the quality of being

"*Afrikaans-onbewus*" (unaware) was most likely to be found in families where the woman had abandoned her *volksmoeder* role.[66] Thus, girded by a strong sense of purpose, by 1954 nearly all SAVF branches were undertaking "*gesinsorg*" (family care visits).[67]

Much like the social workers, reformers, and politicians of the 1920s who were committed to "saving" and "improving" the children of poor whites, so too the Afrikaner nationalist movements of the early apartheid years staked a great deal in "saving" the children of a generation that was in danger of cultural dissolution, despite the NP occupying power. A significant part of this concern involved their support for Afrikaans *kleuterskole* (nursery schools). Afrikaans nursery schools had their origin in the Armstrong-Berning house, established in Pretoria in 1906 as a shelter for unmarried mothers. After Union in 1910, the Department of Welfare began to use it as a place of committal for white children under the age of six. Physically, the children were well cared for, but the nursing staff had little insight into proper educational care for young children. In 1940, Mrs. Eudora Hauptfleisch, then a member of the Armstrong-Berning Board, argued that a school for preschool infants was needed. The board agreed, and that year, the Eudora Hauptfleisch school was established as the first Afrikaans nursery school in the Transvaal. The following year the Transvaalse Vereeniging van Kleuteropvoeding (Transvaal Union of Infant Education) was established with the goal of "advancing nursery schools as a significant part of the education of the Afrikaner child." During the 1940s these schools expanded across the Witwatersrand, and also in the Free State.[68] By the early 1950s, as more and more children, especially in towns, were left without the full-time care of their mothers, support for a local nursery school had become the major task for SAVF branches, and by 1958 there were 74 SAVF-supported *kleuterskole* in the Transvaal alone—a legion of *Duimpies*.[69]

There are at least two factors that account for the energy and resources that the SAVF allocated to *kleuterskole* in the 1950s. First, the SAVF women stuck firmly to the belief that, in industrial society, infants needed to be "physically and spiritually developed for the *volk*."[70] There were existing nursery schools, but not only did these cater primarily to English-speaking children, they were also often run by Roman Catholic nuns. Although seldom "liberal," English-medium schools hardly valued the idea of the *volk*, and in the 1950s Catholic nuns were leading a fighting retreat against school segregation.[71] The SAVF therefore insisted that Afrikaner children should experience their first contact with the "outside" world in their own language, immersed in their own culture, and that their early childhood education should be informed by a Protestant ethic.[72] Secondly, although some critics

Figure 6.1 A Black domestic worker and her charge, a little white boy, early 1960s. Author's personal collection.

among the *volk* did see *kleuterskole* as dumping grounds where lazy mothers left their children, Mrs. Hauptfleish insisted that this was a far better alternative to leaving them in the care of African women domestic servants who, she claimed, knew little about, or cared little for, Afrikaner culture.[73]

As the decade progressed, more women found full-time jobs, and white household incomes increased. Although an established practice on farms and among wealthier whites, the employment of Black female domestic workers only became common among working-class whites in the 1950s. This development introduced all sorts of new racial, sexual, domestic, and child-rearing relations into white homes. The implications of these relations, played out behind the closed doors of the home, prompted a wave of anxieties in the SAVF, the self-appointed custodian of white Afrikaner domesticity. Chief among these concerns was the one expressed by Mrs. Hauptfleish: the danger that white women were abdicating childcare to the Black women whom they employed. In a similar vein, "South Africa relies too much on servants, and this is a great pity for our children," declared an article in *Vrou en Moeder* in 1960.[74]

Archly, if disingenuously, given the meager wages paid to Black domestic workers, a contributor to *Vrou en Moeder* asked whether the cost of domestic labor made it worthwhile for white women to take on employment.[75] But of deepest concern to the women in the SAVF were the types of "unnatural intimacy" that could potentially develop. Contrasting "old style" house servants, seen as paragons of trustworthiness—fondly, nostalgically, and yet patronizingly characterized in this instance as "Outa [Aunt] Doi"—a Mrs. E. S. L. Bell complained that "these days" it was a difficult task to manage Black servants, who were hired off the street, were likely to abscond, and lacked Outa Doi's loyalty and decency.[76] She advised strongly that even if she worked all day, the woman of the house should be the one who "instructed" the domestic worker, and that the rest of the family should avoid developing close relations with the domestic.

The 1950 Immorality Amendment Act, which strengthened prohibitions on sex between "Europeans" and "non-Europeans," along with a growing commitment to enforcing it—particularly against white men—could be interpreted as a means of protecting women's place in patriarchal white household. Indeed, this "unnatural intimacy" identified by Mrs. Bell clearly raised several troubling specters for the SAVF, for it returned to this theme regularly, being covered by *Vrou en Moeder* four times in thirteen issues between December 1960 and December 1961. And these specters introduced a new figure into racialized sexual discourse. Hitherto the focus of such panic and calls for stricter urban segregation and pass laws had been the Black male—manifest for instance in a 1946 article in *Vrou en Moeder* on crime and attacks on women and girls where the SAVF called on the government to tighten influx control on African men and to "evict vagrant natives," urging white household heads to arm themselves.[77] Now African women, who worked in conditions of "unnatural intimacy," became the focus of paranoia, and in December 1961 a Dr. L. Strating coyly urged women to ensure that they returned home before their husbands. African women in domestic service were known as "girls," often dressed in a maid's uniform and robbed of any name except a convenient, easy-to-pronounce "Christian" (actually, Afrikaans or English) one; these customs might be seen as attempts to infantilize them and deactivate their sexual potential.[78] The ways that African women were conscripted into the phantom legions of those threatening apartheid whiteness were related directly to the rise of white women's work, mainly in the *staatsdiens* and the employment of African women in white homes.

The "New" White Woman, the State, and the Nation

Like other intellectual brokers of Afrikaner nationalism, Prinsloo disapproved of the "spirit of individualism" and the freedoms associated with it. For Prinsloo, the *volk* was more important than the individual, and the germ of "individualism" was incubated most dangerously and widely among women by wage labor. Her disapproval represented simultaneously a rebuke of the "dissolution" rippling through western societies and a claim—repeated by her peers until at least the 1980s—that apartheid South Africa was the proper standard bearer of westernism.

Under Afrikaner nationalism, the state was deployed in service of the nation. But the "state" itself was ambiguous about the growth of women's wage labor in the *staatsdiens*. Political office-bearers were uneasy about the ways that women's work picked at the threads of the established order of things—symbolized by the *volksmoeder* concept. Their knee-jerk response was to disclaim the emergence of new gender dynamics in the public service labor market and to reiterate the abiding relevance of the *volksmoeder* idea that Hyslop has shown was central to the NP's populist rhetoric and mobilization.[79] Yet the burgeoning apartheid state needed the labor of these women for its expanding bureaucracy, and senior bureaucrats in the PSC saw things slightly differently. These officials had to balance the ideological and cultural concerns of the political classes (and no doubt, of male PSC officials themselves) while simultaneously meeting the needs of a growing bureaucracy. Senior officials never went as far as considering seriously the kind of proposal made by Prinsloo for the establishment of a Bureau of Female Labour. But just as they incorporated women into the *staatsdiens*, they collected copious statistics, with the obvious implication that the employment of women represented a trend that required careful management. Thus, while the PSC oversaw the mass employment of women in the *staatsdiens*, it did so in ways carefully designed to avoid tipping gender hierarchies. And as much as possible, it limited the permanent employment of married women, thus maintaining a shard of the fiction that its response to the demand for labor was not intended to disrupt families.

Histories of women's work in the *staatsdiens* make us reflect on how racialized ideologies of both nation and gender operated in the apartheid state. Working women transgressed the boundaries of white Afrikaner femininity, which was articulated under the rubric of the *volksmoeder*. This disruption in turn upset elite Afrikaner nationalist ideas about the nation, the *volk*. As Prinsloo's alarm, the minister of labor's bumbling comments, and the SAVF's interventions all indicate, women's entry into wage labor ignited considerable anxiety. The ways that white Afrikaner femininity was renegotiated were reminiscent of how pressures from the labor market, especially during the Second World War, led first to the working girl, then the working wife, and then the working mother, accepted in parts of American culture a decade earlier—and similarly, without any concession to the central idea of patriarchy.[80]

Ironically, just as work in fact presented these women with slivers of the "freedom" described with such disdain by Prinsloo, it exposed them to multiple forms of regulation, management, and, on occasion, discipline. As elsewhere in the mid-twentieth century world, there was evidence of how "the nation" as a historical project was not only able to draw on state resources, but also how it locally had its own ideological framework and channels for regulation outside of the state, and how it contained potent gendered elements. These were developed largely but not solely by the SAVF, and Afrikaans women were much more vulnerable than other, non-Afrikaans whites as the SAVF restaked the parameters of what it meant to be white, Afrikaans ("*Afrikaans-bewus*"), respectable, and a working woman. In so doing, it limited the social possibilities available to these women.[81] Furthermore, it backed up these principles and the standards of behavior assigned to Afrikaans women through its program of *huisbesoek* and its network of amateur social workers operating through branches—the numbers of which expanded in working-class neighborhoods. The new common sense, spelled out and enforced by the SAVF and through educational initiatives like *moederkunde* and the *kleuterskole*, represented a formidable means of policing Afrikaans women from the working class and subaltern sections of white society as they were able to penetrate the intimate domains of everyday life.[82] Thus, the lives of working white women—in the case of this chapter, public servants—were not only ordered by the formal regulations and unwritten codes of the *staatsdiens,* but those who were Afrikaners were also subject to the blandishments and sometimes unsubtle coercion of the SAVF.

Clearly the tasks of shaping and ordering white subaltern femininity demanded cooperation between the state and other bodies. While the Afrikaner nationalist women's movements were quite critical in this regard, they were not the only ones with an interest in policing white women's conduct in apartheid society; the liberal elite shared a similar degree of complicity. And Afrikaans women were not the only objects of such surveillance. The fate of "a lovely Irish girl" from Durban illustrates these points. Although not a public servant, she was a working-class woman, employed as a "shop girl" somewhere in Durban and presumably without connections in the city because she lived in a hostel owned by an organization known as the Durban Bachelor Girls' Club.[83] The club was established after the First World War to "assist the small wage-earner who, through their inadequate wages, start life condemned to undesirable circumstances and overwhelming temptations."[84] Its founding members were drawn from Durban's middle classes, women who would hardly claim any affinity with Afrikaner nationalism. Indeed, at one point during the 1920s, frustrated at the ways in which younger people, especially women, were excluded from decision-making positions in branches of the South African Party (SAP), then in opposition to the NP, members of the club went ahead and formed their own SAP branch. Sometime in the early 1950s, it came to the attention of the Bachelor Club committee that a "lovely Irish girl" had fallen in love with a "fine strapping native" and it was "a hopeless task to keep them apart." So the gentlewomen who managed the Bachelor Girls' hostel hatched a plan, collaborating with the captain of a freighter sailing to Liverpool (himself a "fine old Scot, a father of six"). They kidnapped the girl, packing her into a car and taking her straight to the Durban docks, where they bungled her aboard the ship, after which the gangway was immediately raised before the ship sailed. At Liverpool she was met by representatives of the Girls' Friendly Society and sent on to Ireland.[85] While the girl's parents wrote a "warm and friendly" letter of thanks to the Bachelor Girls' Club, her passion was rather more resilient than her parents or the Bachelor Girls would have liked, and her friends in Ireland set up a subscription to send her back to her "Native admirer." Hearing news of this defiance, the Bachelor Girls went immediately to the chief magistrate of Durban and prevailed upon him to declare the girl a prohibited immigrant.[86] Much like their peers in the SAVF, the Bachelor Girls thus showed themselves to be not only energetic and formidable defenders of apartheid legislation but also willing to police white femininity—brutally in this case—when it was challenged, especially by working-class women.

NATIONALISM, WHITENESS, AND CONSUMPTION

7

The Boom Gate at the Yacht Harbor

Dick, my father, loved walking. When he had leave days from work, nothing put him in a better mood than the prospect of a half-day's walk. He would set off early and preferred to walk with his shirt off, a quirk for which the neighbors sometimes called him "Tarzan." If he had enough money, he would sometimes stop for a few beers along the way, either at a working man's hotel similar to the one where he worked for many years or at one of the bars, reserved strictly for white men, that were a feature of apartheid-era railway stations. Dick's favorite destination was the Durban port, about five miles from our home. The city's picturesque yacht harbor, while part of the port, is separated from the main esplanade by a busy railway line. There was a manually operated boom at the entrance to the harbor that was raised and lowered when a train approached. Of course, until the 1990s the boom operator was always a white man. This man sat in a small shelter similar to those assigned to security guards and the job was probably a legacy of the civilized labor policy that had provided Karel/Charles with his employment as a toilet attendant sixty years earlier. For more than twenty years, Dick coveted the boom operator's job. More than anything, he wanted to be the one to raise and lower the boom and look at the yachts. Depending which one was on duty, he would pause in his walk and spend time with the boom operator, sharing a cigarette and a cup of tea. Sometimes on a weekend he would invite me to ride the bus with him to look at the yachts, an excursion that would invariably involve stopping and chatting with the boom operator, sometimes raising and lowering it a few times "just to get the feel of it." When he and I left Durban for distant Mafikeng in 1992, he insisted we pass by the yacht harbor, protected by its boom, "just for old times' sake." It was the last time he ever saw it.

The boom represented Dick's sole ambition, while the image of him strolling the streets of hot, tropical Durban with his shirt off offers a glimpse of his aesthetic. This manner of aspiration was certainly not the kind that the state sought to cultivate among whites, particularly men, during the 1950s and beyond.

Afrikaner Nationalism and the Wages of Whiteness

One of the historic missions of the Afrikaner nationalist movement in the first four decades of the twentieth century was to address the legacies of poverty among Afrikaners. This mission included ensuring that Afrikaners could reach and maintain the white *ordentlike* (respectable) lifestyle vis-à-vis Blacks described by de Kiewiet while also addressing their presumed cultural inferiority with respect to English-speaking whites. By the beginning of the Second World War, those Afrikaners who could be described as poor whites had virtually disappeared, although the profile of urban Afrikaners, approximately two-thirds of the total Afrikaner population, was predominantly working-class. Speaking at the opening of the Voortrekker Monument in December 1949, Prime Minister D. F. Malan hearkened back to the dangers of dire poverty among whites. Hermann Giliomee is of the opinion, however, that Malan was "still living in the first three or four decades of the twentieth century."[1]

By 1950, Malan was more confident that Afrikaners could "get a place in the economic sun."[2] Artfully, he reminded them that they should not rely too heavily on state support to advance their interests. While the NP government intended to privilege and protect all whites, Afrikaners should utilize their own ambition and hard work to make headway in both public and private sectors.[3] From a point where Afrikaner poverty and poor whiteism had deeply scarred the collective Afrikaner psyche to a mood of gathering confidence in the early 1950s, these optimistic trends accelerated through the decade to a rather bizarre juncture in the early 1960s when there was a concern among certain Afrikaner nationalist elites that Afrikaners were getting too rich.[4]

It is pretty straightforward to plot the growth of income among whites during the 1950s and to demonstrate how, as a subset of this pattern, the income levels of Afrikaans speakers demonstrated particularly rapid acceleration. It is also not too difficult to account for the roles of the state in this process, taking Malan's commitment to protecting and supporting white privilege more seriously than his disclaimer that the government would not favor Afrikaans speakers over English speakers. Also, the material and cultural features of this new prosperity are not too difficult to discern. For instance, Albert Grundlingh explains this for the 1960s, although cultural changes set in motion by economic growth did in fact begin in the previous decade.[5] If, however, we consider rising white affluence and the types of consumption that it spurred from a wider analytic lens and use it as another entry point to investigate the bonds that held together apartheid society, then several questions emerge.

In the early 1990s, David Roediger published *The Wages of Whiteness*, which argued that in the United States, white workers' cash wages were supplemented by psychological, social, and public or infrastructural "wages of whiteness." Despite sporadic criticism, his thesis has aged remarkably well, and part of it is of abiding value to the scholar of white apartheid society, where growing white affluence and a widening wage gap between Black and white workers represented very real "wages of whiteness" and a substantial foundation for complicity and accommodation. Wealth was a clear indicator that poor whiteism had finally ended, as the erstwhile white poor were incorporated into and promoted within the *staatsdiens* or made their way in a booming private sector, where they commanded cash in addition to psychological and social wages. But if we are to go beyond wealth and accumulation, and consider the associated histories of consumption, taste, and aspiration—historiographic entry points that were not commonly utilized when Roediger wrote in the early 1990s—an altogether more complex, contested, and ambiguous picture of elite attempts to manage and regulate whites emerges. For one, frictions that emerged from the material successes of Afrikaner nationalism and apartheid for Afrikaans speakers and whites more generally caused alarm among influential figures in the state, the church, and the academy in the late 1950s and early 1960s. To this end, killjoy Afrikaner national elites tried to intervene to "divert" aspiration and leisure toward what they considered more wholesome ends. Necessity dictates, therefore, an evaluation of the effectiveness (or lack thereof) of the moral, ideological, and disciplinary seawall against the rising tides of affluence that drew whites, especially Afrikaans speakers, away from the sacred duties of the *volk*—or at the very least, "acceptable" norms of everyday life, if not away from the privileges of whiteness.

The absorption of large numbers of hitherto poor whites into fairly well-paid state, parastatal, and private sector work created private household incomes that disrupted the forms of Afrikaner culture imagined by Afrikaner nationalist intellectuals like Geoffrey Cronjé, Jannie Pieterse, and Maria Prinsloo. These whites spent money and indeed were encouraged to do so. However, blacklisting for nonpayment of accounts became widespread, and some whites entered into credit relationships that undermined the very foundations of white supremacy. Some developed an unseemly interest in the occult, meaning that just as the state, a self-proclaimed Christian state, was being made, the nation was being unmade. Yet prosperity and gathering interaction with Western culture—its styles, subcultures, and Cold War psychoses—provided the grounds for coherence of apartheid whiteness that transcended but never eliminated the hoary distinction between Afrikaans and other whites.

White Wages under Apartheid

The best accounts of the political economy of white wages during the 1950s, particularly but not exclusively in the state sector, the *staatsdiens*, and the burgeoning parastatals, remain those produced in the 1970s by Marxist historians. These historians were interested in white wages as part of their broader concern to understand the operation of racial capitalism in South Africa.

After the Second World War, whites experienced something of an economic reversal, one that was however always relative in the context of segregated South Africa. Living costs for whites had increased sharply: on an index set at 100 points in 1938, living costs had risen to 133 in 1945 and 146 by 1948.[6] Moreover, the number of unemployed white men had risen from 76,000 in 1945 to 130,000 by 1948, reflecting the number of returned war veterans unable to settle into regular work. Conditions were thus ripe for some white male wage earners, though by no means all of them, to become quite receptive to the NP's brand of ethnic mobilization by 1948.

Robert Davies writes that electoral support from the white wage-earning classes was central for the NP as it assumed power in 1948, and the importance of this class for the party remained consistent as it consolidated power over the next decade. B. J. Vorster, MP for Nigel (and later, prime minister) declared in 1956: "The white worker in South Africa has brought the National Party to the position it occupies today and . . . will keep it in that position in future."[7]

One of the primary means by which the NP sought to address the economic situation of Afrikaners was through various forms of statism, a political philosophy that held that the state itself should control and contribute to economic development and social policy.[8] The state's role in advancing the interests of white workers had several dimensions across various sectors of the economy. Most significant was the dramatic increase in the number of people, mainly Afrikaans speakers, employed by the state itself. The five years from 1950 to 1955 saw the fastest growth to that point in the state's staff establishment, as numbers increased from 481,518 in 1950 to 798,545 in 1955, an annual increase of 6 percent.[9] O'Meara contends that the major beneficiaries of expansion were Afrikaans-speaking males, reflected in the fact that their numbers employed in the *staatsdiens* nearly doubled. Unlike earlier decades, when the state sector had been used to absorb white men in the most nominal unskilled capacity to provide them with some form of income, principles of "civilized labor" were applied more strictly to the public service than to any other part of the economy, as whites were reassigned from labor to supervisory positions. As an example, the number of white "railworkers"—laborers—decreased, in absolute terms, by 5,276 between 1948 and 1959.[10] In addition, the early postwar years saw the creation of "literally hundreds" of parastatals. The staffing complement of these bodies was "thoroughly Afrikanerized," and posts in these parastatals came with higher salaries than those paid in the public service more generally.[11]

In the private sector, similar processes unfolded. During the war years, reorganization of the labor process in the manufacturing and engineering industries received a boost under cover of meeting the demands of the wartime economy, but as Davies remarks, in the early apartheid years, restructuring took place in an increasingly greater number of companies and in more sectors of the economy. As industry expanded and mechanized, growing numbers of machine operative posts went to Blacks, while whites moved into "supervisory and mental" jobs, characterized by what Davies calls petty bourgeois work. He adds that "industrial capital" sought not so much to eliminate the racist hierarchy in industry during the transition of early apartheid, but to relocate it to a "higher level." Industry spokesmen were at one with the government in asserting that "the leading role of the white race should be maintained" and that the "natural economic process" should contribute to this objective.[12] These developments, driven by various statist interventions, saw the index of real white wages increase by 10 percent during the first five years of apartheid rule, while those of Blacks dropped by 5 percent.[13] By 1960, a broad white middle class had emerged with considerable purchasing power and particular tastes.

New Domestic Economies

Focused as they are on the organization of work and the operation of the political economy, these histories fail to recognize the kinds of white domestic economies that emerged during these years. There were at least two major changes to white household-scale economies. First, the expansion of work in the private and (especially) public sector saw a big increase in the number of women who were employed, meaning that for the first time there were double-income families. Second, the public service drive toward professionalization, along with its preference for Afrikanerization, enabled a wave of university-educated Afrikaans speakers to enter the *staatsdiens* at higher levels than their generational predecessors.

The most obvious evidence of aspirant middle-class status among working whites was the development of new residential neighborhoods, and the idea of a single white family living in a single-family dwelling was also central to the Afrikaner nationalist vision of the orderly family. The desire among whites to own houses was supported by the state, though the means of making this a practical reality remained regulated. Historically, for members of the white wage-earning classes struggling to establish and consolidate their status as *ordentlik* (respectable), the ideas of "home" and a house were closely intertwined. Sometimes, though, the house would be part of a semidetached row and, from about the 1920s, circumstances sometimes diverted families to flats, especially in cities like Durban, Johannesburg, and Cape Town.

There was, however, a long history of shortage when it came to housing for working class whites, stretching back to at least the end of the First World War.[14] From the mid-1940s, this shortage was exacerbated by industrialization, the demobilization of white veterans, and, in the words of NP Member of Parliament D.G. Conradie, housing regulations that favored "big builders and influential people," making it difficult for the "smaller builder and the smaller man who was able to help himself in the past."[15] After the Second World War, a variety of land purchase schemes and soft loans aimed specifically at white male veterans saw the development of new ex-service neighborhoods like Victory Park, Roosevelt Park, and Montgomery Park in Johannesburg, and Woodlands in Durban.[16] But beyond these developments, the political importance of the Afrikaans-speaking wage earners for the NP's electoral success, the rising affluence of that class, and the cultural significance of housing meant that it was hardly surprising to see a spurt of new housing for whites from the late 1940s. As an NP Member of Parliament put it to the House, between 1945 and 1948, the United Party government built 23,510 houses for whites at a cost of £23,500,000, while in its first two years in office, the NP administration built 31,256 houses at a more economical £26,500,000.[17]

The development of new neighborhoods took place most substantially in those cities with a heavy concentration of public servants: Cape Town, Pretoria, and, to a lesser extent, Bloemfontein. Thus, the 1950s saw the growth of new white neighborhoods, including Waverley, Rietfontein, Villeria, Gezina, and Wonderboom to the north of the city in Pretoria; and Parow, Bellville, and Durbanville in Cape Town, also to the north of the city behind what became known as the *boerewors-gordyn* (boerewors curtain).[18] As the director of housing explained earnestly to NP Member of Parliament W. A. Maree, apartheid principles *were* being implemented in new housing schemes.[19] Well after the formal abolition of apartheid, the director's meaning remains clear: it is stark how effectively these new neighborhoods were developed as white enclaves, separated from Black townships and even high-rise white neighborhoods, by physical barriers like mountains, major highways, or industrial areas. In this respect, apartheid-era neighborhoods developed with white wage earners in mind were very different from older city neighborhoods where lines of racial demarcation were often grayed and arbitrary.

Housing assistance was available to all whites under a scheme whereby the National Housing Commission provided guarantees and a subsidy of up to 30 percent when applicants approached a building society for a loan—although an opposition member of Parliament, H. Davidoff, grumbled that the real beneficiaries were building societies who charged an interest rate of 6.5 percent. If a homeowner took a loan over the standard twenty years, he (only men qualified for support) paid more than the capital. "That is too much," declared the MP.[20] Public servants fared better, as they received a subsidy of up to two-thirds, but only if they bought new houses. Effectively, therefore, the state was capitalizing these new public servant neighborhoods. The state also believed that it was investing in the stability of the social order. As the National Housing Commission reported: "From the national point of view home ownership is a stabilizing influence and one of the major bastions against communism and other social ills."[21] Anxieties about communism may have been misplaced, but an effect of these enormous housing subsidies was to add a substantial increment to the wages of whiteness enjoyed by a particular sector of white society.

Predictably, in the self-consciously regulated world of Afrikaner nationalist governance, the central state tried to manage architecture and urban planning in the new neighborhoods, and the National Housing Commission paid the South African Council for Scientific and Industrial Research (CSIR) £10,000 to undertake research into the best design and materials for white housing. Ultimately, though, it was really the (subsidized) market that drove the architectural aesthetics of these neighborhoods. "A home of his own," declared the Servitas Housing Corporation, tapping cannily into the importance of housing for the aspirant middle class, adding for good measure, "A decent house for the family man is key."[22] Servitas, which had branches in Johannesburg, Durban, Bloemfontein, Port Elizabeth, and Cape Town, was one of the many corporations vying to build houses in the new neighborhoods. Its prospectus offers a snapshot of white middle-class housing aspirations in the early 1950s. Houses would have two or three bedrooms and one bathroom. Floors would be of hardwood or tile, and the kitchen would be tiled. There would be a garage for one car.[23] The house would cost between £400 and £1,000, depending on the number of bedrooms and the interior fittings. By 1953, Servitas claimed to have already built more than 1,500 houses in what it optimistically described as "garden villages," and the houses were of a fairly standard design, clear today even after years of modification and gentrification. Each new neighborhood was planned to include a clinic, sports field, library, schools, and churches. Besides being sensitive to the cultural value of housing—or more accurately, particular types of housing—for the aspirant white middle class, Servitas was also sharply aware of the bureaucratic steps needed to help these whites realize their dream home (and for the company to realize a profit). Thus, it promised to help prospective buyers arrange financing though the National Housing Commission and also, if they qualified, subsidies through their employers.

As the new neighborhoods developed, the Suid-Afrikaanse Vrouefederasie (SAVF), that watchdog of the *volk*, expressed approval of their design and facilities. It was not just the layout and physical aesthetics of the neighborhoods that attracted interest and concern from these guardians of Afrikaner nationalism, but also questions of the neighborhoods' cultural character. Revealing an instance of unease that would recur among Afrikaner nationalist elites through the decade during which poorer Afrikaners would drift away from the cultural values of the *volk*, the SAVF announced in September of 1947 that new SAVF branches had been opened in the new Pretoria suburbs of Rietfontein and Villeria.[24] These branches had ten and eleven members respectively, but the extent to which their progress was monitored in the columns of *Vrou en Moeder* is noteworthy. By the mid-1950s both had expanded, although growth was slow and several years of recruiting in these predominantly Afrikaans-speaking, public service neighborhoods had only pushed up membership in each case to the low twenties. Contrary to the confident assertions made by the director of housing in 1953 that apartheid was being implemented, the planning vision of apartheid's senior bureaucrats was not always as cut-and-dried in the geographies of urban neighborhoods. In 1953, for instance, the NP member for Langlaagte, a working-class area in Johannesburg, reported that, despite the provisions of the 1950 Group Areas Act, the cornerstone of urban apartheid in his constituency, "European and non-Europeans are living cheek by jowl."[25] This apartheid anomaly was noted with alarm by the SAVF.[26]

Housing, especially in the new suburbs, represented the aspirant edge of Afrikaans-speaking middle-class consumption and pride at having shaken off the stain of poverty and economic inferiority in relation to English-speaking whites. But the housing occupied by those whites unable to capitalize as successfully on the apartheid dividend was a cause of distress to middle-class Afrikaner nationalists whose vision for white—particularly Afrikaans-speaking—society under NP rule was decidedly middle class. From the 1920s, high-rise apartments to accommodate whites had begun to feature in South African urban landscapes, most particularly in Johannesburg and Durban. The social history of white flatland in South Africa remains unwritten, although from early on these large, high-rise housing blocks were viewed with some distaste by the staunch women of the SAVF, quite plausibly because apartments, especially those occupied by working-class white people, tended to attract a motley and eclectic mix of tenants.[27] By the 1950s, the SAVF would declare unambiguously that "flats did not make appropriate homes for the *volk.*"[28] Consistent with its broader concerns during the decade, the SAVF framed its disapproval around child-rearing—that flats represented an unhealthy and unwholesome environment for children who required "activity and exercise." This was an opinion shared by veteran United Party MP Vernon Shearer, who warned that the development of flatlands was part of a bigger phenomenon indicating the erosion of family life: "what are we finding in this country? We find that the tendency is to move away from family life; the erection of big blocks of flats where man and wife are going out to work. We find that in this country, because of the policies followed by this and other Governments family life is fast disappearing."[29] Not all whites were able to take advantage of housing subsidies to purchase their own homes or even rent houses or flats at market rates. By the end of 1957, nearly 5,000 "railway houses," allocated to married white railway men at a nominal rental, had been built.[30] Squat, solid, and red-brick, with a characteristic small front veranda and a fenced yard, these houses remain a common feature of South African cities, rural towns, and former railway junctions. In those cities with a revenue base large enough to afford them, substantial subeconomic housing estates were developed to provide safe and affordable housing to working-class and unemployed whites. Nominally, entry into these followed a referral by a social worker, but this was not always the case.[31] White subeconomic housing usually constituted blocks of flats, both low-rise and high-rise. In Durban, for instance, Kenneth Gardens was made up of 286 flats, spread over thirty blocks, while Flamingo Court, built in 1958, was a thirteen-story block with 200 flats. Even at the time, these estates acquired a distinct reputation for disorder and immorality, attracting not only the official attention of social workers but also derogatory nicknames (in the case of Flamingo Court, "FL Court").[32]

In 1947, when the crisis of postwar housing shortage was still developing, the SAVF was full of praise for those municipalities that invested in these subeconomic housing estates for whites, commending them for stemming the "flight to backyards."[33] But by 1949, it was urging urban branches to direct their *huisbesoek* activities to housing estates.[34] The echoes of poor whiteism were never far away. Clearly concerned about possible moral and cultural lapses among Afrikaans speakers resident in subeconomic housing, the SAVF's *huisbesoek* thus added further surveillance to that experienced by these poorer white communities. This was in addition to the professional social workers who directed their attention there, and seldom, if ever, to the well-heeled and respectable communities in the new public service neighborhoods.

Home ownership featured prominently in the aspirational horizons of whites joining the new class of public servants. But neither home ownership nor the (lesser) respectability that came from private rental were universal ambitions among all whites, all Afrikaners, or all public servants. The archive suggests that during the course of the decade, whites took advantage of subeconomic housing, draining state and municipal coffers and also frustrating intentions of the NP, the state, and Afrikaner national elites to foster a respectable homeowning class of prosperous Afrikaans speakers. The Department of Health and Welfare felt obliged to send a memorandum to all municipalities in 1962 that reminded them that subeconomic housing had to be developed on strict "racial lines," suggesting that this apartheid protocol was not always followed, and moreover emphasizing that income limits should be enforced. No family should pay more than one-fifth of their income, or twenty-two rand, a month.[35] This housing was thus nominally reserved for families earning R110 a month.[36]

Perhaps the most distressing sign during the early apartheid years that not all whites were able to drag themselves out of poverty (or more appropriately, into respectability) was demonstrated by the presence of those who continued to occupy accommodation established for poor whites in the interwar years. Going back to the gendered nineteenth-century histories of proletarianization and working-class formation in South Africa, there were long traditions of white working men occupying bachelor quarters. These histories also meant that as women left the rural areas to seek work, mainly in factories, single quarters were established for them, too, in Pretoria, Johannesburg, the east and west Rand, and Durban. Instead of disappearing as working-class populations became more stable, this type of accommodation became more common with the onset of the Great Depression. Coinciding with the most comprehensive years of civilized labor interventions during the 1920s and early 1930s, gangs of poor white men were mobilized and put to work on labor-intensive projects like building roads or dams, often far from their homes.

There they were housed in the most rudimentary single-sex quarters, sometimes tents—a perverse mirror image of the single-sex compounds built for Black migrant workers. As these poor whites were incorporated into permanent jobs in the public service, usually in the very low grades, these temporary quarters became institutionalized, subsidized by the state as a meager wage of whiteness. In 1947, the NP member of Parliament for Wonderboom, Mr. M. D. C. Nel, expressed his indignation that railway workers in Maquassi in the western Transvaal were "forced to live in hovels." He seemed particularly outraged that there was "not a single bath for the lot of them."[37]

Single-sex quarters did not vanish overnight, although the quality of the establishments did improve during the early years of NP rule; these improvements were not funded exclusively by the state but also by Afrikaner nationalist welfare organizations and, increasingly, capital from successful and confident Afrikaners. Thus the SAVF and its provincial affiliates, for instance, managed homes for working women: Harmonie, Sonskyn, and Brixton in Johannesburg, and the Christelike Dameshuis in Durban. The latter was situated in the upper-class Glenwood area of the city.[38] In addition, reflecting greater liquidity and (*volks-*) capitalization than other sectors that employed mainly Afrikaans speakers, some Afrikaner corporations like Sanlam established comfortable hostels for their single male employees, to all accounts similar to studio apartment buildings, although there were communal dining rooms and strict regulation governing the men's conduct.

Perhaps single-sex accommodation could be excused on the assumption that it was temporary, for young workers who were not yet married. But rural work camps that became semipermanent family settlements for road gangs represented an uglier blot—more so because road workers were in fact part of the public service. By way of structure and design, these camps carried an air of impermanence. They were prefabricated, often without connection to services like electricity or sewage, and they were usually situated some distance from established *platteland* towns. In December 1959, *Vrou en Moeder* carried a poignant article on women's way of life in the road camps. The wife of the road worker, it commented, was forced into a nomadic existence. She was shunned and isolated from local communities who looked down on road worker families. Road camps, the article declared in a rare note of criticism, were an affront to the reputation of the Afrikaner and the government's duty to care for its own: the *"moeder"* (mother) who lives in a road camp "also deserves to have her dreams and hopes."[39] Road camps were far from the style of housing that Afrikanerdom's elite envisaged for the *volk* under an NP government, and other whites, even public servants, looked down upon those who lived in these camps. One informant who spent several years living in a camp while working on a construction project in the northern Cape Province wearily recalled an annual joke among public servants that at Christmastime all the men in the camps should be rounded up to claim their children.[40]

A final word on housing, or more particularly, the types of housing that working class whites occupied, and the neighborhoods where they lived. These questions mattered in the work life of the public servant. One of the questions in the public service merit assessment asked for a short but precise description of the candidate's address and living conditions, further testimony to the bureaucracy's intention to surveil and manage the lives of the white *beamptes* and the importance of housing within these ambitions.

Credit and a New Wave of *Volkskapitalisme*

While housing was at the center of new patterns of aspiration and consumption among whites, especially public servants with access to generous housing subsidies, aspiration, consumption, and taste were influenced and accelerated by new sources of consumer credit. Grundlingh writes that there was a general appeal to Afrikaners during the 1950s to "save for stability" and that the drive to "spend for success" came only in the 1960s.[41] There is however evidence to indicate that this periodization was not so clear-cut, and that credit-fueled spending by whites took off in the 1950s.

If earlier waves of Afrikaner nationalist *volkskapitalisme* (people's capitalism) had witnessed the mobilization of Afrikaner savings toward investment in Afrikaner financial and manufacturing industries, a subsequent wave that has attracted much less attention was the rise of consumer credit.[42] This type of credit was a significant driver in the emergence of an Afrikaner middle class, initially in the wake of the Great Depression, and it could well have been a symptom of an unwillingness on the part of Standard Bank and Barclays Bank, the major commercial banks at the time, to fund those whites considered risky borrowers.[43] Moreover, as Cape nationalist and later cabinet minister T. E. Donges commented to the Ekonomiese Volkskongres (National Economic Congress) convened by the Federasie van Afrikaanse Kultuurverenigings (FAK) in 1939, Afrikaner farmers, workers, and the tiny Afrikaner middle class all saw urban capitalism and finance, and banks in particular, as the personification of "imperialism" and the epitome of the power of *Hoggenheimer*.[44]

Thus, in 1938, Samba was opened as a "buy aid society"—as distinct from a building society which funded the purchase of fixed assets like housing. With its head office in Bloemfontein, Samba had branches in the rural heartland of central South Africa: in Kimberley, Aliwal North, Graaff-Reinet, Cradock, and Port Elizabeth. It "combined the power of a group of consumers to bargain for discounts," which it passed on to its members.[45] It also offered personal loans to its members, including fairly substantial amounts for the purchase of motor vehicles. In 1947, the Koophulpvereniging vir Staatsdiensamptenare [Buying aid society for civil servants] was established in Cape Town, while a year later Koopkrag, with its head office in Pretoria, was founded to cater to the large and growing population of urban Afrikaans speakers in the Transvaal.[46] These societies operated on similar principles to Samba and all sought to develop their client base among white public servants—in the case of the Koophulpvereniging, exclusively so. With their emphasis on buying and consumer credit, and their willingness to include in their business those whites otherwise deemed unworthy of commercial credit, these societies gave significant impetus to the emergence of middle-class styles of consumption. It was a perfect match between institutions willing to bargain for lower prices and to extend credit and Afrikaners with access not only to housing, but to more household capital than ever before. Once credit agreements were entered into, these contracts built in added layers of compliance because white credit consumers depended on stable employment. For public servants already subject to workplace regulation, credit not only added another subtle layer as they had to retain their jobs to retain the credit, but also invested white public servants more deeply in the race, class, and gendered privileges of apartheid society. These "buy aid" and consumer credit societies were however not universally welcomed within the corridors of Afrikanerdom. As O'Meara writes, they represented a challenge to Federale Volksbeleggings (Federal Volk's Investments, or FVB), established as an Afrikaner credit company by the FAK in 1940.[47] In 1941, for instance, the Ekonomiese Instituut (Economic Institute) of the FAK tried to stop Koopkrag from competing with the FVB campaign to secure investment from *wage-earning Afrikaner investors*. However, not all whites were able to afford formal credit, not even that extended by sympathetic credit societies and Afrikaner banks.

Umzinto is a little town on the KwaZulu-Natal South Coast, and from the early 1950s it began to enjoy a decade of expansion due to its importance as a railway junction. It saw an influx of unskilled white railway workers, who occupied the lowest bands of wage work available to whites on the railways. This was precisely the stratum of whites unable to secure access to credit, even via "softer" sources established particularly to assist white public servants. The social pressures they, like other whites, experienced to consume— furniture, a car, clothing—and the need for credit sometimes initiated developments that ran counter to the trajectories of apartheid society. Then, in about 1953, Mr. I. Belim, a devout Muslim of Indian origin, opened a small general dealership in Umzinto. Belim had set off to study law at the University of Fort Hare where he was taken by the spirit of the Defiance Campaign against Unjust Law in 1952. He refused to take a course in Afrikaans, which was then a prerequisite for a law degree. Unable to graduate, he returned home to Umzinto and opened his shop. Part of his business involved selling furniture, clothing, and, later, appliances to white railway workers on credit. A kindly and generous man, Belim became immensely popular with them. He never demanded that they sign any formal credit agreement—"it was done on trust, over a handshake"—and because his business was run on Islamic principles, customers were not gouged by interest.[48] Sometimes debts were held over for years. Relationships forged between Belim and white railway workers are now, in some cases, into the third generation. While there was an element of mutual interest in these histories across the color line, they are nonetheless poignant and transgressive, as they developed against the odds, at a time when the government was implementing measures like the 1950 Group Areas Act (applied harshly in Umzinto), which aimed to eliminate competition to white-owned businesses and to minimize all kinds of contact between people of different races.

Trying to be an honest broker between "buy aid societies" and organizations like the FVB, and alert, perhaps, to the kinds of relations developing between people and individuals like Belim, the government sought to regulate credit during the early 1950s with the introduction of a Hire Purchase Bill in 1954. A series of exchanges in Parliament reflected disparate interests and suggested that the NP itself seemed divided about credit, the benefits of hire purchase, and the role of the state in protecting citizens from the ravishments of indebtedness—a recurring horror in Afrikaner nationalist politics. Introducing the bill, Minister of Economic Affairs E. H. Louw declared that "the main object of this Bill—the primary object—is to promote general economic conditions in the Union."[49] He pointed out that goods, especially motor cars, were much more expensive than a decade earlier, making it very difficult for wage earners to buy in cash. While the Chambers of Commerce and the Federation of Industries complained that the bill would be used to restrict credit, the minister countered that they did not appreciate how it could in fact also be used to stimulate buying, particularly at times of recession when cash was in short supply—a not implausible assertion during the economically volatile 1950s. A supportive backbencher went so far as to describe hire purchase (or layaway) as a "new type of capital formation."[50] The minister added that the bill was not intended to rein in spending and that "if a man wishes to live beyond his means, he can do so." He reiterated his point by concluding that "It is not the purpose of [the bill] to start a moral or social crusade. That is the function of the churches. That is the function of the welfare organisations."[51] Nico Diederichs, member for Randfontein (and

Figure 7.1 Maydon Wharf, Durban. Apartheid's political, cultural, and religious elite feared that whites were living beyond their means. Cars and motorcycles were popular purchases among working-class whites. Author's personal collection.

later state president), weighed in with an uneasy response that indicated a struggle to simultaneously toe the party line in Parliament and express his own concerns, forged in a different era of Afrikaner nationalism and class formation. Beginning with a convoluted distinction between hire purchase, which he characterized as "future saving" (when it was used to buy capital or durable consumer goods), and "extravagance," he moved on to an apocryphal, if rather bizarre, anecdote. In Cape Town, he declared, a "very large number" of typists and clerical assistants were suffering from tuberculosis. This was because they seldom had proper meals, as they "have so many debts under the hire purchase system . . . that they cannot afford to have a proper meal everyday."[52] He rearticulated the NP's position in respect to the bill—and in doing, mildly contradicted the minister—by insisting that the bill was not intended to promote growth in ways that could result in reckless spending, but was instead meant to protect the *volk*.[53]

The goods that white public servants bought on credit helped to entrench their status as an emergent—indebted—middle class. Each month the Public Servants' Association (PSA) published a magazine called *The Public Servant*,

Nationalism, Whiteness, and Consumption   145

and the advertisements that it carried yield useful perspectives on the types of credit-driven consumption common among white public servants, as well as the aesthetics and aspirations which propelled their spending. Even for those unable to buy their own homes or afford market-related rents (like railway workers who enjoyed the benefit of heavily subsidized railway housing), furniture and household goods were the most common form of credit purchase. Very often, furniture shops advertised deals where buyers could purchase a complete household of furniture, with repayment terms especially tailored for public servants.[54] Appliances like refrigerators and electric cooking ranges were also regularly advertised, but the item which carried the highest aspirational value was a piano. "A gracious home is incomplete without a piano," declared the Century Radio and Tube Company in a June 1949 advertisement.[55] Adulterating its copy with a measure of flattery, it invited "you, the connoisseur of music" to call for a demonstration; and once again, special terms were offered to public servants. These instruments were costly, and the number of suppliers advertising pianos in *The Public Servant* is quite striking. The magazine also carried occasional articles on aesthetics and taste. "Not all of us can have real Aubusson carpets or Napoleon furniture," wrote Susann, who edited the women's page. Even a small flat or a room could become a woman's "most satisfying way of expressing [her] own personality and character." After commenting on how a "beautiful, elegant woman" had made her Johannesburg flat a "perfect background for her own exquisite appearance" by making little red-and-white awnings to hang over the windows above the curtains, she turned her attention to a rather more humble setting, addressing "the girl who lives in a tiny flat consisting of only a bathroom and L-shaped room." Her advice to this girl was rather more forced, as she recommended that she "curtain off the niche in which the personal belongings are kept," hanging swaths of bright cloth over the curtain. Behind the very triteness of Susann's decorating ideas lay a strand of prudishness: women should ensure that in their bathrooms, the bath itself was hidden behind a "lovely curtain" while the rest of the bathroom could be styled "just like a powder room."[56]

Besides furniture, advertisements for clothing featured prominently in *The Public Servant* over the years, and these advertisements provide commentary on the emerging domestic economies among the class of whites employed in the public service, as well as the drive for upward mobility, particularly among men for whom such opportunities were more readily available. Thus, in a particular testimony to white household arrangements, Evercheap, a shop in Pretoria, offered "ladies, kiddies and maids under- and outer-wear."[57] Another advertisement for men's clothing placed by an outfitting shop called Hepworth's ("Tailored suits for men with small budgets") enticed potential customers by pointing out that "good appearance made for a good impression and contributed to promotion."[58] Not all white public servants prioritized household goods and clothing. Especially among younger single men, cars and motorcycles were more common purchases, even when these were beyond their means.[59] Credit spending also had its downsides. Confirming Deiderich's fears, it was reported in the *Pretoria News* with some alarm in 1953 that 500 whites were being credit blacklisted per month.[60] Presumably, in a city dominated by the *staatsdiens*, a significant proportion of these were public servants.

Global (Sub)Cultures, Afrikaner Nationalism, and Whiteness

Just as white affluence was on the rise in South Africa, giving substance to new ambitions and aspirations, these trends collided with other global trends as the cultural landscape of Western society experienced a seismic shift in the 1950s. White South African youths, for instance, were increasingly exposed to youth subcultures from other parts of the world, particularly Britain and the United States. Young people in Britain and the United States who identified with these subcultures were defiantly antiestablishment, but just as their use of drugs was often liberal, their attitude to race relations was anything but; this was especially true for British youths. David Kynaston has produced a magnificent sociocultural history of Britain in the 1950s in which he colors in the brilliance and the pastels of a society undergoing rapid change. Most obviously, the 1950s brought new vitality to consumerism so that it became the ethos of the day. He suggests that the "shared reference points" of the day shifted from the church and the political domain to popular culture, particularly sound and vision. The new modernity, he comments, "may have meant different things to different people and the pace of change would have varied considerably from place to place, but by 1957 it was undoubtedly becoming the dominant *zeitgeist*—dump the past, get up to date, and embrace a gleaming, functional, progressive future."[61]

The 1950s was an age when practices previously taboo became increasingly public—although not uncontroversially so. Homosexual scandals became more common and featured in the media more prominently than before, exemplified by media and public interest in the affairs of Ian Harvey, a rising Tory MP and junior minister in the Foreign Office, who was caught "performing an act of gross indecency with another male person." These incidents seemed to suggest that "unnatural practices" were becoming more open to public discussion.[62]

A. W. DAVIS

for

Distinctive Furniture

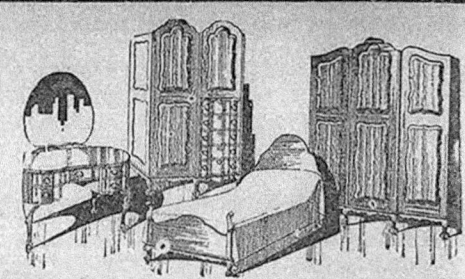

This 7-piece selected kiln-dried Imbuia Bedroom Suite (as illustrated) comprises: lady's 5 ft. Robe, two-thirds hanging space, one-third fitted with shelves and three drawers. 4 ft. Dressing Chest with 5 drawers and mirror. Gent's 3 ft. 6 in. Robe. Complete with two 3 ft. beds with springs and inner spring mattresses. CASH PRICE **£179-10-0**
Easy Terms arranged.

7-Piece solid Imbuia Dining Room Suite (as illustrated) comprising 5 ft. x 3 ft. Table, 4 ft. 6 in. Sideboard and six Chairs. CASH PRICE **£74-11-6**
Easy Terms arranged.

4 EQUAL MONTHLY PAYMENTS TREATED AS CASH

3-Piece, 3-division Lounge Suite with loose inner spring cushions. Covered in attractive and durable tapestry to choice. CASH PRICE **£77-10-0**
Easy Terms arranged.

PRETORIA'S FAVOURITE FURNITURE STORE

Solid Imbuia Chest (as illustrated) fitted with attractive brass handles. A useful and attractive addition to your home. CASH PRICE **£25-0-0**
Easy Terms arranged.

A.W. Davis
AND COMPANY LIMITED
A GEEN & RICHARDS STORE

250 CHURCH STREET, PRETORIA.   Phone 3-2618

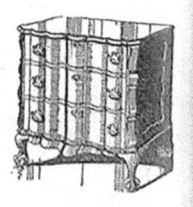

Figure 7.2 and Figure 7.3 From *The Public Servant*, March 1951 and March 1952, respectively. The availability of credit fueled consumption among whites in the 1950s. Furniture shops regularly advertised deals whereby white public servants could purchase an entire household of furniture on easy credit terms. Images courtesy of Public Servants Association of South Africa.

KOM BESIGTIG
ONS NUUTSTE
KLAVIERE!!

STEL NIE UIT TOT MÔRE NIE; BESOEK ONS RUIM VERTOONKAMERS NOG VANDAG. SIEN DIE RYKE VERSKEIDENHEID VAN KLAVIERE EN ANDERE MUSIEKINSTRUMENTE. EN AS U ONS NIE KAN BESOEK NIE, PLAAS U BESTELLING MET DIE VOLSTE VERTROUE. U SAL TEVREDE WEES.

BELANGRIK!

1. Alle klaviere word verskaf op maandelikse paaiemente (ook buite Pretoria).
2. Vry aflewering, Pretoria, of Vry op Spoor, Pretoria, verpakking ingesluit.
3. Skriftelike waarborg vir 10 jaar.
4. Gratis Stemkontrak vir één jaar.

KEMBLE — WELMAR — BUCKLAND — ACROSONIC — BALDWIN GULBRANSEN — STORY AND CLARK — MINI ROYAL — BRINSMEAD ENS.

Ons het ook 'n groot voorraad deeglik herboude Duitse klaviere en vleuels.

Century
RADIO & TUBE CO. S.A. (PTY.) LTD.

Telefoon 2-3636 (3 lyne)
Telegramme "Allwave"

VERTOONKAMERS KERKSTRAAT 240, PRETORIA.

Figure 7.4 and Figure 7.5 From *The Public Servant*, August 1947 and December 1948, respectively. Class formation among white public servants in the 1950s involved cultivating ambitions to respectability and gentility—such as owning a piano (available on credit). Images courtesy of Public Servants Association of South Africa.

And subcultures became more visible than ever they had been before. The most notorious group to emerge in 1950s Britain was the Teddy Boys, youths characterized by their dress, zoot suits and brothel creepers, and their insolent disregard for established norms of dress, behavior, and authority. Some Teddy Boys (and girls) followed the fashion trends, but others formed themselves into gangs. They fought with each other and were also responsible for violence against the general public, most notoriously, in the Notting Hill area of London in 1957. There, Teddy Boys estimated at about 2,000 strong assaulted new Black immigrants, demonstrating an "atavistic dislike of black men with white girlfriends."[63] Riots escalated as African and West Indian immigrants responded by taking the law into their own hands.

Of course, Britain was not South Africa. But it was one of white South Africa's reference points, and many influential Afrikaner nationalist elites of the day had strong ties with Europe—particularly the "Hollanders," those who had pursued graduate study in the Netherlands. These trends, the rise of consumerism, the turn from the churches, growing licentiousness and immorality, defiant youth cultures and, not least, lynch-style racial violence, would all have alarmed them. Although these trends were not all attributable to growing wealth, they were all features of the new modernity that threatened the ideas of the nation, engineered so carefully around the idea of a respectable, stable, and cohesive white middle class anchored in the *staatsdiens*.

Locally, these dangerous tendencies were manifest in the ducktail subculture among white youths in the early 1950s. Part of a new youth phenomenon in Western societies based on the pursuit of leisure and impelled by the expansion of popular culture and consumerism, the ducktails were a South African equivalent of Britain's Teddy Boys.[64] The term "ducktail" originally referred to a hairstyle, where hair was molded into a point at the back reminiscent of a duck's tail. This tail was usually accompanied by a coif pulled down over the forehead and sideburns. As a new and unlikeable feature on the South African cultural landscape, the term "ducktail" was first used by the press in the early 1950s, and the presence of ducktail gangs was felt in all major cities by the mid-1950s.[65] As a subculture, ducktails were hedonistic and rebellious with little respect for law, order, or work. Katie Mooney categorizes ducktail activities as either social or antisocial. Social activities included frequenting cinemas, dancehalls, billiard rooms, bars, and public parks, where they drank and smoked *dagga* (marijuana). Antisocial activities included gate-crashing, vandalism, temporary theft of cars for joyriding, assaulting innocent bystanders, intergang street fighting, molesting women, and assaulting homosexuals and Africans.[66]

The ducktails' style, thuggery, and criminality were a cultural and judicial affront to society as a whole. But, in addition, ducktail culture represented a challenge to the ways that Afrikaner nationalism understood order in apartheid society on at least three levels. First, ducktails were "known" to have sex across the color line, a point made by Louis Freed, a psychiatrist from the University of the Witwatersrand who was interested in the "medical" dimensions of crime and author of an alarmist book on crime in South Africa.[67] Second, ducktails regularly performed racial assaults—"kaffir bashing" in the crude and unselfconscious argot of white apartheid society. This of course ran counter to the idea that racial violence was institutionalized, sometimes juridical, and always the preserve of the state. And third, they made a virtue of idleness. Mooney describes a case where three ducktails lived in a room: "a work schedule gets drawn up. Number one will work from January to April and support his two friends. Then he will retire. Number two will then work accordingly until the end of August and will support the other two. Thereafter number three gets his turn to work."[68] As we have seen, idleness among white men in particular was seen by local psychologists, criminologists, and sociologists as a condition of moral weakness, and it had been the subject of the first systematic foray in a unified South Africa after 1910 to discipline white men.

Elite Afrikaner nationalist responses to this dissident offshoot of Western consumer culture ran true to form. These responses were not that different than reactions prompted by earlier demonstrations of white dissidence, nonconformity, and defiance. There was foremost a moral outrage driven powerfully by the likes of Freed, who stood outside of Afrikaner nationalism. Freed was socially conservative and especially concerned about moral lapses among whites. In this sense, his entry points into sociology and welfare work coincided with those of the intellectual and cultural guardians of Afrikaner nationalism. Freed had a history of engagement with what he believed were social pathologies among whites and had, for example, produced in 1939 a "Report on [white] homosexuality" that had a strong emphasis on lesbians.[69] Now he aimed his sights at ducktails, highlighting their propensity to frequent "brothels in African areas . . . [where] they meet African tsotsis [thugs] . . . and their black molls dressed in 'Suzie Wong' skirts . . . We were informed that the experience was supposed to represent a 'new sort of thrill for the degenerates of both sections of the population.'"[70] Freed also highlighted the dangers that ducktails represented to respectable and vulnerable sectors of white society: "A group of 200 defenceless children, while returning from a swimming gala at Ellis Park, was attacked for no reason by a gang of young thugs, brandishing knives and knuckle-dusters."[71] The ducktails were also viewed as a threat to public morality: "It is not uncommon to find the Ducktails and their molls locked in passionate embraces in full view of passersby."[72] There were often violent confrontations between ducktails and the police, leading to the deployment of the flying squad and plainclothesmen, appeals for harsher punishment for ducktails, and measures to restore order and discipline among white youths. It is noteworthy though that ducktails were not sent to the work colonies for "rehabilitation." Perhaps the sentiment was that these young men needed punishment and discipline before reform could be effective. It is uncertain how widely Freed's work was read, but he nevertheless lent scholarly credence and gravitas to the idea that ducktails were more than a nuisance and instead represented a substantial social ill: a disorderly and self-destructive offshoot of consumer culture.

Cronjé and Pieterse weighed in with a major scholarly study.[73] Like earlier Afrikaner intellectuals and social reformers who had concentrated not so much on poor or newly urbanized whites, but instead on their children, Cronjé and Pieterse focused on youth. In typical Cronjé fashion, he managed to get himself commissioned to undertake a study by the Nasionale Jeugraad (the National Youth Board), one of the myriad bodies under the umbrella of the FAK. Although Cronjé and Pieterse's study was meant to add a spine of independence and academic detachment to the understanding of white youth, it revealed a deep concern, at once emotive and future-oriented, common in Afrikaner nationalist circles in the late 1950s and 1960s: namely that youth, not having endured the hardships that their parents had suffered, might too easily relinquish the gains of the long Afrikaner nationalist struggle and the 1948 NP victory by succumbing to "outside" cultural influences.[74] Although their report did not deal with the ducktailism per se, it did insist very strongly that efforts to sustain the ideological and cultural purity of white South African youths, Afrikaners especially, needed to be strengthened. Cronjé and Pieterse predicted that the assaults on young Afrikaners from salacious and disorderly Western popular culture would increase. Indeed, this conclusion was probably central in prompting Cronjé's career move from sociology to *dramatologie* ("dramatology") and his late-life passion for the ideological, cultural, and educational value of youth radio drama.

There is also evidence that some white public servants sought solace in the realm of the supernatural. In the late 1940s and the first half of the 1950s, we encounter a series of long-running advertisements in *The Public Servant* placed by one Victor Rabie who hailed from Langlaagte, Johannesburg, and called himself "*Die Wit Yogi*" (The White Yogi): these advertisements featured Eastern mysticism, appropriately sanitized for white public servants in a racist society. He promised to reveal to his clients the psychic secrets

Figure 7.6 From *The Public Servant*, December 1948. "Die Wit Yogi" regularly, for more than a decade, advertised in *The Public Servant*. Image courtesy of Public Servants Association of South Africa.

of the East and to expel the "devil of drink" from afflicted individuals. He offered hypnosis, Prana, Raja, and Hata, and treatment for illnesses such as dyspepsia, epilepsy, high blood pressure, rheumatic pain, and "women's problems."[75] While it is difficult to gauge why, or precisely how many, white public servants consulted *Die Wit Yogi*, the fact that he advertised in the magazine for such a long period suggests that he had some following among this constituency. This in turn highlights cracks in the edifice of apartheid-era whiteness: that there were streams of existential anxiety running through sections of white society—which may have been in part caused by growing pressures related to lifestyles and or debt—as well as a certain disillusionment with not only the churches but Western medicine.

In 1964, Piet Cillié, editor of *Die Burger*, morosely wondered whether "we shall see the day when we shall come to curse our highly praised prosperity."[76] His comments targeted the growing prosperity of South African society as a whole, how economic growth drew bigger numbers of Afrikaners into towns, and the implications of this trend for apartheid's emerging geographies. But he also tapped into sentiments, current in Afrikaner nationalist circles from the 1950s, that whites were becoming "too wealthy," too entangled in an alien consumer culture that was inimical to the purposes of the Afrikaner civil religion. It was argued that the youth had lost the older generations' devotion to the *volk*, tempered by hardship and poverty. These dangers were made starkly visible by the ducktails, but were not limited to them.

Clearly Cillié's sentiments were shared by influential figures in the Afrikaner nationalist establishment, as the state sought to manage the contradictions he had highlighted by diverting white interest to what it considered more wholesome ends. In 1952, for instance, it invoked Afrikaner heritage in an attempt to drum up patriotic fervor. That year was the tercentenary of Jan van Riebeeck's arrival at the Cape, and a festival committee was established under the FAK to arrange and coordinate festivities nationally.[77] In grandiloquent (and obsequious) flight, a government backbencher nonetheless captured something of the festival's significance within the upper reaches of Afrikaner nationalism. Praising the "highest officials in the country and the State," he declared that they had all contributed "in this proud period to show some affection for . . . our cultural life, to fondle it and show that measure of devotion which is due to it."[78]

Yet while the idea of celebrating van Riebeeck's landing was supported at the very highest political level, local organization fell to town and city councils where budgetary constraints and diverse levels of commitment meant that the festival had a very uneven feel to it and consequently failed to capture the public imagination. Cape Town, which was designated as the focal

Figure 7.7 and Figure 7.8 Working-class whites at leisure, Natal (now Kwazulu-Natal) south coast, early 1950s. A day at the beach and a trip on a narrow-gauge railway. Author's personal collection.

point for the tercentenary, was accused in Parliament of "forgetting South Africa"—a claim that Cape Town mayor Fritz Sonnenberg angrily denied.[79] Enthusiasm for the festival in other parts of the country was even more underwhelming than in Cape Town.

There were also substantial state resources allocated toward establishing subsidized holiday resorts for whites at dams, in the mountains, and at the seaside. It was Afrikaners, in particular, who were targeted. Most of these resorts were created under the auspices of the Afrikaanse Taal en Kultuurvereniging (AKTV), although the Transvaal Onderwyse Unie (TOU) also developed a resort for its members at Leisure Bay on the Natal South Coast. That these resorts were an initiative of the AKTV provides an indication of both their purpose and their ambience. Above all, they represented a place where families could experience a wholesome holiday that would reinvigorate Afrikaners' loyalty to Afrikaner nationalism. Thus, during their holiday, families could expect to participate in a range of activities—singing, tug-of-war, *jukskei* (an Afrikaner folk sport)—and to attend religious services, poetry readings, and plays designed to strengthen their attachment to the *volk*. They could also listen to lectures on such topics as health, history, and current affairs. Other branches of the state also understood the value of these Afrikaner nationalist holidays. Notably, the PSC negotiated with the railways to offer annual travel concessions to public servants and their families if they could prove that they were visiting one of the AKTV resorts.[80]

Whiteness Reconfigured

As whites, especially Afrikaners, became wealthier, they began to loosen the cultural tethers of Afrikaner nationalism. But this loosening was not only a product of affluence leading to individualism and feeding a sense of cultural complacency, since whites were becoming more integrated into a new type of "globalized" Western cultural world, marked by consumerism and the growing visibility and prominence of popular culture. The ducktail subculture represented the sharp edge of this shift, and Afrikaans speakers were no less immune to it than other whites. Although the evidence is slightly outside of this volume's chronological frames, Grundlingh points out that in the mid-1960s, more Afrikaans-speaking youths (48.5 percent) listened to LM radio, the major local source of rock and roll music, than English speakers (46.7 percent).[81]

Shifts in the political and cultural economies, beginning ironically enough soon after the NP won power, marked the onset of changes in the ways that white South African society was imagined by Afrikaner nationalist elites and in the ways that whites were managed. High-profile celebrations like the van Riebeeck tercentenary, conceived with polemic purpose in mind, may with hindsight have marked a last hurrah for approaches based exclusively on appeals to the Afrikaner *volk*—although these would inevitably continue right up to the 1980s.

The limited efficacy and range of appeals to loyalty to the *volk* spurred the rise of new techniques of regulation, which were also significant grounds for compliance among whites. These were based on the lure of prosperity and stability and on the need for security at a time when mass defiance of apartheid was gaining force. This triad was able to transcend narrow ethnic politics, and it included non-Afrikaner whites substantially and comprehensively in the apartheid project. Significantly, from the 1960s, growing numbers of English speakers voted for the NP, a shift demonstrated in the 1966 general election (and in every apartheid-era election after that).

My father Dick's sole ambition to operate the boom in Durban's harbor not only left him outside of these major trajectories of white working-class formation. The absence of any real interest to buy, build, possess, or consume left him relatively untouched by one of the major frames that bound white people to apartheid society. Examples such as his must surely have exasperated the state. He was free: instead of a web of debt and repayment obligations (benign, to be sure), he died in 1998 with R400—about US $26—in his bank account and no will, testament, or assets to portion or distribute. His was a small, personal act of rebellion against the patterns of consumption that began to emerge among whites from the 1950s and the desire for upward social mobility that drove them. Perhaps the disparity between my father's lifestyle and the ambitions that were taking root among white men, a distance that he was either unable or unwilling to bridge, were a consequence of his experience as a soldier. For some of his comrades, not only in South Africa but elsewhere, the vigorous pursuit of worldly success no longer mattered that much after five or six years of fighting fascists and Nazis. His was by no means a full-blown revolt against apartheid's fundamental hierarchies, although he certainly had little respect for the kind of macho white masculinity that gained traction under apartheid, with its embrace of military conscription and gun culture.

The rhetoric of security certainly did provide more than the ideological, financial, and human resources to expand the military and police, for it also offered a means to discipline and resocialize white male malcontents and transgressors. Already in 1956, H. J. Venter, a criminologist at the University of Pretoria, had begun urging "compulsory full-time military training from one to two years for all boys" to beat youth crime.[82] This was to be achieved, presumably, by increasing the numbers of soldiers and policemen, and by subjecting "youth criminals" to military discipline. These criminological appeals for conscription coincided with other appeals originating from figures close to the security establishment, who had an interest in expanding the apartheid state's military and police capacity in the face of increasingly militant opposition to apartheid. Through the 1960s and 1970s, conscription for white men was progressively extended.

Thus, the very success of the NP and supportive Afrikaner nationalist organizations in state-making was a factor in unmaking the Afrikaner nation as it was conceived from at least the 1938 Great Trek centenary and through the 1940s by Afrikaner nationalist intellectuals, especially economists, sociologists, and theologians. However, these contradictions and this partial unraveling initiated the formation of a new "nation" forged around whiteness, rather than Afrikaner-ness, as well as around new methods of surveillance and regulation. The wages of whiteness, or, more precisely, the kinds of cultural change they drove, the lifestyles and ambitions and tastes they inspired, did, after all, help hold together the ideological and political bonds of apartheid culture. Exposure to global cultures and participation in histories across the color line did not in any way mean that white South Africans lost their racial consciousness. While the Umzinto railway workers were happy to accept Belim's credit and kindness, there was not one objection from a white person when he and other people of Indian descent were evicted from their homes and business premises under the Group Areas Act in the late 1950s: testament perhaps to the observation that while there were many currents of racial supremacy in apartheid South Africa, and that some of these jarred, few whites were either immune or hostile to racist ideologies.

ALCOHOL AND SOCIAL ENGINEERING

8

A Fragment, and a Problem

In the early 1950s, a wave of panic washed through certain influential reaches of white South African society: that whites were drinking too much. The alcohol panic was driven by Geoffrey Cronjé. He fostered anxiety about white drinking into a type of hysteria within circles of Afrikanerdom by forcefully placing it onto and moving it up agendas of cultural and professional organizations, state bureaucracies, and commissions of inquiry. It was an odd panic, which resonated not so much in the press or in the chambers of public opinion, but within the bureaucracy, activating a range of state and bureaucratic processes. In the wake of this anxiety there emerged new state responses to white drinking, at once broader and less obviously punitive than what had hitherto pertained.

Globally, we know little about the history—much less the comparative history—of drinking and nationhood.[1] This is also true for South Africa and extends to the ways that alcohol served to both mark the boundaries of race and shape the content of "acceptable" white behavior. How the "the nation" was framed (and the cluster of issues around which this prevailing question was resolved) had consequences for the shape of all sorts of other ideologies and policies.

A fragment of history represented by a 1950s–vintage anxiety about white drinking yields several lines of inquiry.[2] This fragment is useful since it allows us to consider several genealogies as well as nascent themes and continuities in the ways that alcohol, "the nation," policing, and care were understood, each rendered visible from the beachhead of the alcohol panic. These themes include elite white ideas and debates about alcohol and alcoholism, which whites were considered "useless"—a blight and a threat to white society—and which were deserving of care, medical attention, and rehabilitation.[3] Also revealed are how new ideologies about order, race, delinquency, and rehabilitation had taken root, and where in the state these were located. Further, there were of course implications for the ways in which whites were managed. In seeking some of the ways that whites, especially working-class whites, responded to these measures, we gain insight into how they transgressed, the limits of this transgression, and the ties that bound them into apartheid society.

Of course, drinking was not the only way in which working-class whites and white *skirminkels* (lowlives) posed challenges to state- and nation-making. Certainly, Cronjé must have been well acquainted with the very range of delinquency, the tenor of defiance that rippled through white society. With a style reminiscent of *West Side Story*, these themes featured in the colorful prose of Louis Freed, the psychiatrist with an interest in Johannesburg crime and street life, especially where these social interactions crossed the color line. Freed would later go on to complete a doctorate in social work at the University of Pretoria under Cronjé's supervision.[4] Cronjé was interested primarily in alcoholism and its social, cultural, and economic ramifications during this phase of his career as a social worker, sociologist, and policymaker. The alcohol panic, along with the social engineering and ideological and disciplinary architecture in its wake, shaped something of the complexities of white everyday life.

Cronjé was the central figure in the alcohol panic, and more generally, in policy and scientific debates about whites, alcohol, and alcoholism during the early apartheid years. He drew on both penal and welfarist traditions as well as on medical models of treatment to develop a battery of responses to manage heavy drinking among whites. For the time, Cronjé was quite innovative in the ways that he was able to marshal both state and private resources to this end. Indeed, his new system to identify, monitor, and police whites who drank excessively was well suited to the evolving class and social structure of white society from the 1950s into the 1960s. While he also reformed and reorganized the work colonies—which had fallen into disuse during the Second World War—during the 1950s, the majority of white drunks were more effectively treated as patients, sometimes (but not always) voluntarily, than as detainees.

New Patterns of Drinking and Treatment

During the early Union years from about 1911 until the late 1930s, the primary state response to heavy white drinking entailed assigning *leeglopers* (idlers/loiterers/loafers)[5] and men who were seen to be chronic drunks—in other words, those who displayed their drunkenness publicly—to the work colonies.[6]

However, the Second World War stimulated a surge of African urbanization, and it also witnessed an increase in cases involving drunkenness across the board. Between 1938 and 1947, cases involving "Europeans" increased by 97 percent, "Coloureds" by 130 percent, "Asiatics" by 140 percent, and "Natives" by 76 percent.[7] This trend sparked concerns about white drinking that transcended the earlier focus on *leeglopers* and chronic alcoholics. These new developments, rooted in particular moments of industrialization and class formation, highlighted the potential of drinking to upset the most fundamental arrangements of South African society. In 1943, for instance, the Suid-Afrikaanse Vereniging vir Maatskaplike Dienste (South African Association for Social Services) published a pamphlet called *Blanke-Vroue, Naturelle-Mans en Drank* (White women, native men and alcohol).[8] Worrying that dense and disorderly urbanization could lead to "European women drinking with Natives," the pamphlet presented a number of alarmist case studies, including one where, early one morning, a drunken white woman was found wandering around a Johannesburg location wearing only a flimsy nightdress. The *Vereniging* noted with alarm that the number of white women convicted for drunkenness in Johannesburg, "mainly those whose husbands are in the army," had increased to nearly half of all "European" convictions for alcohol-related offenses.[9] The following year, a similar pamphlet pointed out that there was moreover a danger that "a European woman under the influence of liquor solicits Natives for immoral purposes"— that is, that unchecked drinking by white women could erode the segregated order of things.[10]

From the 1930s, there was also a growing interest, particularly in the United States, in the scientific understanding of alcoholism and its medical treatment. An interdisciplinary Institute of Alcoholic Studies was established at Yale University, which ran a summer school, while the American Association for the Advancement of Science sponsored a Research Council on Problems of Alcohol.[11] Like the Alcoholics Anonymous (AA) movement with its voluntary fellowship devoted to the rescue and spiritual upliftment of the alcoholic, scientists urged that alcoholism should be treated as an illness rather than a symptom of moral or psychological weakness.[12] Unlike AA, scientists believed that the "most effective means of rehabilitating the alcoholic is through the clinic in which physicians, psychologists, and other trained specialists work cooperatively with each patient."[13]

These new American ideas on the medical rehabilitation of alcoholics, working in collaboration with AA, were far more sophisticated than prevailing South African state responses to alcoholism, or even British ones that were otherwise some of the more common reference points for the introduction of international ideas to South Africa.[14] There is evidence to suggest that the American innovations gained currency in at least some influential medical, public health, and social welfare circles in South Africa during the late 1940s. UP Member of Parliament Dr. Vernon Shearer had a deep interest in alcoholism, and both sides of the House recognized his expertise. Between 1946 and at least 1950, he was in regular correspondence with both American and South African doctors, with the latter eager to learn about the treatment protocols being developed in the United States. Shifts in South Africa toward more humane medical treatment of alcoholics were accompanied by a resurgence of social welfare interest in the chronic drunk—an interest that was not always particularly humane.

Unlike earlier waves of social welfare activity, this interest in the treatment of alcoholism was activated by concerns about alcohol abuse by white women. On the Witwatersrand, from the mid-1940s, the Women's Section of Toc H, a Christian service movement, led the charge, gathering allies from the local medical fraternity, other welfare organizations like the Rand Aid Society, the YWCA, the Social Welfare Division of the Johannesburg City Council, and the National Council of Women.[15] While emphasizing the extent of white drinking, especially among women, and the value of AA, it seemed that the major focus of the coalition led by Toc H was to persuade the state to "subsidise treatment homes for inebriate females"—this meaning white females, of course.[16] This coalition also sought legislation that would enable involuntary committal to these institutions.[17]

During and after the Second World War, fears that alcohol abuse, especially among white women, could test the boundaries of a segregated society already under stress combined with innovations in scientific thinking about the treatment of alcoholism. These interests created an environment for the emergence of initiatives aligned more closely with public health and social welfare than with penal philosophy. Various responses from the state and white elites existed alongside each other. Some were inclined to punish and discipline miscreants, while others were oriented more toward community-based interventions, with institutionalization as a last resort for habitual cases.

Geoffrey Cronjé and New Approaches to Drunkenness and Alcohol

Problem drinking among whites was not confined to the preapartheid years, nor to those on the fringes of respectable white society. An unsolicited letter to Prime Minister Malan by one Gael Fraser captured the very essence of anxiety about white drinking when he harangued Malan that "alcoholism must be cured now, if White Civilization is to survive in South Africa."[18] Even institutions of state, where whiteness was both produced and managed, were not immune to problem drinking. Although they yield just a snapshot, returns from police disciplinary tribunals are illustrative: of the seventeen dismissals from the South African Police during the months of June, July, and August 1949, fifteen were for drunkenness.[19] With the growth of wage work for white women under apartheid, questions about the use of alcohol, the possibility of excessive drinking, and workplace productivity received fresh impetus. Furthermore, as the decade of the 1950s unfolded, there was growing alarm among the new generation of efficiency-oriented public service managers that excessive drinking by public servants, even if this only took place on weekends, would undermine workplace productivity.[20]

These were matters close to Cronjé's heart. He never completely abandoned the idea of forced confinement represented by the work colonies and the practice of assigning white men who were deemed to be not only drunkards but also idle and delinquent to these institutions. Cronjé did, however, begin to favor other approaches that sought instead to manage alcoholism and problem drinking across a far wider spectrum of the white population. His own change of mind revealed an evolving response within Afrikaner nationalist circles toward white drinking that was more in line with the welfare impulses popular during the late 1930s and 1940s than with the penal orientation of the early Union years. Cronjé's growing preference for welfare and medical approaches was no doubt spurred by changes to the class structure of white society, particularly among Afrikaans speakers. For much of the century poor whites were considered a problem and seen as legitimate subjects for punishment when they failed to respond favorably to the coercive types of "improvement" imposed upon them. But by the 1950s, destitution among whites was a thing of the past as white society became more widely middle-class. A more appropriate approach for the management of whites now included methods that would not disrupt the fiction of "respectability," nor the still-tenuous trajectory of upward social mobility. However, the threat of penal sanction never entirely disappeared, and this represented a nascent style of governance for the management of whites that spread to other domains of their lives.

The early apartheid years saw Cronjé assume a new modus operandi, whereby he functioned not so much as a university-bound scholar but as an intellectual who was also an arch bureaucrat and quintessential gray eminence. During the late 1940s and through the 1950s, he was able to generate concern across bureaucracies and among powerful political brokers about white drinking.

While chairing the Commission of Inquiry into Family Life, convened in August 1951 by Minister of Health and Social Welfare Karl Bremer, Cronjé ensured that alcohol was marked and discussed as a significant challenge to white family life.[21] At about the same time, Bremer summoned a national conference on social work, which he ordered explicitly to "confine itself to European problems."[22] Once again, Cronjé was appointed chair, reflecting no doubt his status as head of the academic department that trained the majority of the country's white social workers. This event was significant for several reasons. First of all, delegates identified alcohol abuse as a major focus for social work. There were papers by Cronjé and by Dr. Key, who was the physician-superintendent at Valkenberg psychiatric hospital in Cape Town, and who would later become a major adversary to Cronjé on the treatment of alcoholism.[23] Second, social work was organized and oriented professionally in a fashion that would equip it in new ways to tackle the problems—whether existing or potential—of alcohol abuse. Delegates also specified care of the alcoholic as a special focus group.[24] Additionally, they prepared a resolution for Minister Bremer to recognize social work as a profession and to award professional status to social workers, a trend that had gathered momentum since the work of the Carnegie Commission in the early 1930s as more "scientific" approaches to social work found favor and as more social workers were trained in the universities, especially Pretoria. Yet they also urged the minister to extend funding support to voluntary, often amateur social welfare associations that undertook service to the white poor. These included organizations like the Rand Aid Society, but by far the most significant group preferred by conference attendees were those that fell under the Afrikaner nationalist umbrella, the provincial Vroue Federasies (Women's Federations).[25] A major outcome of the conference was a recommendation to the minister that he convene a national conference on alcoholism—white alcoholism, of course—and establish a "permanent, representative Committee on Alcoholism."[26] Bowing to the opinion of the social workers, Bremer agreed that such a conference should be called and set a date for November 1951. In his statement he expressed the hope that the conference, as well as the permanent committee, would improve the nation's "alcohol hygiene."[27]

When he opened the conference a few months later, Bremer pointed out that alcohol abuse was too big a burden for the state to carry on its own, and that it needed the support of associations that "come from the heart and soul of the community." He clearly approved of the idea flighted at the recent social work conference that voluntary social welfare organizations—the most well-established of which were firmly Afrikaner nationalist—be supported, and also coopted for state-driven campaigns. He ended by stating that "it is no use trying to combat (alcohol abuse) merely by saying it is a nasty thing that must stop. We have to arrive at positive measures."[28] This was a statement open to interpretation, but it must surely have been music to the ears of those in the audience inclined to social engineering.

The central question at the conference was one that had played out in the evolving protocols for the treatment of white drunks since the enactment of the 1911 Prisons and Reformatories Act. This was whether alcohol abuse was symptomatic of idleness and other types of moral regress or whether it was an illness. Delegate Mr. K. Malt put it perfectly when he posed the question: "Is it a sickness or is it a sin?" This was more than a semantic question, one of purely academic interest, for the way that it was answered would inform the ways that the state and other protagonists responded to white drinking. Dr. Key led the charge for those who saw alcoholism as a medical condition. He began by commenting that "alcohol psychosis was particularly severe among European males," a circumstance he ascribed to the fact that "the European is largely a brandy drinker, 42 per cent [alcohol] content." Key's preferred method of therapy incorporated three main approaches: conditioned reflex aversion treatment, referral to Alcoholics Anonymous, and the prescription of Antabuse (Disulfiram). "Thirty years' experience of dealing with alcoholics in mental hospitals" convinced him that the mental hospital was the wrong place for the treatment of most alcoholics. Although some alcoholics might need short-term hospitalization in the case of "acute alcoholic episodes"—delirium tremens—he believed that outpatient clinics were best-suited to their needs. Key did, however, concede that there were "irrecoverable cases" and those "from whom no co-operation can be expected." These were the individuals, he believed, who should be consigned to the work colonies which, as we shall see, were revived in the late 1940s. A representative of Alcoholics Anonymous lent his weight to Key's analysis, describing alcoholism as an "allergy-like condition."[29] In parliament, just a few months earlier, medical doctor and veteran campaigner for the compassionate treatment of alcoholics Dr. Shearer weighed in with his support of this view. In the previous year, 83,000 cases of drunkenness, drawn from all sectors of the population, had come before the courts, but he pointed out that these were "skidrow" types, "human derelicts," while those who abused alcohol in the comfort of their homes or with friends seldom saw the inside of a court. The real number was thus probably far higher than 83,000, with him speculating that it might be something in the region of 500,000 across all race groups. Insisting that alcoholism was not a "deviation from morality" and that work colonies were outmoded and "blatantly unfair" because "chronic drunks are treated like common criminals and thrown into gaol," he pointed out that alcoholism nonetheless caused severe "social erosion." Yet provincial hospitals—presumably here he was referring to those for whites—showed no interest in treating alcoholics. "In fact," he would state, "one learns that various provincial administrations are passing ordinances prohibiting admissions of alcoholics into provincial hospitals."[30]

At the conference, however, Cronjé advocated the opposite view, one more consistent with his sociological training and his intellectual and ideological habit of constantly defining the undesirable and the abnormal and trying to enclose them. He made a point, which he would reiterate regularly, about the need for systems of classification supported by appropriate legal and administrative structures: alcohol was not a sickness, but without a legal framework it could not be addressed as a social work issue. *Dominee* (Reverend) de Beer, public morals secretary of the Nederduitse Gereformeerde Kerk, supported Cronjé's position that alcoholism was a moral matter, a subject for social work, and that it required management, in some instances correction, rather than medical intervention. He pointed out that "you cannot divorce the problem of alcoholism from the drinking of alcohol . . . The conference should attend more to preventative measures." In a moral injunction to monitor carefully those sections of the white population vulnerable to the seduction of alcohol, he then proposed: "This conference resolves that the alcoholic should be rehabilitated along religious and scientific lines; admits that many alcoholics have become so by various mental maladjustments and psychological attitudes that predispose them to alcoholism, but does not accept the dictum that alcoholics are such persons who are in no way responsible for their condition." His motion did not receive majority backing at the conference, and the differences between medical and sociological approaches remained unresolved. The delegates did, however, agree on a lesser issue: to establish a "temporary standing committee" on white alcoholism.[31]

The temporary committee met a year later, in November 1952, and true to form Cronjé exercised a heavy hand in its deliberations.[32] That committee generated a substantial set of recommendations that testified to a broader welfarist approach to the question of white drinking and community-based rehabilitation, acknowledged the need for medical care in some instances, and concomitantly shifted emphasis away from the penal ideologies of the work colonies. It is, however, salient that elements pioneered in the work colonies were incorporated into the new framework for the management of white alcoholism. In a sense, then, these recommendations represented something of a synthesis of the opinions expressed at the previous year's conference.

From the outset the committee was clear that regulations needed to be drafted for particular race groups—and that it would confine itself to white drinking. It then stated that a premise for any set of guidelines had to be that "the alcoholic can be helped and is worth helping," precisely the language of enlightened reformism employed some years earlier by Shearer and which, in turn, was at the core of new philosophies about interdisciplinary treatment of alcoholism that had gained popularity in America during the Second World War. In a gesture to Afrikaner nationalist ideas about social cohesion, and reflecting the arguments that Cronjé, De Beer, and others had made the previous year, the committee acknowledged further that while alcoholism was a health problem for the individual, it was equally a "social problem . . . by virtue of the fact that every alcoholic, directly or indirectly, affects the living of other persons in the community." Consequently, it mooted a more substantial role for social workers in "alcohol cases" before the courts, in the treatment of alcoholism in the community at large, and in responding to the social problems associated with drinking. It also recommended that lecturing tours be undertaken by "suitably trained staff"—in all likelihood, University of Pretoria-trained social workers—to raise public awareness about the dangers of excessive drinking.[33]

The committee viewed white drinking from a strongly social scientific foundation, manifest in its insistence that standards be developed to determine what precisely constituted "abnormal" or "excessive" drinking, and how alcoholism might be defined. Cronjé's influence was apparent, for the appeal for "standards" was supported by the recommendation that these be underpinned by methods that, as we shall see, he had developed for men in the work colonies, notably the medical, psychological, and sociological examination.

Alcoholics Anonymous found favor with the committee, which also advocated support for "buffer institutions," private homes and retreats for the treatment of alcoholism, like Cottesloe House in Johannesburg. Moreover, it was argued that hostels, for which provision was made in the 1949 Work Colonies Act, discussed below, be established. The committee hoped that treatment and rehabilitation in these institutions, free from the stigma of the psychiatric hospital, the prison, or the work colony, would help to "restore confidence and get the party back into circulation."

Over the next few years, the idea that alcoholics should not be routinely institutionalized gained traction in influential government circles. As early as 1954, in a press release on supplementary budgets, Minister of Finance Eric Louw pointed out that there were probably 80,000 white alcoholics, and that while a miniscule proportion of these had to be accommodated at great cost in the work colonies, this system was fundamentally ineffective: "An alcoholic could not be cured by a penal method."[34] He added that he had hoped to fund the activities of Alcoholics Anonymous—before learning that its principles prohibited it from accepting money from nonmembers. Reflecting not only his distaste for the work colonies, but the growing clamor for productivity in state circles, he moreover allocated a sum of money to the Rehabilitation Board, then responsible for the care of whites injured on duty, to "devote attention to the rehabilitation of alcoholics after they have received [medical] treatment under the aegis of the Department of Social Welfare."[35] Other approaches, borrowed from the work colonies and demonstrating sometimes particular Afrikaner nationalist concerns as well as Cronjé's hand, also featured in the committee's prospectus. It advocated "labour therapy" and also insisted that religious guidance was a critical component in both prevention and treatment of alcoholism. Finally, it affirmed its debt to American scientific approaches to alcoholism when it proposed the establishment of a faculty of alcoholism at a South African university—probably the University of Pretoria—modeled on the Center for Alcohol Research at Yale.

The guidelines enunciated at the 1952 Conference provided a blueprint for subsequent treatment and rehabilitation of alcoholism among whites. In 1956, the committee that had come together under Cronjé's intellectual and bureaucratic guidance in 1952 morphed into the South African National Council on Alcoholism (SANCA). By the end of the decade, SANCA had fostered the organization of a network of constituent societies across the country, and it was in negotiations with the University of Pretoria for the establishment of a "summer school" to "enable both professional and laymen to ... obtain a diploma on "the subject of alcoholism and/or the treatment of alcoholism.""[36] In 1962, the Retreats and Rehabilitation Bill went before parliament. This legislation enabled the establishment of alcohol retreats for women, which represented a significant lacuna in previous regulations.

The foundations laid by the 1952 Conference's discussions, recommendations, and resolutions for state reactions to white drinking are significant. Although work colonies would survive until the early 1960s, these deliberations marked a shift from earlier models of policing and discipline (best represented by the procedures in the work colonies and the ideologies that underlay these), which were by definition limited in scope to those detained in the colonies. The new and evolving techniques of management and surveillance targeted the health of the white population as a whole and permitted the monitoring of a far broader swath of society: women in particular.

The List for the Train

While so many white South Africans were establishing themselves in steady jobs, buying houses, and taking up credit during the late 1940s and early 1950s, Dick and Vic Roos battled to reintegrate into postwar civilian society. Neither of the brothers was able to find steady work, and they drank too much and larked around with their comrades from the war (often to the chagrin of owners and managers of night clubs, bars, and billiard saloons). Neither married; they lived some of the time with Charles and Grandmother Roos, and sometimes in cheap boardinghouses. By the end of the war, they were in their mid-twenties and, had they served in other, later wars, would probably have been diagnosed with post-traumatic stress disorder.[37] In 1945, when they were demobilized from the Union Defence Force, they were regarded as heroes. "Homes fit for heroes" screamed newspaper editorials and United Party (UP) politicians (although, to be sure, the "heroes" were invariably white and they were male). Yet by 1950 these two young men were on the list of names for transportation by train from Durban to the work colony at Sonderwater.

When writing to each other about men sent to the work colonies, it was not uncommon for senior work colony officials to refer to them with a kind of offhand callousness as "*blanke tsotsis*," a racially-loaded term implying that they were not-quite-white thugs.[38] In the space of five years, men like Dick and Vic were thus transformed from returned war heroes to *blanke tsotsis*, deserving of internment in a work colony. The almost diametrically opposing ways in which they featured in the official imagination may be partly explained by the change of government in 1948. The UP, strong supporters of South African participation in the Second World War, occupied office to that point. After the 1948 general election, the NP, always ambivalent and lukewarm in its attitude to the war and the white South Africans who enlisted, won power. This shift prompts us to ask further questions about the ways in which the state itself changed, what new ideologies about order, race, delinquency, and rehabilitation had taken root, and where in the state these were located. Of course, these political changes had implications for the ways in which whites, particularly men of a certain class and social background, were managed.

Dick and Vic's silence on this was in all likelihood rooted in shame. Detention in a work colony was not that different from a prison sentence, and their status as white men was held up to scrutiny, even if this was done by a measure of frivolity and insult. They were not alone in remaining silent about experience in the work colonies. Few of my other informants volunteered any detail about the work colonies or even acknowledged knowing about them. Work colonies do not feature in any of the secondary literature on South Africa during the apartheid years.[39] Tellingly, when I approached one of the few surviving work colony superintendents in 2009 with a request for an interview, he awkwardly declined, saying that work colonies were "ancient history" and "a closed book"; banal clichés that perfectly matched some of the banal ambitions of apartheid elites to engineer South African society and the banal rationalizations they routinely deployed.

It was these silences and the very erasure of the history of the apartheid work colonies that initially piqued my interest in the ways in which apartheid society policed and disciplined its white subalterns. These silences also raise questions about how and to what extent we might read the social histories of these white men as they rode the train from South African cities to work colonies like Sonderwater and subsequently disappeared into the non-world of these institutions.

Retaining the prewar focus on white men who were "problematic," state work colonies in the apartheid years played a role in how the authorities set about engineering a particular type of white society. Whereas in the prewar years, state work colonies were quasi-prisons or labor camps, they were now transformed into institutions that sought to radically resocialize individuals by isolating them from the outside world, reeducating them and regulating every aspect of their lives. During the early years of apartheid, work colonies remained places of confinement and correction, although new internal procedures were introduced to reeducate detainees. Surveillance of inmates continued after release from the colonies to ensure that they remained precisely the sort of white citizens that the state sought to cultivate. Under apartheid, bureaucrats responsible for the work colonies were at pains to distinguish them from the penal regimes of the past, but their reforms nonetheless enabled the state to punish these men on the cultural margins of white society without the stigma of a criminal record and in ways calculated to minimize recidivism.

Work Colonies in Apartheid Society

In its first full parliamentary session since coming to power, the NP passed the Work Colonies Act of 1949. Significantly, control of work colonies shifted from the Ministry of Justice to the Ministry of Social Work, beyond the close oversight of the judicial system. A work colonies advisory board was appointed and for most of the 1950s was headed by none other than Geoffrey Cronjé. As part of the state's drive to promote the development of a new, respectable white middle class, the 1949 act focused on a far broader category of white men who were deemed "socially maladjusted." The act declared that the "aim of the work colonies is to teach detainees their community responsibilities and how to live as well-adjusted members of the community."[40] The work colonies would "offer instruction in industry, respectability, and good citizenship," and "so bring the maladjusted to better insights."[41] In addition to its intention to discipline and reeducate white men identified as "miscreants," the 1949 act also sought to restore them to stable family life. Read together, these aims reveal another layer of Afrikaner nationalist thought: that the family was the core social unit of the *volk*, and that men were the rightful supporters and heads of families.

Compared to the 1927 Work Colonies Act, the 1949 act gave far greater capacity to monitor men sent to the work colonies beyond the terms of their immediate detention. Previously, detainees had to be convicted of specific offenses (usually idling or drink-related); now, the minister and his bureaucracy had wide discretion to elaborate conditions of "maladjustment" and to commit white men to work colonies after investigation by a social worker. The maximum term of detention was three years and, crucially, upon release, the ex-detainee was subject to regular reports by a social worker serving as a probation officer. The ex-detainee had to sign an agreement to remain under the supervision of a social worker, refrain from using alcohol and drugs, find work, maintain his family, and not associate with persons "known to have a bad reputation."[42] In turn the probation officer had to report on the ex-detainee's employment, church attendance, dwelling, and his "adjustments . . . and sense of values and responsibility."[43] If, in the social worker's opinion, the ex-detainee again showed signs of "maladjustment," he could be recommitted. Upon a second committal, detention could be indefinite, and this innovation placed considerable pressure on former detainees to toe the line and conform to the cultural and social mores emerging during the early apartheid years for white people.[44]

Reorganization of the Work Colonies

By the early 1950s, the NP had begun to elaborate architectures of control, most obviously for Black South Africans, but also for whites. Work colonies, one element of the apartheid mechanism, were reorganized. Existing colonies at Eersterivier and Swartfontein were retained but transformed. A new work colony, which would eclipse the older institutions in size and significance and leave the most detailed archival record, was opened at Sonderwater, a former military base.

During the Second World War, the number of committals to work colonies increased significantly in the wake of Proclamation 133 of 1941, which authorized the compulsory detention of white male drunks.[45] Existing facilities were inadequate, and there were discussions between the Department of Social Work and the Departments of Lands, Public Works, and Defence on where white men sentenced to confinement under Proclamation 133 should be housed. In March 1947, after years of intermittent negotiations—and well after the end of the war—the permanent secretaries for social work and

Figure 8.1 The railway siding at Sonderwater (sometimes spelled "Zonderwater"). By removing certain categories of white men from society and confining them in out-of-the-way places, work colonies like Sonderwater contributed toward reconstituting a version of white society where certain categories of "miscreant" white men were neither present nor visible. This kind of erasure extends in part to the archive, and I have been unable to find any photographs of Sonderwater or other apartheid-era work colonies—just a bleak, flaky sign at the railway siding.

defense agreed that part of the Sonderwater military camp, now in excess of military requirements, would be turned over the to the Department of Social Work for establishing a new work colony. This portion of land contained hutments capable of housing several staff and at least 200 inmates.[46]

Sonderwater was located about thirty miles from Pretoria near the small town of Cullinan. The military base was isolated and secluded, and, with a certain bureaucratic élan, the new work colony simultaneously accomplished several objectives. First, those detained for "rehabilitation" in the country's biggest work colony would effectively be removed from the public eye. It was expedient to make miscreants disappear from the cultural geography as apartheid's reformers sought to imaginatively reconstitute white society around the ideal of middle-class respectability. Second, the colony was organized in ways that reduced the burden on a fiscus beginning to feel the strain of the burgeoning apartheid infrastructure. Twenty hectares of agricultural land was transferred to it, contributing to the Department of Social

Work's objective of "making the Work Colony as self-sufficient as possible."[47] It is not clear whether the other colonies were able to develop similar cost-cutting schemes. Third, the Sonderwater colony provided sheltered work for "semi-educated" (*halfgeskoolde*) whites in a suitable out-of-the-way location where they could be monitored and, if necessary, disciplined.[48] The social distance between these low-level public servants and the inmates was narrow indeed. Eight *halfgeskooldes* were appointed to Sonderwater in February 1947. They described themselves as carpenters, builders, or plasterers. However, as the chairman of the Work Colonies Advisory Board, Cronjé commented dryly a few years later that whites who ended up in the work colonies (or in this case, sheltered employment) often claimed a trade when in fact they had only worked as laborers in that occupation.[49]

Correspondence between the Departments of Social Work and Labour suggests that the identification of suitable forms of sheltered work for *halfgeskoolde* whites as well as those unable to otherwise participate in the labor market—due, for instance, to injuries sustained in the war—was a state priority during the late 1940s.[50] The project was not greeted with unmitigated enthusiasm by the managers of the work colonies. The superintendent of Sonderwater, for instance, complained regularly that he lacked adequate staff to maintain order and supervise inmates, and in 1950 he was obliged to use several *halfgeskooldes* for this purpose. Preempting by some years the sentiments expressed by Buys that the post office was not a welfare service for the absorption of *halfgeskooldes*, he wrote a strongly worded letter to the secretary of welfare. Reminding the secretary of the high purpose of the work colonies, the superintendent insisted that this situation was unacceptable and demanded the immediate appointment of the "right type of people," stating bluntly that "weaklings from other departments cannot be dumped here."[51]

Soon after the passage of the 1949 act, men were committed for detention in Eersterivier and Swartfontein work colonies, and by early 1950, Sonderwater was ready to receive its first "European" inmates. Once admitted, they were taken to a nurse for medical examination, followed by an appointment with the district surgeon on his next visit.[52] Cronjé, however, was concerned that little was known about the background of inmates, making "treatment" difficult. To this end, doubtless reflecting Cronjé's sociological zeal, the Work Colonies Advisory Board drew up a scheme for a threefold medical, psychological, and sociological examination.[53] The sociological examination focused on moral and religious values, including questions about sexual conduct and even masturbation, demonstrating Cronjé's obsessive fear that public morality and the future of the *volk* itself could be eroded by desire and sexual license, borne by the *insluiper*. Another set of questions, regarding religious denomination and church attendance, evoked the Afrikaner nationalist assumption that the health of the family and *volk* were linked under God.[54]

Inmates were classified to "promote and facilitate [their] specialised treatment."[55] The First Annual Report of the Work Colonies Advisory Board stated that "devising of a classification scheme should go hand in hand with the planning of methods of treatment."[56] Inebriates and "won't works" who were otherwise not guilty of any crime and were deemed physically healthy and mentally "normal" were sent to Swartfontein and Eersterivier, although Eersterivier also accepted those who needed special medical attention. The "worst alcoholics, mental deviates, the anti-social, hoboes, etc."—to the Board, the "most serious cases"—were sent to Sonderwater.[57] Once classified and assigned to the most appropriate work colony, detainees were subject to the following regime:

1. Their physical health was attended to as best possible;
2. Efforts were made to build the spiritual and moral components of his constitution;
3. Through hard work he would learn the value of productivity;
4. He would become a more disciplined person, so that upon release, he could live a more disciplined life;
5. If estranged from his family, efforts would be made to reunite them;
6. Efforts would be made to develop "normal" insights and social behaviours.[58]

With group therapy, spiritual guidance, and individual counseling, detainees were expected to work 48.5 hours per week in a variety of vocationally-oriented fields—in Cronjé's idiom, "labour therapy."[59] The Board's Third Annual Report announced proudly that a "large variety of employment" was offered, in fields such as dairy production, transport, clerical work, masonry, welding, cooking, and painting.[60] Inmates were paid a modest wage, depending upon their classification.[61] An informant, however, dismissed this official description of a regime of correction and improvement: while acknowledging that he received a small wage, he claimed that "labour therapy" was in fact hard labor closely monitored by brutal *halfgeskooldes*. He compared its pointlessness to the initial training he received in the military early in the Second World War: dig a hole one day and then fill it up on the next.[62] In this respect, not much change had occurred in the everyday routine of the work colony from that of the 1920s.

Active leisure was encouraged. Sonderwater inmates played rugby, soccer, and *jukskei* (an Afrikaner folk sport), and sometimes matches were arranged with outside teams from nearby eastern Transvaal towns, although these always took place in the work colony. In something of an unguarded insight into how administrators regarded inmates, the Sixth Annual Report describes how in all three work colonies inmates were organized into "houses"—much like schoolchildren throughout the Anglophone world. This, the report noted, ensured that "during the year, a healthy spirit of rivalry prevailed."[63]

In addition to providing "treatment," social workers tried to locate the detainee's family.[64] This created additional opportunities to penetrate and patrol white households and was one of the ways that white women in "vulnerable families" were subject to the state's attention. This gaze focused on how women looked after themselves, their children, and their households and kept their behavior within the limits expected by social workers. An ever-present threat was that children could be removed and placed in foster care or orphanages if social and moral norms were not maintained.

Detention in apartheid-era work colonies was planned above all to punish. But in the ideological climate of Afrikaner nationalism and under the guiding hand of Cronjé (who believed in the potential of social engineering), there was a commitment to correcting and reeducating inmates that was far more multidimensional and all-encompassing than the earlier, simple use of physical labor as moral corrective. Most significant, however, in transforming apartheid-era work colonies into more effective disciplinary mechanisms than their predecessors was the introduction of probation. An informant emphasized that fear of the probation officers' scrutiny demanded ongoing, often small-scale self-regulation on the part of the ex-detainee. Van, like Dick and Vic a war veteran, spent time at Sonderwater work colony during the 1950s. In the late 1940s, he drank heavily and drifted from one employer to another, lived in a boardinghouse, and battled with his rent. In 1951, he was assigned to Sonderwater work colony, which he described as the "*dronkplaas*" (drunk's farm)—a term that reflected his own road to Sonderwater. He spent two years at Sonderwater and was then released early. Given a suit and a travel voucher to return to Durban, he sold his suit at the nearby Cullinan railway station, got drunk, and tried to exchange the travel voucher for cash. Re-detained that very day, he served another eighteen months. When it was time for his release, a social worker found him a job as a clerk in a government motor pool in Durban. Here Van was subject to a supervisor who was a strict disciplinarian. The probation officer visited the garage regularly for two years—but always spoke to Van's boss, not Van. Van's boss was a member of the NP, and in election years, until about 1966, cajoled Van to help with putting up posters and driving voters to polls. Even when his boss was transferred elsewhere, Van continued with these election chores.

He never drank again after leaving Sonderwater for the second time.[65] Van's story demonstrates how a fairly mundane practice like probation connected large-scale mechanisms of social regulation, represented by the work colony, with practices of internal supervision and bound him to apartheid's political structures. In addition to the privilege that all whites enjoyed, his complicity was based partially on his own sobriety and partially on his desire to avoid a return to the work colony.

Detainees

Cronjé's board kept detailed statistics on apartheid-era work colonies. In 1950, about 600 white men were detained in the three work colonies; numbers peaked at around 1,300 per annum in the mid and late 1950s, and then declined until 1960 when work colonies were closed.[66] Nearly all inmates were Afrikaners with average levels of formal schooling of about eight years.[67] Most had some employment history and were from urban areas.[68] "Drinking is the predominant problem of the work colonies," said the Second Annual Report, and throughout the 1950s, the largest percentage of inmates were committed for "inebriety."[69] This attention to alcohol abuse indicates how drunkenness was perceived as a major social danger among whites in the early apartheid years. Chronic drunkenness was a condition that could erode the coherence and integrity of the new, respectable white family emerging from the political and disciplinary economies of apartheid.[70] The second largest category of inmates was committed for "not supporting family," which emphasized Afrikaner nationalist assumptions that men should be breadwinners.[71]

Such statistics, formally presented in the board's annual reports, were part of the rationale deployed by Cronjé's board to develop and sustain work colonies as institutions of discipline and control for white men of certain classes. A careful reading of the archive offers further insight into how the apartheid state detained whites who were considered "miscreant" at certain junctures—those who it considered worthy of rehabilitation. For instance, in 1949, the nominally liberal Johannesburg City Council wrote to the ministers of justice and social work asking that "European homosexuals and other submerged individuals be rounded up and sent to work colonies."[72] Shortly after interracial sex was prohibited in 1949, there are references to detainees who were in mixed marriages—although it is unclear if this was the basis for their detention.[73]

There is also archival evidence of extensive attention by bureaucrats, social workers, and judicial officials to the question of who was or was not suited for "rehabilitation" in a work colony. Most agreed that "hardened" criminals were not appropriate for work colonies, a sentiment expressed frequently by Sonderwater superintendent ?. ?. Hauptfleisch in correspondence with his superiors. "Hardened criminals," he insisted, had no place in the work colonies and could exercise a bad influence, especially on young inmates categorized as miscreants, not criminals.[74] According to Hauptfleisch, such criminal white men were responsible for bringing *dagga* (marijuana) into the colony. He had a "strong suspicion" that some of them were involved in "sexual goings-on" with Black women, exposing a vein of racial anxiety that white male criminality might be associated with interracial sex.[75]

Individual cases illustrate some of the ways that the authorities interpreted and negotiated issues of criminality and the possibility of rehabilitation. Following an interview with Superintendent Hauptfleisch in 1949, one Jack Sanderson was recommended for eventual transfer from prison to the Sonderwater work colony. We know little about Sanderson's crime, but Hauptfleisch considered him "the type of person who would adapt himself to the Work Colony . . . and would not abuse the liberty which the Inmates enjoy." Apparently, the major reason why Hauptfleisch approved Sanderson's transfer was that he had a young wife and baby daughter, and "his future intentions are to go straight and make an honest living for his wife and daughter."[76] ?. ?. S. Pienaar was convicted in 1951 of exposing himself to two white women in Church Street, Pretoria, and of selling "11½ bottles of brandy to a native." Evaluation by the deputy medical superintendent of Weskoppies Mental Hospital revealed that he had a mental age of twelve. Despite his four previous convictions, the doctor, a social worker, and Hauptfleisch agreed that Pienaar could not appreciate the wrongfulness of his actions, could not be held criminally culpable, and was thus not a candidate for prison. Most reluctantly, Hauptfleisch accepted him at Sonderwater for a trial period, although he was anxious to point out that Pienaar's chances of "rehabilitation" were slim.[77] In 1949, a Mrs. van Wyk wrote desperately to the secretary for work colonies, appealing for her twenty-two-year-old son to be transferred from Pretoria Central Prison to a work colony. She worried that her son would not be able to find work after a term in prison and asked that he serve his sentence in a work colony which would give him the chance to "rehabilitate."[78] However, he fitted exactly the profile of persons described by Hauptfleisch as "unsuitable for detention at a Work Colony"—young men between twenty and thirty with a list of previous convictions.[79] Van Wyk lived with his mother, and it was left unsaid that unlike some of those transferred from the prison to the work colony, he had no family depending on him who could provide focus and motivation for his rehabilitation. An official from the Department of Social Work informed Mrs. Van Wyk that her request for her son's transfer to the work colony was denied, and he would have to serve his sentence of three years with hard labor in Pretoria Central Prison.[80] Evidently then, though work colonies sought to punish certain categories of white men, the authorities regularly reiterated the distinction between "hardened criminals" and those who were suitable for detention in the colonies. In short, the latter included white men who, due to excessive drinking or other causes, were not supporting their family or whose domestic arrangements fell outside the Afrikaner nationalist ideal of the white family, united in wedlock.

In addition to those who were actually sent to the work colonies, dread of these institutions exercised a surveilling influence over a larger swath of white society. Work colonies were largely, and quite effectively, occluded from the cultural imagination of respectable middle-class whites. When work colonies did feature, they were sanitized as institutions for adult vocational education or as "model" training centers for men.[81] However, knowledge and fear of these places seeped through other echelons of white society deemed "at risk" and vulnerable.[82] This fear was circulated and sustained through the activities of social workers and *dominees* (clergy) who spent much time visiting poor neighborhoods, quizzing the neighbors of potentially "maladjusted" men. Visits of this kind emphasized that no one in these poor white and working-class communities was ever far from the attention of the state. One poignant example illustrates how the work colonies were feared and loathed. In 1957, a Pretoria woman reported her husband to the police, claiming that he did not support his family. A social worker visited and gave him two weeks to mend his ways. Little changed, and the man was notified that he would be taken to a work colony. On the appointed day, as the police came to arrest him, he drank ant poison and died before the ambulance arrived.[83]

Desertion and the Closure of the Work Colonies

In an institution designed to make those white men detained in work colonies disappear from the physical and cultural landscape of apartheid South Africa, it is difficult to ascertain much about their social history. Indeed, the purpose of their detention and rehabilitation was to mute the subversion and miscreancy they represented before reintegrating them into community life. Letters in and out were heavily censored and we have few inside perspectives on the work colonies.[84] Despite Pieterse's insistence that work colonies should not be seen as "punishment camps," detention differed very little from a prison sentence.[85] Both at the time and later, ex-detainees like Dick and Vic tended to conceal their time in the work colony.

Signs of detainees' agency are only evident in fragments of transgression. Perhaps the most obvious indication of agency was desertion. In its Third Annual Report, the Work Colonies Advisory Board noted that "absconding continues to be a serious problem in the work colonies, especially at Sonderwater where the most difficult cases are kept."[86] Desertion represented an act of defiance against state initiatives to punish and reform detainees in a harsh penal setting. By the late 1950s, around 30 percent of detainees were listed as "absconded" at any given time. These percentages increased around weekends.[87]

Work colonies were fenced but only loosely guarded, usually by *halfgeskooldes*, who had little investment in the success of the colonies. This desultory carceral regime meant that it was easy for detainees to run away, and desertions led to a fruitless game of cat-and-mouse between detainees, work colony staff, and social workers. The board debated whether, upon their capture or voluntary return to the work colony, deserters should be imprisoned.[88] In one instance the Sonderwater superintendent insisted upon the construction of a swimming pool, arguing that swimming had significant health benefits for inmates and would also keep them occupied on weekends, when most absconding occurred. Nonetheless, many still fled. My informant told me that those who deserted "couldn't get government jobs, but they didn't come back." Most worked initially on farms or in smaller family-owned firms.[89] Social workers or police were unlikely to track them down, especially when the suppression of anti-apartheid resistance demanded increasing state resources. As early as 1953, the board began conceding defeat when it agreed to consider whether "untraced absconders should be removed from the register after a specified period."[90] In the late 1950s, there was no shortage of work for white men in the segregated labor market, and eventually most deserters were probably reabsorbed into the mainstream economy. Not all of those consigned to the work colonies viewed the prospect with dread, however, and while many focused their energies on absconding, some saw the colonies as an opportunity for winter shelter. In 1950, there were reports that the majority of men sent from Durban were in fact *landlopers* (hoboes) from the Witwatersrand who had moved to Durban "during the season"—were Dick and Vic unwittingly gathered up with these *landlopers*? These "old lags" from Johannesburg and other Transvaal towns actively sought committal to the work colonies, and in spring or summer, would simply abscond.[91] Contrary to the idea of confinement and improvement, entry into the work colonies from some places, Durban in particular, was so easy that some men were able to use them as "winter retreats."

During the late 1940s and early 1950s, the work colonies had provided Geoffrey Cronjé with a laboratory for social experimentation. However, his experiments were not successful, and his hopes for the work colonies went unfulfilled. In 1961, the work colonies were closed.[92] Desertions and the resistance of detainees were factors; so too were new ideas about the treatment of alcoholism, which opened possibilities for social engineering of white society on grander scales. Significantly, though, the scheme for expanding work colonies was never a project wholly endorsed by the political establishment, and the work colonies began to attract strong criticism from powerful figures in the cabinet. By 1956, for instance, the work colonies had lost the backing of Minister of Finance Louw, who again voiced his distaste for them. In a strong letter to a local representative of Alcoholics Anonymous (AA), Louw wrote that "methods used up to the present, e.g. by sending alcoholics to Work Colonies had not met with... success." While he was willing to provide a supplementary budget estimate to provide funding for the rehabilitation of alcoholics, his appetite to fund the work colonies had clearly diminished.[93] Perhaps more importantly, in the 1960s, military conscription for white men was extended.[94] Military conscription provided the state with extensive repressive capacity when the anti-apartheid struggle was intensifying and developing strategies of armed resistance. In addition, conscription extended the state's capacity to surveil, discipline, and reeducate from a focus on the maladjusted, those men who would otherwise have ended up in work colonies, to all white men.

Ideas favoring confinement did however remain embedded in the Department of Social Welfare's institutional approach to white alcoholism.[95] As late as 1962, when work colonies had in fact already closed, the department declared in its memorandum on the treatment of white alcoholics that year that there "are always those cases in society where social services cannot be rendered without an element of compulsion." These cases included "some alcoholics and other maladjusted persons such as won't works."[96] This line of thinking emphasized clearly the abiding significance of moral and punitive considerations in the treatment of white drinkers. It also reflected Cronjé's obsessive quest for a clear distinction between "normal" and "abnormal" behavior by insisting that places like work colonies were perfect to accommodate those whites who were not "normal"—and therefore should not be accorded the freedoms of "normal" *ordentlike* people—but did not meet the requirements for detention in a psychiatric facility under the Mental Disorders Act. What was noteworthy about the 1962 memorandum—in addition to its obsolescence on the work colonies—was the importance that it attached to retreats for women. Provision for these was made in the 1949 work colonies legislation, but resources and energy had gone exclusively to the work colonies for men at the expense of women's retreats. As the work colonies were closed and as women became increasingly visible in the working life of apartheid South Africa, especially in the *staatsdiens*, their drinking habits inevitably became more visible. For Afrikaner nationalists who assigned such value to the coherence of the family and the role of the mother, this increasing visibility was also more alarming: it was argued that these women ought to be detained until they "once again appreciate civic responsibilities."[97]

In an early-1960s twist, when the state was trying simultaneously to reduce its financial obligations to white alcoholics and to build private-public partnerships for care of the alcoholically stricken, it licensed private institutions to detain those who might otherwise have been sent to work colonies or retreats.[98] While the Rand Aid and other approved associations would house detainees—for no longer than three years—the Department of Social Welfare retained control of probation services, much the same as it had done under the work colonies system.

Conclusion: A Sobering Effect

The alcohol panic points to a number of ways in which whites were managed. Increasingly, the energies of the state were directed more toward cooperation between individuals, community organizations, volunteers, state social workers, and medical professionals. New ideas about self-care and social work reached a larger section of the white population and, unlike the work colonies, women. These new ideas additionally stretched the resources of the state further and laid a platform for partnerships between the state and multiple private welfare agencies. These new approaches were, moreover, unlikely to raise defiance in ways that committal to the work colonies did among the *blanke tsotsis*. However, sanction remained and this was mainly through the threat that children would be removed, either permanently or temporarily, to places of safety or to remote rural boarding schools.[99]

Geoffrey Cronjé was the most significant figure behind the emergence of this new system for the treatment of white alcoholism. These arrangements were the product of a panic fanned by him, albeit a thoroughly bureaucratic one. In a state that was elitist and increasingly bureaucratic, however, the panic generated enough momentum in some official circles to give Cronjé the leverage and institutional space to elaborate a new regime with which to address white drunkenness. Seldom was he as direct as Fraser in the manner that he presented white drinking and white alcoholism as a "threat to white civilization," but of course this alarm was implicit and quite plausible in the ideological climate of apartheid South Africa in the 1950s. Further, white drinking was an issue that was central to his trepidations about white society, particularly his qualms about the potential immoral undercurrents in working-class society and its ability to harbor "*insluipers*."

In her analysis of the development of influx control during the first phase of apartheid between 1948 and 1961, Posel suggests that social engineering only emerged as a prominent feature of state planning in the 1960s.[100] However, Cronjé's attempts to control white drinking and those whites seen as undermining the coherence and moral logics of apartheid society indicate its earlier use in apartheid society. Furthermore, these attempts indicate several methods of social engineering, ranging from approaches that sent men to work colonies to others that targeted wider populations, and which drew on a range of liberal welfare antecedents as well as on permutations of transnational ideologies and disciplinary practices. As techniques of state evolved and became more sophisticated, greater numbers of whites were included within its scope of surveillance. The objective was to detect alcohol abuse, but alcohol was often understood as a harbinger of all manner of other social, cultural, psychological, domestic, and medical dangers. Just so, the imminent threat of drinking was enough to attract the attention of the swelling regiments of social workers, professional and amateur, who kept an eye not only on drinking but also on other social pathologies, including those that were unique to the ideological climate of apartheid, like interracial sex. Indeed, the bureaucratic work and resources mobilized by the alcohol panic suggest that there was a constant fraying at the edges of the cultural model imagined for whites by Cronjé and other figures close to the project of Afrikaner nationalism.

Revealingly, it was almost exclusively working-class whites who received official attention around questions of drinking. Those occupying the more affluent reaches of white society were subject to other kinds of less formal scrutiny by peers, professional societies to which they belonged, and perhaps *dominees* (clergy). The white men who did end up in work colonies were themselves few in number, never more than about 1,300. This was about 0.07 percent of the white population and about 0.13 percent of the Afrikaner population, making the work colony system a substantial investment in a small section of the population. More important is what this elaborate infrastructure tells us about apartheid society and how it was reproduced and reengineered by making certain categories of individuals disappear from society with a view to reeducating them. The history of apartheid-era work colonies reminds us that punitive mechanisms existed to bind white people to apartheid society in ways designed to produce compliance and acceptance of authority. Moreover, through these mechanisms (including, significantly, the use of probation), apartheid ideals were instantiated into some of the basic interactions of white everyday life.

Even as inmates resisted the discipline of the work colonies, they accepted the privileges of whiteness, a pattern we have seen played out in numerous settings across apartheid society during the late 1940s and the 1950s. Indeed, upon release it was common for ex-detainees to find work as low-grade public servants at the bottom layer of an oppressive social system.[101] The little dramas played out by detainees, dramas of defiance and desertion, *dagga*-smoking and "sexual goings-on," were humble features of South African history, particularly when mass resistance to apartheid, the 1960 Sharpeville massacre; and the move to armed resistance dominate our understanding of the period. These dramas are, however, important for the ways that we conceptualize historical processes and for historiographies of compliance and defiance in apartheid society. First, these men's miscreance, their incorrigibility, and their resilience to the discipline of the work colonies, helped shape the apartheid state. Most pertinently, the type of challenge that they represented to apartheid society forced the state to maintain its investment in the work colonies for more than a decade, in the face of Louw's growing opposition. Second, despite their defiance of the evolving racial, cultural, ideological, and gender norms of the day, their indocility could not, by any stretch of the imagination, be interpreted as challenges to the growing sturdiness of apartheid culture, to the apartheid state, or to the logics of separate development.

9

THE END

South African white middle-class funerals are bleak affairs. A short sermon, the coffin whisked away to the undertakers, and thence the crematorium. They're followed by a few minutes of contrived chatter over tea and biscuits in the church hall.

In 2017, I travelled to KwaZulu-Natal to attend the funeral of a favorite uncle who was also the last of my parents' generation, the generation that has been the focus of this book. This very personal loss was accompanied by an epistemic one. Those archives of the intimate, my entries into which had raised so many historical and moral questions, were now closed.

After the funeral, I drove to a small village on the KwaZulu-Natal South Coast to visit the scene of another passing and, indeed, the site of my first encounter with death. Derrick Smythe-Jones had killed himself here forty-six years earlier, in 1971.[1] As I drove south, it was like driving back into history. I was in elementary school when Derrick died, and I learned of his demise from my friends at school. My parents never spoke to me about the death of this kindly, rather reserved, middle-aged man whom I had known for much of my childhood. At that stage I knew very little about his death except that Mr. Smythe-Jones "got killed by the train."

I gave his story little thought until the early years of the millennium, when writing a history of white South African servicemen who volunteered to serve in the Second World War. I learned then that Derrick was a decorated fighter ace. I learned too that he tried out for arguably the most famous Springbok rugby side to leave South African shores. I was told that he had been a certainty for selection, but on the eve of the final trials, he succumbed to a drunken bender, which left him virtually incapacitated on the day.

That book on servicemen was about whiteness. While working on the book I also discovered that Derrick, a single man, a bachelor, had fallen in love with a young Black woman from Magwaza, a nearby location. This type of love, of course, was prohibited under Section 16 of the 1957 Immorality Act, which made it an offence to have sex across the color line.[2]

The story of the love affair emerged in shards and fragments over many decades as I spoke to family members and people who have lived in the company village on the then-Natal South Coast. Derrick's story was never quite told but instead only hinted at. It was a secret, a particularly *apartheid* secret (much like the work colonies), and in a sense it replicated one of the founding premises of white everyday life in apartheid society, that it was subject to a kind of moral inversion of the sort described by Hannah Arendt. Here was a man, finding love in middle age, but instead of it being celebrated and honored, it became shameful; a secret that led to the destruction of this love and to Derrick's violent end.

Derrick had been the manager at the Archibald's Hotel, one of the few establishments in the village not owned by "the company." On the eve of his death he had invited a large group of local white men, including my father, to share drinks with him in the bar of the hotel. Derrick paid, and the men would later pick on this point because Derrick was well known for his tight-fistedness. In those days, hotel bars were obliged to close by ten o'clock, and one cannot know how Derrick passed the hours that followed. All one knows is that Derrick's suicide was planned. Possibly, he feared imminent arrest. Sometime in the reaches of the night, he left the hotel where he lived in one of the rooms and walked into the darkness. He would have crossed the road and stepped onto the rail tracks. There would have been a chilly breeze off the sea. Despite the darkness, the railroad ties would have measured his steps as he walked north to meet the train.

I stood outside the derelict Archibald's Hotel. It was only a short distance from the now rusty, disused railway line. On the left were rundown railway houses, sold off to private owners in the late 1990s. There were remains of an "Indian barracks," which had once housed the sugar company's Indian workforce, segregated in grim quarters. I walked north along the railway sleepers, wondering if I would be able to identify the place where Derrick met his fate. When I reached a bend, I knew immediately that that was the only place on the stretch of the railway line where someone would choose to kill himself.

Color bar legislation meant that the unsuspecting train driver would have been a white man, probably an Afrikaans speaker, perhaps the father or uncle or grandfather of the "railway children" I was forbidden to play with. Hitting and bloodily killing Derrick on that lonely stretch of railroad in the predawn hours was surely traumatic for this man, and he would have had to carry the scars of this experience for life, probably unacknowledged.

The End

For working-class white people like the train driver and Derrick, there was little by way of escape from complicity or accommodation with apartheid society and its most fundamental ideologies. Like my grandfather Karel (Charles), in his struggles with authority in the 1920s, their options and destinies were limited and circumscribed by their location within a racist society. For Derrick, his own destruction was the only path out of the conundrum in which apartheid and love had left him. And while Derrick's death was an unheralded tragedy of apartheid society, another equally pertinent one was the fact that we know nothing about his love, her fate, or even her name.

Derrick's act of defiance would not have marked the train nor put a dent in the system that drove him to suicide. This represents a parable for the ways in which we write histories of whites. If we are to avoid narrating the social histories of these people with E. P. Thompson's "enormous condescension of posterity," we must understand how they were policed, disciplined, and reformed.[3] But we also need to ask when, where, and how they transgressed the interlocking ideological, legal, and moral codes of an increasingly authoritarian state and the limitations of such transgression. They were not heroic figures. Further to this, as Alf Lüdtke points out, we have to avoid writing their history with boundless sympathy.[4] There is no room for apologia when writing the histories of a racist society like apartheid South Africa.

In this volume, we have seen traces of indocility, defiance, and even histories across the color line, although these were fragile and short-lived. The ordinary whites who feature defy the particular *form* of the apartheid state, rendering particular versions of it meaningless. However, they seldom confronted, opposed, or even acknowledged the order of racial supremacy of which apartheid was one ideological, bureaucratic, and disciplinary iteration. That is one of the reasons why so many whites were later able to claim that they never supported apartheid. It afforded whites a way they could simultaneously accommodate and oppose apartheid. These histories also remind us that race, in this case apartheid-era whiteness, was made not only from the top, but also from the bottom.

As we reflect on the histories of whites as a whole, they go further than "no escape." Sometimes there was active collaboration with the apartheid state, even among those who would describe themselves as "anti-nationalist," or, from about the early-1990s, "opponents of apartheid": the librarians in Johannesburg, Durban, and Cape Town, for instance, or the Bachelor Girls. These histories remind us of the self-absorption that shaped white everyday life and also the pervasive ways in which ordinary white people were policed and bound into apartheid society. It held whites captive through economic interests and privilege, particular types of social scientific knowledge, and the sense that they were being watched—a fear almost certainly more imagined than real, as the state was never as efficient and well-coordinated as it claimed.[5] These permutations played out in different ways in ordinary people's lives.

Although the historical scales are vastly different, the historian of ordinary and subaltern whites is thus faced with a similar kind of dilemma to the social historians of Nazi Germany. Strong ties bound people to apartheid society, but we cannot write their history in ways that eliminate these people's agency and deflect moral blame to convenient scapegoats like powerful politicians, important bureaucrats, or murderous policemen.

NOTES

Foreword

1. C. L. R. James, *The Black Jacobins*, 2nd ed. (New York: Vintage Books, 1989), 283. Emphasis added.

I. Compliance and Defiance in the Making of White Apartheid Society

1. This phrase is attributed to Gillie Ford. See Neil Roos, "The Torch Commando, the 'Natal Stand' and the Politics of Inclusion and Exclusion," in *Natal in the Union Period*, ed. Paul Thompson (Pietermaritzburg: University of Natal Press, 1988), 12.

2. Work colonies are discussed further in chapters 3 and 8 of this book. See also Neil Roos, "Work Colonies for White Men and the Historiography of Apartheid," *Social History* 36, no. 1 (February 2011): 54–76.

3. The Comrades Marathon was an annual ultramarathon race of about 89 kilometres (56 miles) between the cities of Pietermaritzburg and Durban in KwaZulu-Natal. It was inaugurated in 1921, and my father competed in the 1950s. Comrades Marathon website, accessed May 20, 2017, http://www.comrades.com.

4. John Dugard, "Convention on the Suppression and Punishment of the Crime of Apartheid," *Audiovisual Library of International Law*, 2008. In 1966, the General Assembly of the United Nations declared apartheid a "crime against humanity."

5. All quotes here from "TRC Final Report: Summary and Guide to Contents," accessed February 14, 2017, https://www.justice.gov.za/trc/report/.

6. Truth and Reconciliation Commission of South Africa Report, Volume 4. Accessed February 14, 2017.

7. A point made by Michael Geyer, a historian of Nazi Germany. See Michael Geyer, "Introduction: Resistance Against the Third Reich as Intercultural Knowledge," in *Resistance Against the Reich*, ed. Michael Geyer and John Boyer (Chicago: University of Chicago Press, 1994), 8.

8. Richard J. Evans, "From Hitler to Bismarck: 'Third Reich' and Kaiserreich in Recent Historiography," in Richard J. Evans, *Re-thinking German History: Nineteenth Century Germany and the Origins of the Third Reich* (London: Allen and Unwin, 1987), 90.

9. The Cape province retained its nominally "color-blind" male franchise, in place since 1853. Under this system African and colored men were entitled to vote if they met property and literacy qualifications. In 1910, the qualified franchise permitted around 22,784 of a total number of 155,221 African and colored men in that province to vote. White women were given the vote in 1930.

10. Eventually ten ethnic "homelands" were developed: Bophuthatswana, Ciskei, Gazankulu, KaNgwane, KwaNdebele, KwaZulu, Lebowa, QwaQwa, Transkei, and Venda. Four of these became independent: Transkei (1976), Bophuthatswana (1977), Venda (1979), and Ciskei (1981).

11. Dan O'Meara, "The 1946 African Mineworkers' Strike and the Political Economy of South Africa," *Journal of Commonwealth and Comparative Politics* 13, no. 2 (1975): 146–73. See also Bill Freund, *The Making of Contemporary Africa: The Development of African Society since 1800*, 2nd ed. (Boulder, CO: Rienner, 1998), 167–203.

12. These congresses were the African National Congress, Coloured Peoples' Congress, Congress of Democrats, South African Congress of Trade Unions, and South African Indian Congress.

13. At a recent seminar at Stellenbosch University, I was asked precisely this by a graduate student: When some of the pressing issues in South Africa are the exclusion of poorer—Black—students from universities and the "decolonization" of the university curriculum, why bother with the study of whites?

14. See Frederick Cooper, "Conflict and Connection: Rethinking Colonial African History," *American Historical Review* 99, no. 5 (December 1994): 1522; Terence Ranger, "White Presence and Power in Africa," *Journal of African History* 29 (1979): 463–69. Many, but not all, of these scholars were part of what was known as the "Ibadan school." See Joseph Ki-Zerbo, ed., *General History of Africa (Abridged Edition) I. Methodology and African Prehistory* (Paris: UNESCO, 1989), 10–28.

15. The division between African and South African history was largely self-created by scholars of South African history who tended to focus on developments in twentieth-century "white" South African politics, arguing that these were of an entirely different order than "colonial" politics and anti-colonial struggles elsewhere on the continent.

16. For one of the more original and better-known arguments on "theory from the south," see John Comaroff and Jean Comaroff, "Theory from the South: or, how Euro-America Is Evolving Towards Africa," *Anthropological Forum* 22, no. 2 (2012): 113–14. On the links between anti-colonial history and literature on the one hand, and contemporary commentary and history-writing on the other, see Robert Young, who insists that any history that claims to be "postcolonial" must be grounded in analyses of the historical and contemporary effects of colonialism—including racism. These perspectives come through powerfully when one includes the kinds of work undertaken by anti-colonial scholars, a point addressed in more detail later in this chapter. See Robert J. C. Young, *Postcolonialism: An Historical Introduction* (Oxford: Blackwell, 2001), 180.

17. Belinda Bozzoli and Peter Delius, "Radical History and South African Society," *Radical History Review* 6/7 (1990): 13–46, 31.

18. Geoff Eley, *A Crooked Line: From Cultural History to the History of Society* (Ann Arbor: University of Michigan Press, 2005), xii–xiii.

19. W. E. B. Du Bois, *The World and Africa: An Inquiry into the Part Which Africa Has Played in World History* (New York: International, 1965), 18–21. In a recent study, Jonathan Metzl shows how racial resentment has literally led to increased mortality rates among poorer white communities in parts of the United States like Tennessee and Kansas. See Jonathan Metzl, *Dying of Whiteness: How the Politics of Racial Resentment Is Killing America's Heartland* (New York: Basic Books, 2019).

20. In *The Political Mythology of Apartheid* (New Haven: Yale University Press, 1985), Leonard Thompson identifies and analyzes myths organizing and perpetuating twentieth-century Afrikaner nationalism. For examples of the way white Afrikaners are portrayed through a contemporary Afrikaner nationalist lens, see, for instance, AfriForum, accessed April 28, 2017, https://www.afriforum.co.za/home/.

21. Jonathan Jansen, *Knowledge in the Blood: Confronting Race and the Apartheid Past* (Stanford, CA: Stanford University Press, 2008), 114–43, esp. 114–16.

22. A point also made by Frantz Fanon in *Black Skin, White Masks* (New York: Grove Press, 1967).

23. Nell Painter, *Southern History Across the Color Line* (Chapel Hill: University of North Carolina Press, 2002), 2.

24. Eley, *A Crooked Line*, 9–10, 190.

25. Hannah Arendt, *Eichmann in Jerusalem: A Report on the Banality of Evil* (Harmondsworth: Penguin, 1977 [1963]).

2. Whites and South African History

1. W. M. Macmillan, *The South African Agrarian Problem and Its Historical Development* (Johannesburg: Central News, 1919); W. M. Macmillan, *Complex South Africa: An Economic Foot-note to History* (London: Faber and Faber, 1930). See also Jeremy Krikler, "William Macmillan and the Working Class," paper presented to "The Making of Class," University of the Witwatersrand History Workshop, February 9–14, 1987.

2. C. W. de Kiewiet, *A History of South Africa Social & Economic* (Oxford: Clarendon Press, 1941), 216.

3. This comment was attributed to the NP candidate in the Wakkerstroom by-election. See *The Natal Witness*, June 27, 1952.

4. Arguably the best study in this vein is Ann Laura Stoler's account of "race and the intimate" in the Dutch East Indies. See Ann Laura Stoler, *Carnal Knowledge and Imperial Power: Race and the Intimate in Colonial Rule* (Berkeley: University of California Press, 2002). See Catherine Hall, "Review of *Carnal Knowledge and Imperial Power: Race and the Intimate in Colonial Rule* by Ann Laura Stoler," *Social History* 29, no. 4 (2004): 532–34.

5. Painter, *Southern History Across the Color Line*, 2.

6. The histories written by Macmillan and de Kiewiet represented notable and early exceptions.

7. R. Silverstone, "Complicity and Collusion in the Mediation of Everyday Life," *New Literary History* 33, no. 4 (2002): 761–80.

8. David Roediger, "Critical Studies of Whiteness, USA: Origins and Arguments," *Theoria* no. 98 (December 2001): 72–98; James Baldwin, "On Being 'White'... and Other Lies," in *Black on White: Black Writers on What It Means to Be White*, ed. David Roediger (New York: Schocken Books, 1999), 177–80; Du Bois, W. E. B., "The Souls of White Folk, 'The Riddle of the Sphinx'" in *Black on White: Black Writers on What It Means to Be White*, ed. by David Roediger, 184–203 (New York: Schocken Books, 1999).

9. Solomon T. Plaatje, *Native Life in South Africa Before and Since the European War and the Boer Rebellion* (London: Laurence King, 1917), http://www.gutenberg.org/ebooks/1452.

10. Steve Biko, "Black Souls in White Skins," in *I Write What I Like: Selected Writings*, ed. Aelred Stubbs (Johannesburg: Picador Africa, 2004), 20–28.

11. Nelson Mandela, *Long Walk to Freedom: The Autobiography of Nelson Mandela* (Boston: Little, Brown 1995).

12. Three volumes of essays edited by Belinda Bozzoli, each with a substantial thematic, theoretical, and methodological introduction written by her, indicate how the workshop developed during its heyday from the late 1970s until the early 1990s. See Belinda Bozzoli, ed., *Labour, Townships and Protest* (Johannesburg: Ravan, 1978); *Town and Countryside in the Transvaal* (Johannesburg: Ravan, 1983); *Class, Community and Conflict: South African Perspectives* (Johannesburg: Ravan, 1994).

13. John Wright commented at the 1999 meeting of the South African Historical Society that the advent of the "new South Africa" had seen the "decommissioning" of history, replaced by heritage. John Wright, "Probing the Predicaments of Academic History in Contemporary South Africa," paper presented to the South African Historical Society Conference, University of the Western Cape, July 11–14, 1999.

14. Deborah Posel, "Social History and the Wits History Workshop," *African Studies* 69, no. 1 (April 2010): 39.

15. Hannah Arendt, *The Origins of Totalitarianism* (New York: Harcourt, Brace, 1966 [1951]).

16. Arendt, *Eichmann in Jerusalem*.

17. Anthony Court, *Hannah Arendt's Response to the Crisis of Her Times* (Pretoria: UNISA; Amsterdam: Rozenberg, 2009), 3–4.

18. Court, *Arendt's Response to the Crisis of her Times*, 4.

19. For Court, this controversy has done much to dissuade serious scholarly engagement with the arguments she raises in *Eichmann in Jerusalem*. See Court, *Arendt's Response to the Crisis of her Times*, 2.

20. Court, *Arendt's Response to the Crisis of her Times*, 2. See also Kathryn T. Gines, "Race Thinking and Racism in Hannah Arendt's *The Origins of Totalitarianism*," in *Hannah Arendt and the Uses of History: Imperialism, Nation, Race and Genocide*, ed. Richard H. King and Dan Stone (London: Berghahn Books, 2007), 69.

21. See, for instance, Ivan Evans, *Bureaucracy and Race: Native Administration in South Africa* (Berkeley: University of California Press, 1997).

22. Arendt, *Eichmann in Jerusalem*, 26.

23. For an account of the emergence and development of subaltern studies written from within the movement, see Dipesh Chakrabarty, "Subaltern Studies and Postcolonial History," *Nepantla: Views from the South* 1 (2000): 14.

24. Vivek Chibber, *Postcolonial Theory and the Specter of Capital* (London: Verso, 2013), 1–2.

25. See Axel Andersson, "Obscuring Capitalism: Vivek Chibber's Critique of Subaltern Studies," *Los Angeles Review of Books* 6 (November 2013).

26. Chibber, *Postcolonial Theory and the Specter of Capital*, 7–8.

27. Partha Chatterjee, "Reflections on 'Can the Subaltern Speak?': Subaltern Studies After Spivak" in *Can the Subaltern Speak?: Reflections on the History of an Idea*, ed. Rosalind Morris (New York: Columbia University Press, 2010), 83.

28. Sumit Sarkar, "The Decline of the Subaltern in Subaltern Studies," in *Reading Subaltern Studies: Critical History, Contested Meaning and the Globalisation of South Asia*, ed. David Ludden (New Delhi: Permanent Black, 2001), 402.

29. Sarkar, "The Decline of the Subaltern in Subaltern Studies," 4; Sumit Sarkar, "The Many Worlds of Indian History," in Sumit Sarkar, *Writing Social History* (Delhi: Oxford University Press, 1997), 13.

30. Gyenendra Pandey, "In Defense of the Fragment: Writing about Hindu-Muslim Riots in India Today," *A Subaltern Studies Reader*, ed. Ranajit Guha (Minneapolis: University of Minnesota Press, 1997) 1–34; Gautam Bhadra, "The Mentality of Subalternity: Khantanama or Rajdharma," in *A Subaltern Studies Reader*, 63–100.

31. Eley, *A Crooked Line*, 162.

32. For an account of the anthropological turn to history and interest in anthropology among historians, as well as the "uneven balance between historians and anthropologists," see Don Kalb, Hans Marks, and Herman Tak, "Historical Anthropology and Anthropological History: Two Distinct Programs," *Fokaal* 26/27 (1996): 6. See also John and Jean Comaroff, *Ethnography and the Historical Imagination* (Boulder: Westviews, 1992), 3–48.

33. Chakrabarty, "Subaltern Studies and Postcolonial History," 24.

34. Cooper, "Conflict and Connection," 1529; 1533.

35. Pandey, "In Defence of the Fragment", 3.

36. David Ludden, "Introduction: A Brief History of Subalternity," in Ludden, *Reading Subaltern Studies*, 19–20.

37. For a strong methodological account of how to take the "pulse of the archive," see Ann Laura Stoler, *Along the Archival Grain: Epistemic Anxieties and Colonial Common Sense* (Princeton, NJ: Princeton University Press, 2009), 17–53.

38. The *Broederbond* was a secret, elite organization of white Afrikaner men. It exercised a significant influence on the NP and on the state bureaucracy.

39. V. van Rensburg, former work colony detainee and public servant. Interview by author, tapes and transcript, Pinetown, July 15, 1998. The Balmoral hotel was a hotel on Durban's beachfront, known locally as "Bad Morals." David Baird, "Watering Holes of My Youth," Facts About Durban (website), accessed November 25, 2017, https://www.fad.co.za/Resources/contribs/dbaird.php.

40. "Coolie" is a derogatory term used largely, but not exclusively, by white South Africans to refer to people of Indian origin.

41. The notion of "souls undressed" refers to W. E. B. Du Bois, "The Souls of White Folk, 'The Riddle of the Sphinx,'" in *Black on White*, ed. Roediger, 184.

42. Sewell addresses the methodological pitfalls of local studies, which may lead to microstudies whose "only valence, politically or otherwise, is one of generalized nostalgia." See William H. Sewell Jr., *Logics of History: Social Theory and Social Transformation* (Chicago: University of Chicago Press, 2005), 6–70; see also Eve Rosenhaft, "Review Article on Geoff Eley and William H. Sewell Jr.," *Social History* 34 (February 2009): 74–79.

43. Comment by Dipesh Chakrabarty at "Subaltern Studies: Historical World-Making Thirty Years On," Australian National University, Canberra, August 3–5, 2011.

44. Hermann Giliomee, *The Afrikaners: Biography of a People* (Cape Town: Tafelberg, 2003).

45. Comaroff and Comaroff, *Ethnography and the Historical Imagination*, 8.

46. Francis B. Nyamnjoh, "Blinded by Sight: Divining the Future of Anthropology in Africa," *Africa Spectrum* 47, no. 2/3 (2012): 70–71. Nyamnjoh explains that the "white others" who feature in the anthropological literature of contemporary South Africa are those "who have failed to live up to the comforts of being white."

47. Paula Hamilton and Linda Shopes, "Building Partnerships between Oral History and Memory Studies," in *Oral History and Public Memories*, ed. Paula Hamilton and Linda Shopes (Philadelphia: Temple University Press, 2008), viii–xv.

3. The Delicacy of Teacups

1. Sheila Roos, "A Thing of the Past . . ." Unpublished memoir, c. 1986.

2. Which became part of the South African Railways after Union in 1910.

3. For a richly textured account of elite settler society and the role of Hilton College in producing this, see Robert Morrell, *From Boys to Gentlemen: Settler Masculinity in Colonial Natal, 1880–1920* (Pretoria: UNISA, 2001).

4. See "Report of Commission in Re Pretoria Indigents" (Pretoria: Government Printer and Stationery Office, 1905). Cited in David Welsh, "The Growth of Towns" in *The Oxford History of South Africa, Volume II. South Africa 1870–1966*, ed. Monica Wilson and Leonard Thompson (Oxford: Oxford University Press, 1975), 116.

5. P. L. van den Bergh, "Miscegenation in South Africa," *Cahiers d'Etudes Africaines* 1, no. 4 (1960): 68.

6. For the emergence of the "poor white problem," see C. Bundy, "Vagabond Hollanders and Runaway Englishmen: White Poverty in the Cape Before Poor Whiteism" in *Putting a Plough to the Ground: Accumulation and Dispossession in Rural South Africa, 1850–1930*, ed. W. Beinart, P. Delius, and S. Trapido (Johannesburg: Ravan, 1986), 120. For an account of the brutal economic struggles that saw both Africans and white Afrikaners dispossessed of their land in the late nineteenth and early twentieth centuries, see W. Beinart and P. Delius, "Introduction," in Beinart, Delius, and Trapido, *Putting a Plough to the Ground*.

7. Rinderpest is a cattle disease that reduced herds in South Africa by between 35 percent (in the Cape colony) and 90 percent (in the Transkei territories). See Francis Wilson, "Farming," in *The Oxford History of South Africa, Volume II*, 116.

8. I refer to "Afrikaans-speaking intellectuals," but more properly they spoke Dutch. Afrikaans only became recognized as an official language in 1925.

9. R. Morrell, "The Poor Whites of Middelburg, Transvaal 1903–1930: Resistance, Accommodation and Class Struggle," in *White but Poor: Essays on the History of Poor Whites in Southern Africa, 1880–1940*, ed. R. Morrell (Pretoria: University of South Africa, 1992), 4.

10. Giliomee, *The Afrikaners*, 319.

11. H. C. Hopkins, *Kakamas – uit die wildernis 'n lushof* (Cape Town: H. C. Hopkins, 1978), 18.

12. Hopkins, *Kakamas*, 15.

13. Hopkins, *Kakamas*, 15.

14. Hopkins, *Kakamas*, 15.

15. Giliomee, *The Afrikaners*, 318.

16. For an account of how ideas about the elect and the righteous translated into late nineteenth-century Calvinist thinking about religious identity, the coherence of social groups, and nationalism, see Irving Hexham, *The Irony of Apartheid: The Struggle for National Independence of Afrikaner Calvinism Against British Imperialism* (New York: Edwin Mellen, 1981), 101–104.

17. In the early part of the twentieth century, there was some dispute among white commentators in South Africa around the definition of a "poor white." These debates tended to follow political fault lines, with Afrikaner nationalists using very broad definitions to emphasize the scale of the problem. The 1932 Carnegie Commission of Investigation on the Poor White Question in South Africa attempted to define the poor white and white poverty in more precise terms. However, it too came up with several definitions. The report spanned five volumes and across the volumes, the terms were described differently, depending on their focus. See Giliomee, *The Afrikaners*, 346–47.

18. Timothy Clynick, "Afrikaner Political Mobilization in the Western Transvaal: Popular Consciousness and the State, 1920–1930," D. Phil., Queen's University, 1996.

19. The school-leaving age varied slightly from province to province. See Ernst. G. Malherbe, *Education in South Africa (1652–1922): A Critical Survey of the Development of Educational Administration in the Cape, Natal, Transvaal and Orange Free State* (Johannesburg: Juta, 1925), 402.

20. E. G. Malherbe, preeminent among South African educationists in the first half of the twentieth century, defined "duly qualified" as a teacher who held an academic and professional qualification equivalent to one year beyond completion of the high school curriculum. See Malherbe, *Education in South Africa*, 403–4. It is noteworthy that in his study, which ran to more than 500 pages, Malherbe did not extend himself beyond the provision and administration of schooling for whites.

21. Malherbe, *Education in South Africa*, 401. The significant increases in the Transvaal and Orange Free State represented the low levels of formal schooling in the former Boer republics.

22. Cited in Francis Wilson, "Farming," 132.

23. Giliomee, *The Afrikaners*, 344.

24. Cited in Welsh, "The Growth of Towns," 228.

25. O. J. M. Wagner, *Social Work in Cape Town* (Cape Town: Maskew Miller, 1938), 13.

26. Wagner, *Social Work in Cape Town*, 31–32.

27. For the contexts of Beattie and Albertyn's remarks, see Giliomee, *The Afrikaners*, 347–48.

28. Wagner, *Social Work in Cape Town*, 14.

29. Wagner, *Social Work in Cape Town*, 22.

30. Morris J. Cohen, "The Epileptic," Unpublished paper presented at the National Conference on Social Work. Empire Exhibition. Johannesburg, 1936, 3–5.

31. Co-operation of Social Welfare Officers and Principals of Schools. SW 176/25. BNS. 1/1/506 38/5/85. State archive.

32. J. R. Albertyn, *The Poor White and Society* (Stellenbosch: Pro Ecclesia-Drukkery, 1932), 106. See also A. Coetzee, *Die Opkoms van die Afrikaanse Kultuurgedagte aan die Rand*,

1886–1936 (Johannesburg: Afrikanse Pers, 1937). Theodore Allen makes a similar point with reference to histories of whiteness in the nineteenth-century United States. See Theodore W. Allen, "On Roediger's 'Wages of Whiteness,'" *Cultural Logic: A Journal of Marxist Theory and Practice* 8 (2001), https://doi.org/10.14288/clogic.v8i0.191856.

33. J. M. Coetzee, "Idleness in South Africa," *Social Dynamics* 8, no. 1 (1982): 4–5.

34. Report of the committee of a hostel for white women, c. early 1920s[?]. Cited in Giliomee, *The Afrikaners*, 344.

35. J. E. Pieterse, "Die ontstaan en ontwikkeling van werk-kolonies in Suid-Afrika," *Tydskrif vir Geesteswetenskappe* 1, no. 4 (1961): 269.

36. L. Chisholm, "Crime, Class and Nationalism: The Criminology of Jacob de Villiers Roos, 1869–1918," *Social Dynamics* 13, no. 2 (1987): 51–56.

37. Pieterse, "Die ontstaan en ontwikkeling van werk-kolonies," 271.

38. Pieterse seems mildly disapproving of this provision, making the point in a paragraph where he discusses the shortcomings of the act. This attitude might reflect the currents of his time, when the apartheid state was expanding its capacity to surveil, discipline, and incarcerate, as well as his position as a sociologist at the highly conservative University of Pretoria.

39. The above detail is drawn from Pieterse, "Die ontstaan en ontwikkeling van werk-kolonies," 271–73.

40. Edward Roux, *Time Longer than Rope: The Black Man's Struggle for Freedom in South Africa*, 2nd ed. (Madison: University of Wisconsin Press, 1978 [1964]), 144.

41. The most substantial account of the Rand Revolt is Jeremy Krikler's *The Rand Revolt: The 1922 Insurrection and Racial Killing in South Africa* (Johannesburg: Jonathan Ball, 2005).

42. Although a staunch segregationist, Smuts believed that a legal color bar represented an admission by white workers that they could compete with Blacks. Cited in Giliomee, *The Afrikaners*, 335.

43. Giliomee, *The Afrikaners*, 341.

44. Report of Committee Appointed to Investigate the Employment of Unskilled European Workers in the Railway Service (UG 29–47), 3. In 1938, the designation "European laborer" was changed to "Railworker."

45. Report of Committee Appointed to Investigate, 14.

46. Report of Committee Appointed to Investigate, 16.

47. Report of Committee Appointed to Investigate, 10.

48. The Union buildings are the seat of the South African government. The Union buildings, completed in 1913, were also the site where Nelson Mandela was inaugurated as South Africa's first democratically elected president in 1994.

49. What was Smith Street is now known as Anton Lembede Street.

50. W. B. White, "Apartheid: The U.P. Reaction." Paper presented at "Structure and Experience in the Making of Apartheid," University of the Witwatersrand, Johannesburg, 1990.

51. For an account of the War Veterans Torch Commando and its role in the white political battles of the early 1950s, see Neil Roos, *Ordinary Springboks: White Servicemen and Social Justice in South Africa, 1939–1961* (Aldershot: Ashgate, 2005), 129–57.

52. In chapter 5, I return more comprehensively to the idea of the *volksmoeder*.

53. H. J. Martin and Neil Orpen, *South Africa at War* (Cape Town: Purnell & Sons, 1979).

4. Insluipers, Geoffrey Cronjé, and Social Policy

1. Others in this vein were criminologist Gerrie Eloff and anthropologist C. W. Prinsloo. Eloff wrote that the "*boerevolk*" represented a new biological type that came into existence as a result of the mixing of European Nordic and Alpine races. See Aletta J. Norval, *Deconstructing Apartheid Discourse* (London: Verso, 1996), 88.

2. J. M. Coetzee, "The Mind of Apartheid: Geoffrey Cronjé (1907–)," *Social Dynamics* 17, no. 1 (1991): 30.

3. See also Norval, *Deconstructing Apartheid Discourse*; Mark Sanders, "Undesirable Publications: J. M. Coetzee on Censorship and Apartheid," *Law and Literature* 18, no. 1 (2008), 101–14.

4. D. Berger, "White Poverty and Government Policy in South Africa, 1892–1934," PhD diss., Temple University, 1983. Farm schools were common on the South African *platteland*. They provided primary education for those white children who lived too far from regular schools to travel daily, and often several grades were combined in one classroom.

5. Professor Geoffrey Cronjé, Curriculum Vitae en Bibliografie. Special Collections, South Africana, University of the Free State. Paarl Boys' High was established in 1868, making it one of South Africa's oldest boys' schools. Known in Afrikaans as *Hoër Jongenskool*, it was also one of the country's most elite schools in Cronjé's day, and it remains so. Some Cape schools, although designated "high schools," accommodated children from all twelve grades.

6. His master's thesis was on Euripides's use of dramatic techniques. *Die Transvaler*, September 17, 1965.

7. Hermann Giliomee, "Cronjé, Geoffrey, 1907–1992," in *Dictionary of African Biography*, ed. Emmanuel K. Akyeampong and Henry Louis Gates Jr. (Oxford: Oxford University Press, 2012), 134. Vrije Universiteit Amsterdam was founded in 1880 as a Protestant university by Abraham Kuyper and a group of influential Protestants. Kuyper was appointed professor of theology and also the university's first *rector magnificus*. George Pavlich has argued that Cronjé's inaugural lecture to the University of Pretoria pointed unambiguously to Cronjé's orientation toward "administrative sociology"—essentially applied sociology—rather than to more classical iterations of the discipline. George Pavlich, "Administrative Sociology and Apartheid," *Acta Academica* 46, no. 3 (2014): 153–76.

8. Robert Czada, "Corporativism," in *International Encyclopedia of Political Science*, ed. Bertrand Badie, Dirk Berg-Schlosser, and Leonardo Morlino (London: SAGE, 2011), 458–63.

9. Antonio Costa Pinto, "Fascism, Corporatism and the Crafting of Authoritarian Institutions in Inter-War European Dictatorships," in *Rethinking Fascism and Dictatorship in Europe*, ed. A. C. Pinto and A. Kallis (London: Palgrave Macmillan, 2014), 87–117.

10. James Sparrow has argued that it also took root in World War Two-era United States. See James Sparrow, *Warfare State: World War II and the Age of Big Government* (Oxford: Oxford University Press, 2011).

11. Peter J. Williamson, *Varieties of Corporatism: A Conceptual Discussion* (Cambridge: Cambridge University Press, 1985).

12. Norval, *Deconstructing Apartheid Discourse*, 7–8, 88. Giliomee points out that in the Transvaal, Afrikaner Nationalism had always taken more republican, anti-capitalist forms than in the "capitalist" Cape. *The Afrikaners*, 442.

13. Fransjohan Pretorius, interview by author, November 24, 2009, Pretoria. Pretorius was a student at the University of Pretoria during the time Geoffrey Cronjé held a chair at that university.

14. Cronjé, Curriculum Vitae en Bibliografie.

15. In the South African academy, a lecturer is roughly equivalent to an assistant professor.

16. C. H. Rautenbach, ed., *Ad Destinatum. Gedenkboek van die Universiteit van Pretoria* (Johannesburg: Voortrekkerpers, 1960), 123.

17. *Rand Daily Mail*, October 10, 1930.

18. Rautenbach, *Ad Destinatum*, 123.

19. F. J. du Toit Spies and D. H. Heydenrych, *Ad Destinatum II, 1960–1982: 'n Geskiedenis van die Universiteit van Pretoria* (Pretoria: University of Pretoria, 1987), 60.

20. Instelling van twee selfstandige departemente om die Departement Sosiologie en Maatskaplike Werk te vervang. May 27,1950. University of Pretoria.

21. Rautenbach, *Ad Destinatum*, 123.

22. Rautenbach, *Ad Destinatum*, 124.

23. Rautenbach, *Ad Destinatum*, 124.
24. These bibliographic details cited in Hermann Giliomee, "Cronjé." See also Crain Soudien, "A Praetorian Sensibility? The Social Sciences and Humanities in Pretoria," ASSAf Humanities lecture and Human Sciences Research Council (HSRC) 50-90-100 Commemoration, Pretoria, August 14, 2019.
25. Coetzee, "The Mind of Apartheid," 17.
26. *Bloedvermenging* is sometimes translated as "miscegenation," but Coetzee prefers "blood mixing" as a closer translation to accord with the broad thrust of Cronjé's arguments in *'n Tuiste*. Coetzee, "The Mind of Apartheid," 9.
27. Coetzee, "The Mind of Apartheid," 17.
28. Arthur P. Wolf and William H. Durham, *Inbreeding, Incest and the Incest Taboo: The State of Knowledge at the Turn of the Century* (Stanford, CA: Stanford University Press, 2004); Polly Morris, "Incest or Survival Strategy: Plebian Marriage within the Prohibited Degrees in Somerset, 1730–1835," *Journal of the History of Sexuality* 2, no. 2 (October 1991): 235.
29. The Transvaal cases are more comprehensively reported. Interestingly, the NGK archives are remarkably silent on incest.
30. M. J. Smit, December 31, 1906, before T. Melborn Duran, JP. LD 1041, AG 307/06. State archive.
31. S. van Vuuren, sworn at the Bierlaagte district, Heidelberg, TLW Shone, JP, June 6, 1906; Lionel Gill, (for) Secretary of the Law Department – The Public Prosecutor, Heidelberg, Rex vs. J. J. van Vuuren: alleged charge of incest, January 27, 1906. LD 1041, AG 307/06. State archive.
32. Cronjé, Curriculum Vitae en Bibliografie
33. Norval, *Deconstructing Apartheid Discourse*, 37, 88.
34. P. Odendaal, Algemene Sekretaris, Federasie van Afrikaanse Kultuurverenigings – Registrateur, UP, 26-3-1944; Registrateur – Prof G. Cronjé, May 23, 1944; Registrateur – Algemene Sekretaris, Federasie van Afrikaanse Kultuurverenigings, June 2, 1944. UP. Translated, the FAK was the Federation of Afrikaner Cultural Organizations.
35. Giliomee, *The Afrikaners*, 487.
36. For an account of the history of the National Party in the 1930s and 1940s, and the emergence of the Herenigde (Reunited) National Party in 1940, see Dan O'Meara, *Volkskapitalisme: Class, Capital and Ideology in the Development of Afrikaner Nationalism, 1934–1948* (Johannesburg: Ravan, 1983), 119–22. See also Dan O'Meara, *Forty Lost Years: The Apartheid State and the Politics of the National Party, 1948–1994* (Athens: Ohio University Press, 1996), 88. The *Ossewa Brandwag* (OB, oxwagon sentinel) was a paramilitary outfit formed in the euphoria of the 1938 Great Trek centenary with the aim of establishing an Afrikaner republic free of "British-Jewish influence."
37. O'Meara, *Forty Lost Years*, 76.
38. Norval, *Deconstructing Apartheid Discourse*, 23.
39. Christoph Marx, *Oxwagon Sentinel: Radical Afrikaner Nationalism and the History of the 'Ossewabrandwag,'* (Pretoria: University of South Africa Press, 2009).
40. O'Meara, *Forty Lost Years*, 76. See also Robert H. Davies, *Capital, State and White Labour in South Africa, 1900–1960* (Atlantic Highlands, NJ: Humanities, 1979), 341.
41. Adam Ashforth, *The Politics of Official Discourse in Twentieth-century South Africa* (Oxford: Clarendon, 1990).
42. R. McLachlan, Sekretaris – Die Direkteur, Buro vir Sensus en Statistiek, August 2, 1951. BNS 248 99/72. State archive.
43. R. McLachlan, Sekretaris – Die Direkteur, Buro vir Sensus en Statistiek, November 28, 1951. BNS 248 99/72. State archive; Notule: Fakulteit Lettere en Wysbegeerte, August 14, 1950. UP.
44. G. Cronjé – Die Rektor, UP, August 14, 1951.

45. R. McLachlan, Sekretaris – Die Direkteur, Buro vir Sensus en Statistiek, August 2, 1951. BNS 248 99/72. State archive.

46. Cronjé, Curriculum Vitae en Bibliografie

47. Notule van Tweede Vergadering van Tydelike Komitee van die Nasionale Konferensie oor Alkoholisme, February 13, 1952. VWN 120, SW 17/81/4. State archive.

48. Peter D. Macdonald, *The Literature Police: Apartheid Censorship and Its Cultural Consequences* (Oxford: Oxford University Press, 2010), 21–82.

49. Macdonald, *The Literature Police*.

50. G. C. Cronjé – Die Rektor, UP, 13/11/53.

51. Macdonald, *The Literature Police*, 21–82; Archie Dick, *The Hidden Histories of South Africa's Book and Reading Cultures* (Toronto: University of Toronto Press, 2013).

52. Macdonald, *The Literature Police*.

53. See, for instance, the Beacon for Freedom of Expression, http://www.beaconforfreedom.org/index.html, accessed April 9, 2021. The list of banned books cited in this section is drawn from the Beacon for Freedom of Expression's website.

54. Office of the Board of Censors. Report of Member or Reader: *A World of Strangers*, Nadine Gordimer. September 30, 1958. Cited in Macdonald, *The Literature Police*. See also *The Literature Police* website supplement, https://theliteraturepolice.com, accessed April 9, 2021.

55. Cronjé, *'n Tuiste vir die Nageslag*, cited in J. M. Coetzee, *Giving Offence: Essays on Censorship* (Chicago, IL: University of Chicago Press, 1996), 173.

56. Registrateur – Prof. G. Cronjé, May 14, 1964; G. Cronjé – Die Registrateur, UP, May 30, 1964; Registrateur – Prof. G. Cronjé, June 15, 1964.

57. In 1949, for instance, he was elected to the Executive of the Nasionale Toneelorganisasie (National Drama Organization), and he eventually served as its chairman. Cronjé, Curriculum Vitae en Bibliografie.

58. Spies and Heydenrych, *Ad Destinatum II*, 42.

59. National Drama Organization.

60. Transvaal Council for the Performing Arts.

61. Spies and Heydenrych, *Ad Destinatum II*, 43.

62. *Skakelblad*, November 1964.

63. Don Rubin, Ousmane Diakhate, and Hansel Ndumbe Eyoh, *The World Encyclopedia of Contemporary Theatre: Africa* (London: Routledge, 1997), 294.

64. *Skakelblad*, November 1964.

65. Spies and Heydenrych, *Ad Destinatum II*, 44.

66. *Die Transvaler*, September 17, 1965.

67. *Skakelblad*, November/December 1965.

68. Pretorius interview, November 24, 2009.

5. Work and Ideology in the Apartheid Public Service

1. Deborah Posel, "Whiteness and Power in the South African Civil Service: Paradoxes of the Apartheid State," *Journal of Southern African Studies* 25, no. 1 (March 1999): 102.

2. *New Era*, May 23, 1946.

3. First Report of Commission of Inquiry into Grievances of Railway Workers, October 1949, UG 9 of 1950, paragraph 154.

4. *Cape Times*, May 15, 1946.

5. *New Era*, May 23, 1946.

6. *Pretoria News*, May 21, 1946.

7. *Cape Times*, October 18, 1946.

8. *Star*, November 26, 1946.

9. *Pretoria News*, March 13, 1947.

10. *Rand Daily Mail*, September 25, 1946; November 8, 1946.

11. *Thirty-Seventh Annual Report of the Public Service Commission*, 1948, UG 33/1949, paragraph 69.

12. The *staatsdiens* incorporated the civil service, referring to individuals in departments directly involved with the daily exercise of administration and governing, while the public service itself was broader and included teachers, scientists, nurses, mechanics, road and railway workers, and all those who were employed by the government and rendered a service to the public. See Posel, "Whiteness and Power in the South African Civil Service," 100.

13. O'Meara, *Forty Lost Years*, 61–62.

14. See Norbert Finzsch and Robert Jutte, *Institutions of Confinement: Hospitals, Asylums and Prisons in Western Europe and North America, 1500–1950* (Cambridge: Cambridge University Press, 2003). For a South African perspective on these processes see Roger Deacon, "From Confinement to Attachment: Foucault on the Rise of the School," *The European Legacy* 11, no. 2 (2006): 121–38.

15. Eley, *A Crooked Line*, 9–10, 190.

16. *Public Service Commission*, 1948, paragraph 46.

17. A. E. Gerhart, D. Eng, M.I.A.-Hon Dr. T. E. Donges, Minister for the Interior, August 2, 1948. BNS 248 99/72. State archive.

18. General Report of the Committee of Enquiry into the grievances of officials of the Department of Post and Telegraphs. August 1949. SDK 4896 vol. 1. State archive.

19. Committee of Enquiry into the grievances of officials of the Department of Post and Telegraphs. The "list" was the Divisional Priority List, which ranked all officials in the public service and established an order for promotion posts.

20. Minister of Posts and Telegraphs – Postmaster General, August 6, 1950. SDK 4896, vol. 1. State archive.

21. *Thirty-Eighth Annual Report of the Public Service Commission*, 1949, UG 26/1950, paragraph 139.

22. *Public Service Commission*, 1949, paragraph 140–41.

23. Hermann Giliomee, *The Afrikaners: Biography of a People* (Charlottesville: University of Virginia Press, 2003), 493.

24. *Thirty-Ninth Annual Report of the Public Service Commission*, 1950, UG 23/1951, paragraph 43.

25. *Public Service Commission*, 1950, paragraph 44.

26. *Public Service Commission*, 1950, paragraphs 44–45.

27. See, for instance, Private Secretary, Agriculture – W.A. Maree, LV, November 12, 1951. PV 55 52/10/1/1/1. State archive.

28. David C. Potter, "The Last of the Indian Civil Service," *South Asia: Journal of South Asian Studies* 2, no. 1–2 (1979): 26.

29. With the exception of teachers and nurses, Black workers were all confined to the general division where they earned considerably less than whites.

30. *Public Service Commission*, 1948, paragraph 88.

31. *Public Service Commission*, 1948, paragraph 104.

32. *Public Service Commission*, 1950, paragraph 203.

33. *Public Service Commission*, 1949, paragraph 17.

34. *Public Service Commission*, 1949, paragraph 61.

35. *Public Service Commission*, 1950, paragraphs 190–91.

36. For an account of the Indian civil service exam, see Ann Ewing, "Administering India: The Indian Civil Service," *History Today* 32, no. 6 (June 1982): 45.

37. *Fortieth Annual Report of the Public Service Commission*, 1951, UG 33/1952, paragraphs 137–138.

38. See, for instance, "Opleiding van Tiksters," Staatsdienskommissie, January 10, 1956, GG 2148 71/294, vol. 1; "Tiksters vir permanente annstelling," Staatsdienskommissie, October 16, 1956, 71/294B, vol. 1. State archive.

39. "Statistics required for annual report," PSC 19/22/F/1 December 12, 1958. GG 2,148, vol. 3. State archive.

40. See, for instance, *Public Service Commission, Forty-Second Annual Report* (1953), UG 28/1954, paragraph 55; *Public Service Commission, Forty-Third Annual Report* (1954), UG 25/1955, paragraph 52.

41. *Public Service Commission*, 1950, paragraphs 297–98.

42. D. Hobart Houghton, "Economic Development, 1865–1958," in *The Oxford History of South Africa, Volume II*, edited by Monica Wilson and Leonard Thompson (Oxford: Oxford University Press, 1975), 36–48.

43. Sometimes, especially in the case of first- or second-generation immigrants, those parts of the private sector that were most accessible were small, family-owned businesses: corner cafés, greengrocers, bakeries.

44. Posel, "Whiteness and Power in the South African Civil Service," 99–100.

45. *Public Service Commission, Forty-Fourth Annual Report*, 1955, UG 16/1956, paragraph 26.

46. *Public Service Commission*, 1955, paragraph 63.

47. *Public Service Commission*, 1955, paragraph 64.

48. Posel, "Whiteness and Power in the South African Civil Service."

49. *Public Service Commission, Forty-Fifth Annual Report*, 1956, UG 17/1957, paragraph 28.

50. *Public Service Commission*, 1956, paragraph 28.

51. *Public Service Commission, Forty-Sixth Annual Report*, 1957, UG 27/1958, paragraph 70.

52. *Public Service Commission, Forty-Eighth Annual Report*, 1959, UG 30/1960.

53. *Public Service Commission*, 1949, paragraph 78.

54. *Public Service Commission*, 1950, paragraph 209.

55. *Public Service Commission, Forty-First Annual Report*, 1952, UG 23/1953, paragraph 32.

56. *Public Service Commission*, 1954, paragraph 55.

57. *Public Service Commission*, 1955, paragraph 62; *Public Service Commission*, 1956, paragraph 45; Staff Clerks' Quarterly Meeting, March 6, 1957, GC 794 13/3051. State archive.

58. *Public Service Commission*, 1957, paragraph 89.

59. *Public Service Commission*, 1958, paragraph 58.

60. *Public Service Commission*, 1958, paragraph 88.

61. A phrase used in Parliament by H. Pockock, an opposition member of Parliament. *Hansard*, vol. 92, 1955, col. 1,228.

62. *Public Service Commission, Forty-Seventh Annual Report*, 1958, paragraph 50.

63. Jon Lewis, *Industrialisation and Trade Union Organisation in South Africa, 1924–1955: The Rise and Fall of the South African Trades and Labour Council* (Cambridge: Cambridge University Press, 1984); Eddie Webster, *Cast in a Racial Mould: Labour Process and Trade Unionism in the Foundries* (Johannesburg: Ravan, 1985).

64. See Albert Wessels, *Farmboy and Industrialist* (Johannesburg: Perskor, 1987), 154–155.

65. Duty Sheets and Procedure Manuals, Forms Z 190 and Z 191. GG 2148 71/294 vol. 1. 1951. State archive.

66. They set out, in a sense, to "provincialize" Europe. For an elaboration of the cultural arguments and ripostes at play, see Dipesh Chakrabarty, *Provincializing Europe: Postcolonial Thought and Historical Difference* (Princeton, NJ: Princeton University Press, 2000), esp. 1–23.

67. *Public Service Commission*, 1950, paragraph 248.

68. CEN 68 E1/1/1, November 13, 1951. State archive.

69. Omsendminuut SDK 2/G. Merietebepaling, January 13, 1956. Sekretaris: Staatsdienskommissie. GG 2148 71/294 vol. 1. State archive.

70. L. E. L. Kleuver, Secretary, PSC-The Commissioner for Inland Revenue, December 30, 1952. SDK 2/G/3 vol. 6, "Inland Revenue." State archive.

71. Inland Revenue Merit Assessment 1952. SDK 2/G/3 vol. 6, "Inland Revenue." State archive.
72. *Public Service Commission*, 1954, paragraph 48.
73. *Public Service Com*mission, 1954, paragraphs 73-74.
74. *Public Service Commission*, 1957, paragraph 90.
75. *Public Service Commission*, Forty-Ninth Annual Report, 1960, UG 27/1961, paragraph 104.
76. *Public Service Commission*, 1960, paragraph 107.
77. *Public Service Commission*, 1953, paragraph 75.
78. *Public Service Commission*, 1955, paragraph 89.
79. *Public Service Commission*, 1949, paragraph 204.
80. *Public Service Commission*, 1949, paragraph 204.
81. *Public Service Commission*, 1954, paragraph 17.
82. *Public Service Commission*, 1954, paragraph 17.
83. *Public Service Commission*, 1958, paragraph 26.
84. *Public Service Commission*, 1958, paragraph 26.
85. *Public Service* Commission, 1959, paragraph 70.
86. *Public Service Commission*, Fiftieth Annual Report, 1961, R.P. 26/62, paragraph 31.
87. *Public Service Commission*, 1961, paragraph 102.
88. Will Jackson, *Madness and Marginality: The Lives of Kenya's White Insane* (Manchester: Manchester University Press, 2013).
89. Robert Davies, *Capital, State and White Labour in South Africa* (Atlantic Highlands, NJ: Humanities, 1979), 341.
90. Davies, *Capital, State and White Labour*, 340-348.
91. *Hansard*, vol. 70, 71, 72 and 73, 1951, col. 5,353.
92. Verslag van die Komitee van Ondersoek na Beskutte Arbeid, Sekretaris van Volkswelsyn. PV 94 1/47/26/1. E. G. Jansen papers. Archive for Contemporary Affairs, University of the Free State (hereafter Archive for Contemporary Affairs).
93. Conference of work colony superintendents, 1957. VWN 1850. SWA 274. State archive.
94. Verslag van die Verrigtinge by 'n Konferensie van Departementele Beheerbeamptes gehou op 5 en 6 Maart 1957, Staff Clerk's Quarterly Meetings, GG 794 13/3051. State archive.
95. *Public Service Commission*, 1956, paragraph 28.
96. *Public Service Commission*, 1957, paragraph 81.
97. *Public Service Commission*, 1957, paragraph 81.
98. *Public Service Commission*, 1958, paragraph 52.
99. T. Dunbar Moodie, *The Rise of Afrikanerdom: Power, Apartheid and the Afrikaner Civil Religion* (Berkeley: University of California Press, 1980 [1975]) 234-235. The idea of the "steel frame" was made famous by former British Prime Minister David Lloyd George, who in 1935 described the Indian Civil Service as "the steel frame on which the whole structure of our government and administration in India rests."
100. Ann Laura Stoler, *Along the Archival Grain: Epistemic Anxieties and Colonial Common Sense* (Princeton, NJ: Princeton University Press, 2009), 18-20.
101. J. H. Basson, Algemene Sekretaris, VSA-Die Sekretaris, Departement van Finansies, March 9, 1952. TES 5175 28/406. State archive.
102. J. L. Jooste, Sekretaris van die Tesourie – Die Algemene Sekretaris, Vereniging van Staatsbeamptes, May 5, 1952. TES 5175 28/406. State archive.
103. "Kleredrag: Beamptes/Werknemers in die Departement van Tesourie," Sekretaris van die Tesourie, une 10, 1956. TES 5175 28/406. State archive.
104. Kleredrag: Beamptes. PSC September 16, 1956. TES 5175 28/406. State archive.
105. Conference of work colony superintendents, 1950. VWN 1850, SWA 274. State archive.

106. Gladys Hall, interview by author, Durban, May 14, 2010. Gladys Hall was a housewife during the period under discussion.

107. Posel, "Whiteness and Power in the South African Civil Service," 99–119.

108. *Hansard*, January 19 to June 22, 1951, col. 1,228, February 14, 1951; January to June 25, 1952, col. 2,647, March 12, 1952.

109. *Hansard*, January to June 25, 1952, col. 2647, March 12, 1952.

110. The informant asked to remain anonymous.

111. Jon Hyslop reminds us that rent-seeking, patronage, and corruption—at all levels—were features of apartheid state-building. See Jonathan Hyslop, "Political Corruption: Before and After Apartheid," *Journal of Southern African Studies* 31, no. 4 (December 2005): 773–89.

112. State Entomologist – Dr. E. Chese Brown, Tower Hospital, Fort Beaufort, December 19, 1952. CEN 65 vol. 1. State archive.

113. ARB 907 1000/21/1/1/10 vol. 6. January 25, 1957–May 27, 1957. State archive.

6. Women, the Labor Market, and the Domestic Economy

1. For an overview of the development of the discipline in the Netherlands, see Anton C. Zijderveld, "History and Recent Development of Dutch Sociological Thought," *Social Research* 33, no. 1 (Spring 1966): 115–31.

2. M. J. M. Prinsloo, *Blanke vroue-arbeid in die Unie van Suid-Afrika* (Cape Town: Nasionale Boekhandel, 1957). Extracts over the following three pages are from *Blanke vroue-arbeid*, 340–50.

3. A concept similar to that described by Foucault as a "technology of the self," a means by which people assess and regulate their own behavior. See, for instance, Luther H. Martin, Huck Gutman, and Patrick H. Hutton, *Technologies of the Self: A Seminar with Michel Foucault* (Amherst: University of Massachusetts Press, 1988).

4. Elsabé Brink, "Man-made Women: Gender, Class and the Ideology of the *Volksmoeder*," in *Women and Gender in Southern Africa to 1945*, ed. Cherryl Walker (Cape Town: David Philip, 1990), 273.

5. Brink, "Man-made Women," 274.

6. Brink, "Man-made Women," 279. Totius was the pen name of Jakob Daniël du Toit (1877–1953). Translated, the title of Postma's book was "Boer Woman: Mother of Her Nation."

7. Louise Vincent, "A Cake of Soap: The *Volksmoeder* Ideology and Afrikaner Women's Campaign for the Vote," *The International Journal of African Historical Studies* 32, no. 1 (1999): 5.

8. These studies are cited in Brink, "Man-made Women," 281–83.

9. Louise Vincent, "Bread and Honour: White Working Class Women and Afrikaner Nationalism in the 1930s," *Journal of Southern African Studies* 26, no. 1 (March 2000): 63–67.

10. Jonathan Hyslop, "White Working-Class Women and the Invention of Apartheid's 'Purified' Afrikaner Nationalist Agitation for Legislation against Mixed Marriages, 1934–9," *The Journal of African History* 36, no. 1 (1995): 57–81.

11. At the time, "mixed" marriages sometimes referred to those between English-and Afrikaans-speaking whites, reflecting contemporary white understanding of the "race question."

12. Hyslop, "White Working-Class Women," 60. For an account of the ways in which white women were seen as untrustworthy and as potential agents of "treason" to racial supremacy, see Lewis Gordon, *Bad Faith and Antiblack Racism* (Atlantic Highlands, NJ: Humanities, 1995). Cited in *Black on White: Black Writers on What It Means to Be White*, ed. David Roediger (New York: Schocken Books, 1999), 305. Historical questions of how white women's sexuality and fertility threatened to undermine the racial order in twentieth-century South Africa have been most comprehensively addressed by Susanne Klausen. She also addresses official responses to the imagined threats posed by white women. See Susanne Klausen, *Race, Maternity and the Politics of Birth Control in South Africa, 1910–1939* (Basingstoke: Palgrave

Macmillan, 2004); *Abortion Under Apartheid: Nationalism, Sexuality and Women's Reproductive Rights in South Africa* (Oxford: Oxford University Press, 2015).

13. Vincent, "Bread and Honour," 67.

14. Cited in Vincent, "Bread and Honour," 67. In Afrikaans, *meid* is a racial slur. African women domestic workers were (and often still are) described by whites as "maids." Naming a white woman a "maid" was to imply that she was not-quite-white.

15. Vincent, "Bread and Honour."

16. Vincent, "Bread and Honour," 78.

17. Nancy Clark, "Gendering Production in Wartime South Africa," *The American Historical Review* 106, no. 4 (October 2001): 1,183. See also Jon Lewis, *Industrialisation and Trade Union Organisation in South Africa* (Cambridge: Cambridge University Press, 1984); Eddie Webster, *Cast in a Racial Mould: Labour Process and Trade Unionism in the Foundries* (Johannesburg: Ravan, 1985).

18. Clark, "Gendering Production," 1,186.

19. Clark, "Gendering Production," 1,190–91.

20. Clark, "Gendering Production," 1,199–1,205.

21. Clark, "Gendering Production," 1,206–07.

22. See, for instance, George Cloete Visser, *OB: Traitors or Patriots?* (Johannesburg: Macmillan, 1977); Charl Blignaut, "From Fund-raising to Freedom Day: The Nature of Women's General Activities in the *Ossewa Brandwag*," *New Contree* 66 (July 2013): 121–50.

23. Blignaut, "The Nature of Women's General Activities in the Ossewa Brandwag," 125–28.

24. Although by the 1980s many of the new public servants were Blacks, employed by the various "homeland" administrations.

25. C. D. Taylor. Notes on the public service, May 29, 1964–July 16, 1967. 1/11/4/9/1 vol. 1. Archive for Contemporary Affairs.

26. *Public Service Commission*, 1948, UG 33/1949, paragraph 135.

27. Staff Clerks' Quarterly Meetings, August 29, 1951. GC 794. State archive.

28. *Public Service Commission*, 1948, paragraph 150. The profession of social work had recently evolved out of welfare work, which was historically undertaken among white Afrikaners by women attached to the Dutch Reformed churches and later, the Afrikaner nationalist women's groups.

29. Tikskole, January 10, 1950. GG 794 13/3051. State archive.

30. Staff Clerks' Quarterly Meetings, August 29, 1951. GC 794. State archive.

31. A. Tyderman, Interview by author, March 1, 2017. Tyderman was a public servant, and later a housewife.

32. *Public Service Commission*, 1948, paragraph 141. Each year the Public Service Commission of Enquiry took on specific matters for investigation.

33. *Public Service Commission*, 1951, UG 33/1952, Annexure B. *Public Service Commission, 43rd Annual Report*, 1954, UG 25/1955, Annexure B; *Public Service Commission, 46th Annual Report*, 1957, UG 27/1958, Annexure A.

34. *Public Service Commission, Forty-First Annual Report*, 1952, UG 23/1953, Annexure G.

35. Deborah Posel, "Whiteness and Power in the South African Civil Service: Paradoxes of the Apartheid State," *Journal of Southern African Studies* 25, no. 1 (March 1999): 99–119.

36. *Public Service Commission*, 1949, UG 26/1950, paragraph 91.

37. *Public Service Commission*, 1949, paragraph 19.

38. *Public Service Commission*, 1950, UG 23/1951, paragraphs 143–44.

39. *Public Service Commission*, 1950, paragraph 92. This, incidentally, was a similar condition to one specified in 1961 for "Bantu Officers," who were expected to take on "leading roles in the administration of their own communities." *Public Service Commission, Forty-Ninth Annual Report*, 1960, UG 27/1961, paragraph 23.

40. See, for instance, *Public Service Commission*, 1950, paragraphs 143–44.

41. *Public Service Commission*, 1948, paragraph 142.
42. *Public Service Commission*, 1954, paragraph 54.
43. *Public Service Commission*, 1952, Annexure G.
44. *Public Service Commission*, 1951, paragraphs 14 and 15.
45. Cost of living allowances were calculated according to where a public servant was based. Those living on the Witwatersrand received the highest allowances, although public servants living in other towns regularly complained that their cost of living was in fact higher than on the Witwatersrand.
46. *Public Service Commission, 48th Annual Report*, 1959, UG 30/1960, paragraph 17.
47. *Public Service Commission*, 1959, paragraph 18.
48. Induction, 5 April 1957. PSC 99/G/4 GG 2148 vol. 2. State archive.
49. C. D. Taylor. Notes on the public service, May 29, 1964–July 16, 1967. 1/11/4/9/1 vol. 1. Archive for Contemporary Affairs.
50. *Vrou en Moeder*, March 1946.
51. *Vrou en Moeder*, June 1947.
52. *Vrou en Moeder*, September 1946.
53. Lynn Y. Weiner, *From Working Girl to Working Mother: The Female Labor Force in the United States, 1820–1980* (Chapel Hill: University of North Carolina Press, 1984), 100–101; Elaine Tyler May, *Homeward Bound. American Families in the Cold War Era* (New York: Basic Books, 1999).
54. *Vrou en Moeder*, April 1954.
55. See Paul Popenoe and Roswell Hill Johnson, *Applied Eugenics* (New York: Macmillan, 1918); Paul Popenoe, *Problems of Human Reproduction* (Baltimore: Williams & Wilkins, 1926); E. S. Gosney and Paul Popenoe, *Sterilization for Human Betterment: A Summary of Results of 6,000 Operations in California, 1909–1929* (New York: Macmillan, 1929).
56. *Vrou en Moeder*, April 1954.
57. *Vrou en Moeder*, April 1954.
58. *Vrou en Moeder*, April 1958.
59. *Vrou en Moeder*, April 1956.
60. *Vrou en Moeder*, September 1944.
61. *Vrou en Moeder*, April 1958.
62. *Vrou en Moeder*, July 1957.
63. A. E. Rossouw and M. L. Spies, *Ons Onthou 74 Jaar: Die C en N Meisieskool Oranje Bloemfontein* (Bloemfontein: Meisieskool Oranje, 1982), 34–38.
64. Welma Mentz, interview by author, Bloemfontein, March 20, 2014. Welma Mentz was a nurse and a teacher.
65. *Vrou en Moeder*, June 1949.
66. *Vrou en Moeder*, September 1959. With the distinctions of *"Afrikaans-bewus"* and *"Afrikaans-onbewus,"* the women in the SAVF pointed to those who lacked commitment to a particular synthesis of Afrikaans cultural values.
67. *Vrou en Moeder*, December 1954.
68. Eudora Hauptfleisch, "Kleuterskole van die SAVF in Transvaal," *Vrou en Moeder*, July 1957.
69. *Vrou en Moeder*, June 1952. "Duimpie" (thumb) and "Klein Duimpie" (little thumb) were very common names for *kleuterskole*.
70. *Vrou en Moeder*, July 1957.
71. Kathleen Boner, *Dominican Women: A Time to Speak* (Pietermaritzburg: Cluster, 1998).
72. *Vrou en Moeder*, July 1958.
73. *Vrou en Moeder*, July 1957.
74. *Vrou en Moeder*, October 1960. Articles expressing similar sentiments also appeared in April 1959 and October 1960.

75. *Vrou en Moeder*, October 1960.
76. *Vrou en Moeder*, October 1960.
77. *Vrou en Moeder*, March 1946.
78. Jacklyn Cock, *Maids and Madams: A Study in the Politics of Exploitation* (Johannesburg: Ravan, 1980).
79. Hyslop, "White Working-Class Women," 57–81.
80. Weiner, *From Working Girl to Working Mother*.
81. Deborah Posel, "The Case for a Welfare State: Poverty and the Politics of the Urban African Family in South Africa in the 1930s and 1940s." Paper presented to a workshop on South Africa in the 1940s, Southern African Research Centre, Queen's University, Kingston (September 2003), 1.
82. David Goldberg makes the point that the more comprehensively the state (or those close to it) is able to penetrate the intimate reaches of everyday life, especially the family, the greater its capacity to "educate" and control a social body. See David Theo Goldberg, *The Racial State* (Oxford: Wiley, 2002), 100.
83. Formation and activities of the Bachelor Girls' Club. KCM 92/12/4/4. Killie Campbell Collections (hereafter Killie).
84. Cambridge House Hostel for Girls, c. 1930, Durban Bachelor Girls' Club, KCM 92/12/4/1. Killie.
85. The Girls' Friendly Society was established in Liverpool under the auspices of the Anglican church to support "friendship and Christian fellowship" among girls from rural areas who sought employment in cities, often as domestic workers. One of its more controversial rules was that members be virgins. See Ellen D. Maki, "Domestic Service and the Girls' Friendly Society," in *Finding Folk: Discovering Ancestors across Time and Place*, March 27, 2016, http://findingfolk.org/2016/03/domestic-service-the-girls-friendly-society/.
86. Formation and activities of the Bachelor Girls' Club. Killie.

7. Nationalism, Whiteness, and Consumption

1. Giliomee, *The Afrikaners*, 489. Giliomee writes that in 1948, Afrikaners constituted 57 percent of the white population and had a 29 percent share of the total income, compared to 46 percent for English-speaking whites and 20 percent for Africans, who made up 68 percent of the total population.
2. Giliomee, *The Afrikaners*, 489.
3. Giliomee, *The Afrikaners*, 489.
4. Albert Grundlingh, "Are We Afrikaners Getting Too Rich? Cornucopia and Change in Afrikanerdom in the 1960s," *Journal of Historical Sociology* 21, no. 2–3 (June 2008): 143–65.
5. Grundlingh, "Are We Afrikaners Getting Too Rich?"
6. Giliomee, *The Afrikaners*, 480.
7. Davies, *Capital, State and White Labour*, 331, 338, 339.
8. Dan O'Meara, *Forty Lost Years*, 76.
9. O'Meara, *Forty Lost Years*, 76.
10. Davies, *Capital, State and White Labour*, 345–346.
11. O'Meara, *Forty Lost Years*, 76; 79. This salary disparity between parastatals and the more traditional sectors of the public service persists today.
12. Davies, *Capital, State and White Labour*, 339–41.
13. O'Meara, *Forty Lost Years*, 78.
14. Lis Lange, *White, Poor and Angry: White Working Class Families in Johannesburg* (Aldershot: Ashgate, 2003), 88–96.
15. *Debates of the House of Assembly*, 1948, vol. 64, cols. 537–39 (*Hansard*).
16. Roos, *Ordinary Springboks*, 103–27.
17. *Hansard*, 1953, vols. 82, 83, col. 372.

18. *Boerewors* is a type of traditional South African sausage that is stereotypically a great favorite of Afrikaans-speaking whites.
19. PV 55 2/10/1/1/1 1956–Nov 20–1966–Des 28. State archive.
20. *Hansard*, 1956, vols. 90, 91 and 92, cols. 5611–12.
21. *Hansard*, 1954, vols. 84, 85 and 86, col. 3661.
22. RB 86. 1953. State archive.
23. Through the 1960s in particular, car ownership among whites soared. By the 1970s, car ownership for whites was surpassed only by that in America.
24. *Vrou en Moeder*, September 1947.
25. *Hansard*, 1953, vols. 82 and 83, col 493.
26. *Vrou en Moeder*, September 1953.
27. Although Clive Chipkin does provide a substantial account of the architectural history of Johannesburg. See Clive M. Chipkin, *Johannesburg Transitions: Architecture and Society from 1950* (Johannesburg: S T E, 2008).
28. *Vrou en Moeder*, April 1954.
29. *Hansard*, 1954, vols. 84, 85, and 86, col. 3653.
30. *Hansard*, 1957, vols. 93, 94, col. 2331.
31. For a history of Kenneth Gardens, see M. Marks, K. Erwin, and T. Fleetwood, *Voices of Resilience: A Living History of Kenneth Gardens Municipal Housing Estate in Durban* (Pietermaritzburg: University of Kwazulu-Natal Press, 2018).
32. Derek Austin, "Memories of Growing Up in Woodlands, Durban," December 2008, http://www.fad.co.za/Resources/memoirs/derek/austin.htm. The nickname "FL" stood for "French letters," a colloquial term for a condom implying that Flamingo Court was a place of great promiscuity.
33. *Vrou en Moeder*, September 1947. Demobilization of war veterans caused considerable housing shortages, especially in cities. A rental market developed around backyard dwellings, sometimes informal structures. In the early postwar years the Springbok Legion, a veterans' movement, led a campaign by white war veterans to "occupy" what they deemed to be underutilized houses in Hillbrow, Johannesburg.
34. *Vrou en Moeder*, June 1949.
35. In 1961, South African currency converted from pounds, shillings, and pence to rands (R) and cents (c).
36. A 272 191 15/11. State archive.
37. *Potchefstroom Herald*, April 11, 1947.
38. *Vrou en Moeder*, June 1947, June 1951.
39. *Vrou en Moeder*, December 1959.
40. B. le Roux (former public servant), interview by author, Cape Agulhas, August 8, 2017.
41. Grundlingh, "Are We Afrikaners Getting Too Rich?," 146.
42. See most notably Dan O'Meara, *Volkskapitalisme: Class, Capital and Ideology in the Development of Afrikaner Nationalism, 1934–1948* (Johannesburg: Ravan, 1983), 119–221.
43. Noting that in the 1950s Afrikaners were still generally poorer than English-speaking whites (although not immigrants, especially Portuguese and Greeks), Sylvester Richards, a former Standard Bank official, commented that Afrikaners tended to lack the confidence to approach large banks like Standard and Barclays for loans. They tended to prefer smaller banks with links to Afrikaner nationalism like Volkskas. Sylvester Richards, personal correspondence with author, December 14, 2016.
44. O'Meara, *Volkskapitalisme*, 134. *Hoggenheimer* was an anti-capitalist cartoon drawn by Afrikaner nationalist cartoonist D. C. Boonzaier. Hoggenheimer was a caricature of a Jewish financier who was always ready to exploit poor Afrikaners.
45. www.samba.co.za.

46. www.ahitygerberg.co.za. Its annual financial statements offer some sense of the range of its activities. See, for instance, Koopkrag Wins- en Verliesrekening vir die jaar geëindig 30 Junie 1956. RB87/SA. State archive.

47. O'Meara, *Volkskapitalisme*, 116.

48. A. Belim, interview with author, Umzinto, November 11, 2016. A. Belim is one of the sons of the business patriarch discussed in the case study above.

49. *Hansard*, 1954, vols. 84, 85, and 86, col. 6528.

50. *Hansard*, vols. 84, 85, and 86, col. 6549.

51. *Hansard*, vols. 84, 85, and 86, col. 6529.

52. *Hansard*, vols. 84, 85, and 86, cols. 6549–53.

53. *Hansard*, 1954, vols. 84, 85, and 86, col. 6556.

54. See, for instance, *The Public Servant*, January 1949; August 1952.

55. *The Public Servant*, June 1949.

56. *The Public Servant*, April 1950.

57. *The Public Servant*, December 1952.

58. *The Public Servant*, April 1956.

59. D. Spies, former public servant, mine worker and mine manager. Interview with author, Bloemfontein, February 22, 2017.

60. *Pretoria News*, July 11, 1953.

61. David Kynaston, *Modernity Britain: Book One: Opening the Box, 1957–1959* (New York: Bloomsbury, 2014), 44.

62. Kynaston, *Modernity Britain*, 251–55.

63. Kynaston, *Modernity Britain*, 169–72.

64. Katie Mooney, "Identities in the Ducktail Youth Subculture in Post-World-War-Two South Africa," *Journal of Youth Studies* 8, no. 1 (2005): 41.

65. Katie Mooney, "'Ducktails, Flickknives and Pugnacity': Subcultural and Hegemonic Masculinities in South Africa, 1848–1960," *Journal of Southern African Studies* 24, no. 4 (December 1998): 754.

66. Mooney, "Ducktails, Flickknives and Pugnacity."

67. L. F. Freed, *Crime in South Africa: An Integralistic Approach* (Johannesburg: Juta, 1963), 83.

68. Mooney, "Ducktails, Flickknives and Pugnacity," 764.

69. L. F. Freed, Report on Homosexuality in Johannesburg, 23/2/1939. A 1212/CK. Historical Papers, University of the Witwatersrand.

70. Cited in Mooney, "Ducktails, Flickknives and Pugnacity," 761.

71. Mooney, "Ducktails, Flickknives and Pugnacity," 763.

72. Mooney, "Ducktails, Flickknives and Pugnacity," 768.

73. J. E. Pieterse and G. Cronjé, *Verslag van die jeugondersoek wat die Departement Sosiologie van die Universiteit van Pretoria vir die Naionale Jeugraad onderneem het* (Johannesburg: Voortrekkerpers, 1962).

74. Grundlingh, "Are We Afrikaners Getting Too Rich?," 153.

75. See, for instance, *The Public Servant*, January 1949; March 1949; February 1950; April 1952.

76. Grundlingh, "Are We Afrikaners Getting Too Rich?," 157.

77. A colonial administrator of the Dutch East India Company, van Riebeeck was commander of the Cape from 1652 to 1662. Notably during the apartheid years, many Afrikaners viewed him as the founding father of their nation.

78. *Hansard*, January 18 to June 25, 1952, vols. 77, 78, 79, 80, col. 6269.

79. Ciraj Rasool and Leslie Witz, "The 1952 Jan van Riebeeck Tercentenary Festival: Constructing and Contesting Public National History in South Africa," *Journal of African History* 34 (1993): 447–68.

80. Holiday Concessions for Public Servants, SDK 4896, 120/G. State archive.
81. Grundlingh, "Are We Afrikaners Getting Too Rich?," 154.
82. Mooney, "Ducktails, Flickknives and Pugnacity," 763.

8. Alcohol and Social Engineering

1. A. Lynn Martin, *Alcohol, Violence and Disorder in Traditional Europe* (Kirksville, MO: Truman State University Press, 2009); Paul Taillon, "'What We Want Is Good, Sober Men': Masculinity, Respectability and Temperance in Railroad Brotherhoods, c. 1870–1910," *Journal of Social History* 36 (2002): 319–320.

2. Gyanendra Pandey noted that a single instance of strife allowed him to delineate many themes salient to the history of modern India. These included the way "nationhood" is naturalized, how the representation of a small section of society is taken as the "national mainstream," and the drive to homogenize the nation's history. These "single instances" are what the subaltern studies group of scholars know as "the fragment," and I use the idea similarly, to look backward and forward and to consider several themes that derive from a single episode. Gyanendra Pandey, "In Defense of the Fragment," in *A Subaltern Studies Reader*, ed. Ranajit Guha (Minneapolis: University of Minnesota Press, 1997), 1–33.

3. See, for instance, Zwia Lipkin, *Useless to the State: "Social Problems" and Social Engineering in Nationalist Nanjing, 1927–1937* (Cambridge, MA: Harvard University Asia Center, 2006). There are of course countless other examples, most obviously from Nazi Germany, the Soviet Union, and Latin America.

4. Louis Freed, *The Problem of European Prostitution in Johannesburg: A Sociological Survey* (Cape Town: Juta, 1949), 83. This book emerged from Freed's D. Phil thesis of the same title. The degree was awarded by the University of Pretoria in 1949. Geoffrey Cronjé as his supervisor.

5. For more on the notion of white male idleness and the anxieties it produced, especially in Afrikaner nationalist circles, see chapter 3.

6. Pieterse, "Die onstaan en ontwikkeling van werk-kolonies," *Tydskrif vir Geesteswetenskappe* 1, no. 4, (1961): 270.

7. *Rand Daily Mail*, November 3, 1951. To be sure, segregationist laws severely circumscribed drinking by those who were not white, and many of the cases cited by the *Rand Daily Mail* may in fact have been related to possession or trade of alcohol rather than drunkenness per se.

8. *Blanke-Vroue, Naturelle Mans en Drank* (Johannesburg: Suid-Afrikaanse Vereniging vir Maatskaplike Dienste, 1943).

9. The *Rand Daily Mail*, November 3, 1951, similarly reported that "in every instance of drunkenness except Asiatics, more women than men were drunk in Johannesburg."

10. "European Women, African Men and Drink: Alarming Revelations by the Johannesburg Branch of the Social Services Association of South Africa, 1944." PV 155 Shearer 194. Archive for Contemporary Affairs, University of the Free State (hereafter Archive for Contemporary Affairs).

11. "Alcoholism Is a Problem of Management," *The Office: Magazine of Management, Equipment, Methods* 30 (December 1949): 6. PV 155 Shearer 194. Archive for Contemporary Affairs; Lyman C. Duryea, Medical Director – Dr. Vernon L. Shearer, February 14, 1947. PV 155 Shearer 111. Archive for Contemporary Affairs.

12. Founded in the United States in 1935.

13. "Alcoholism Is a Problem of Management."

14. In Britain, the breakthrough came with the opening of the alcoholism treatment unit within the National Health Service by Dr. Max Glatt in the early 1950s. Griffith Edwards, E. Jane Marshall, and Christopher C. H. Cook, *The Treatment of Drinking Problems: A Guide for the Helping Professions* (Cambridge: Cambridge University Press, 2003), 13.

15. Toc H was founded as a type of "Everyman's Club" for British and Allied soldiers in Poperinghe, Belgium in December 1915. After the First World War it became an interdenominational association for Christian social service, and it extended through the Dominions. Although initially open only to men, women became more involved in Toc H affairs during the Second World War and organized themselves into the Toc H (Women's Section). Toc H (Women's Section) Post War Work. Minutes of meeting convened by Toc H (Women's Section) in regard to homes for inebriate women, held at Balgownie House, Johannesburg, on 11 May 1950. PV 155 Shearer 111. Archive for Contemporary Affairs.

16. Minutes of meeting convened by Toc H (Women's Section).

17. Minutes of meeting convened by Toc H (Women's Section).

18. Gael Fraser – D. F. Malan, "The Truth about Alcoholism," 16.11.51. VWN 125 SW 17/18. State archive.

19. The Commissioner of the South African Police –The Secretary for Labour, Pretoria, September 15, 1949. BNS 248 96/72 vol. 1. State archive.

20. Geoffrey Cronjé and G. C. van Zyl, *Slagoffers van Drank* (Kaapstad: HAUM, 1959), 18–21.

21. R. McLachlan, Sekretaris – Die Direkteur, Buro vir Sensus en Statistiek, August 2, 1951. BNS 248 99/72. State archive; R. McLachlan, Sekretaris – Die Direkteur, Buro vir Sensus en Statistiek, November 28, 1951. BNS 248 99/72. State archive.

22. Secretary – the Under-Secretary of Social Work, National Conference on Social Work (August 10, 1951). VWN 125 SW 17/81. State archive.

23. Provisional Agenda for National Conference on Social Work (September 24–28, 1951). VWN 1141 SW 17/63. State archive.

24. J. M. Lotter, "Die Geskiedenis van Maatskaplike Werk in Suid-Afrika," Nasionale Buro vir Opvoedkundige en Maatskaplike Navorsing. NRSN N 1/2/35. State archive.

25. Lotter, "Die Geskiedenis van Maatskaplike Werk."

26. Press Statement, Minister for Health and Social Welfare Dr. Karl Bremer, August 16, 1951. VWN 125 SW 17/18. State archive.

27. Minister for Health and Social Welfare Dr. Karl Bremer, August 16, 1951.

28. Report on the National Conference on Alcohol, 1951. Archive for Contemporary Affairs. The following discussion cites points made at this conference and included in the report.

29. Report on the National Conference on Alcohol, 1951.

30. Hansard, 19th January to 22nd June 1951, vols. 74, 75, 76, cols. 9624–26.

31. Report on the National Conference on Alcohol, 1951.

32. Most of the following discussion is drawn from the record of 1952 discussion. Notule van tweede vergadering van tydelike komitee van die Nasionale Konferensie oor Alkoholisme. VWN 126 SW 17/81/4. State archive.

33. My informant was not aware of these tours, and it is uncertain whether or not they materialized. E. Luttig (former social worker), interview by author, Bloemfontein, September 12, 2013.

34. Three Items in Supplementary Estimates to Provide for the Treatment and Rehabilitation of Alcoholics. 44 – 1954. Archive for Contemporary Affairs.

35. Three Items in Supplementary Estimates to Provide for the Treatment and Rehabilitation of Alcoholics. Archive for Contemporary Affairs.

36. Resolutions and subjects for discussion by council at annual general meeting, June 1962, Johannesburg. SANCA national executive. VWN 759. State archive.

37. Ben Shephard, *A War of Nerves. Soldiers and Psychiatrists in the Twentieth Century* (Cambridge, MA: Harvard University Press, 2003).

38. Superintendent, Eersterivier work colony – The Secretary for Social Welfare, December 18, 1950. VWN 1119 SW 486 vol. 2; Sekretaris van Volkswelsyn – Die Superintendent, Werkkorps vir Blankes, March 13, 1951, VWN 119SW 486 vol. 2. See also Direkteur van

Gevangenisse – Die Sekretaris van die Tesourie, July 22, 1953. TES 4915 F28/428 vol. 1. State archive.

39. Neil Roos, "Work Colonies for White Men and the Historiography of Apartheid," *Social History* 36, no. 1 (February 2011): 54–76.

40. Jannie Pieterse, "Die ontstaan en ontwikkeling van werk-kolonies in Suid Afrika," *Tydskrif vir Geesteswetenskappe* 1, no. 4 (1961): 275; *First Annual Report of the National Work Colonies and Retreats Advisory Board*, 1950, U. G. 25–1951. Natal Society Library.

41. Pieterse, "Die ontstaan en ontwikkeling van werk-kolonies," 275.

42. Release on Licence (Regulation 77 (6)). Department of Social Welfare and Pensions, VWN, 61/9, 367. State archive.

43. Department of Social Welfare, Report by a supervisor on an inmate released on license from a Work Colony/Retreat under the Work Colonies Act No. 25 of 1949 (Circular No. 73 of 1951). VWN 61/9, 367. State archive.

44. Pieterse, "Die ontstaan en ontwikkeling van werk-kolonies," 277. Roger Deacon's analysis of histories of discipline is useful to understand how apartheid work colonies represented a more intrusive, comprehensive, and sophisticated method of social control than their predecessors. He argues that discipline tends to evolve towards a more positive approach that aims to make those disciplined "attached" to the values of society by leading them to internalize supervisory practices. Men were punished and disciplined "not less, but better." Roger Deacon, "From Confinement to Attachment: Foucault on the Rise of the School," *The European Legacy* 11, no. 2 (2006): 121–38.

45. Establishment of Sonderwater Work Colony, Doc. 73 VWN 61/15, 367, part 1 – Sonderwater work colony. State archive.

46. Establishment of Sonderwater Work Colony, Doc. 73 VWN 61/15, 367, part 1 – Sonderwater work colony; Secretary for Social Welfare – Secretary for Defence, 14.4.47. Doc 49 VWN 61/15, 367, part 1 – Sonderwater work colony. State archive.

47. Secretary for Social Welfare - Secretary for Defence, 14.4.47. Doc 49 VWN 61/15, 367, part 1 – Sonderwater work colony. State archive.

48. F. J. Basson, Sekretaris van Volkswelsyn – Die Afdelingsinspekteur, Departement van Arbeid, 22 February 1947. Doc 40 VWN 61/15, 367, part 1 – Sonderwater work colony. State archive.

49. F. J. Basson, Sekretaris van Volkswelsyn – Die Afdelingsinspekteur, Departement van Arbeid, 22 February 1947. Doc 40 VWN 61/15, 367, part 1 – Sonderwater work colony. State archive; *National Work Colonies and Retreats Advisory Board. Third Annual Report in Terms of the Work Colonies Act, No. 25 of 1949*, 1953 UG 29/1953. Natal Society Library.

50. F. J. Basson, Sekretaris van Volkswelsyn – Die Afdelingsinspekteur, Departement van Arbeid, February 22, 1947. Doc 40 VWN 61/15, 367, part 1 – Sonderwater work colony. State archive.

51. Superintendent, Sonderwater Werkkolonie – Die Sekretaris van Volkswelsyn (Werkkolonies), October 4, 1950. Doc 187, VWN 61/15, 367, part 1 – Sonderwater work colony. State archive.

52. Superintendent, Sonderwater Werkkolonie – Die Magistraat, Cullinan, July 7, 1952. Doc 183, VWN SW 61/15, 367, part 2– Sonderwater work colony. State archive.

53. Superintendent, Sonderwater Werkkolonie – Die Magistraat, Cullinan, July 7, 1952. Doc 183, VWN SW 61/15, 367, part 2 – Sonderwater work colony. State archive; *First Annual Report of the National Work Colonies and Retreats Advisory Board*.

54. *National Work Colonies and Retreats Advisory Board Second Annual Report in Terms of the Work Colonies Act No. 25 of 1949*, 1951, UG 35/1952. Natal Society Library. The board's interest in masturbation may have reflected broader concerns about "abnormal" behavior among inmates. Although the 1948 Kinsey Report did much to dispel myths about masturbation,

during the 1950s it was not entirely detached from associations with psychiatric and medical illness.

55. *First Annual Report of the National Work Colonies and Retreats Advisory Board.*
56. *First Annual Report of the National Work Colonies and Retreats Advisory Board.*
57. *First Annual Report of the National Work Colonies and Retreats Advisory Board.*
58. Superintendent, Sonderwater Werkkolonie – Die Magistraat, Cullinan, July 7, 1952. Doc 183, VWN SW 61/15, 367, part 2– Sonderwater work colony. State archive.
59. Secretary of Justice – All Officers in the Department of Justice, January 23, 1950. Doc 124, VWN 61/15, 367, part 1 – Sonderwater work colony. State archive; *National Work Colonies and Retreats Advisory Board Second Annual Report.*
60. *Third Annual Report in Terms of the Work Colonies Act.*
61. Secretary for Social Welfare – The Superintendents, Swartfontein, Sonderwater and Eersterivier Work Colonies, nd. Doc 234, VWN 61/15, 367, part 1 – Sonderwater work colony. State archive.
62. V. van Rensburg, former work colony detainee and public servant. Interview by author, tapes and transcript, Pinetown, July 15, 1998.
63. *National Work Colonies and Retreats Advisory Board Sixth Annual Report*, 1956, UG No. 53/1958. Natal Society Library.
64. See, for instance, "Helpende Hande," *The Public Servant*, August 1952, 33–35.
65. Van Rensburg interview.
66. *First Annual Report of the National Work Colonies and Retreats Advisory Board; National Work Colonies and Retreats Advisory Board Second Annual Report; National Work Colonies and Retreats Advisory Board Eighth Annual Report*, 1958. U. G. 22/1960. Natal Society Library.
67. *National Work Colonies and Retreats Advisory Board. Third Annual Report.*
68. *First Annual Report of the National Work Colonies and Retreats Advisory Board, 1950; National Work Colonies and Retreats Advisory Board Second Annual Report.*
69. *National Work Colonies and Retreats Advisory Board Second Annual Report.*
70. J. E. Pieterse, *Drank-misbruikers: 'n Sosiologiese Ondersoek van 250 Aangehoudenes in Werkkolonies* [Alcohol abusers: A Sociological Investigation of 250 Detainees in Work Colonies], (Kaapstad/Pretoria: HAUM, 1959). It is no coincidence that Pieterse, a protégé of Cronjé, prepared his doctoral thesis under Cronjé's supervision, and subsequently became the major authority on drink and the welfare of whites.
71. *National Work Colonies and Retreats Advisory Board Second Annual Report.*
72. Secretary for Social Welfare – The Senior Probation Officer, Johannesburg, February 9, 1949. VWN 61/10 vol. 367. State archive.
73. Secretary for Social Welfare – the Superintendents, Swartfontein, Sonderwater and Eersterivier Work Colonies, 29-11-1949. Doc 234, VWN 61/15, 367, part 1 – Sonderwater work colony. State archive.
74. Superintendent, Sonderwater Werkkolonie – Die Sekretaris van Volkswelsyn (Werkkolonies), October 4, 1948. Doc 187, VWN 61/15, 367, part 1 – Sonderwater work colony. State archive.
75. D. B. Hauptfleisch, Superintendent, Sonderwater Werkkolonie – Die Sekretaris van Volkswelsyn, November 28, 1949. Doc 236, VWN 61/15, 367, part 1 – Sonderwater work colony. State archive.
76. D. B. Hauptfleisch, Superintendent – The Crown Prosecutor, Johannesburg, Report on Suitability for Admission to Work Colony Jack Sanderson, March 25, 1949. Doc 203, VWN 61/15, 367, part 1 – Sonderwater work colony. State archive.
77. Versoekskrif: G. W. S. Pienaar. Doc 228, VWN 61/15, 367, part 1 – Sonderwater work colony. State archive.

78. M. M. van Wyk – Die Sekretaris van Volkswelsyn 18-6-49. Doc 220, VWN 61/15, 367, part 1 – Sonderwater work colony. State archive.

79. D. B. Hauptfleisch, Superintendent – The Crown Prosecutor, Johannesburg, Report on Suitability for Admission to Work Colony Jack Sanderson, 25-3-1949. Doc 203, VWN 61/15, 367, part 1 – Sonderwater work colony. State archive.

80. S. R. Kruger – Mev. M. M. van Wyk, August 22, 1949. Doc 225, VWN 61/15, 367, part 1 – Sonderwater work colony. State archive.

81. "Helpende Hande," *The Public Servant*, August 1952, 33–35; *Die Vaderland*, July 19, 1952. Clipping in VWN 61/15, 367, part 1 – Sonderwater work colony. State archive.

82. N. Grundlingh, former public servant. Personal communication with author, March 12, 2009.

83. Brigadier H. A. Mouton (retired), former police officer. Personal communication with author, January 22, 2009.

84. *First Annual Report of the National Work Colonies and Retreats Advisory Board.*

85. Pieterse, "Die ontstaan en ontwikkeling van werk-kolonies," 275.

86. *Third Annual Report in Terms of the Work Colonies Act.*

87. See, for instance, *National Work Colonies and Retreats Advisory Board Sixth Annual Report*; *National Work Colonies and Retreats Advisory Board Eighth Annual Report.*

88. *Third Annual Report in Terms of the Work Colonies Act.*

89. Van Rensburg interview.

90. *Third Annual Report in Terms of the Work Colonies Act.*

91. Superintendent, Eersterivier work colony – The Secretary for Social Welfare, December 18, 1950. VWN 1119 SW 486 vol. 2. State archive.

92. *National Work Colonies and Retreats Advisory Board Eleventh Annual Report in Terms of the Work Colonies Act, No 25 of 1949*, R. P. 60 /1962. Natal Society Library.

93. Eric Louw – R. Hill, May 3, 1956. TES 8538 131/9/5. State archive.

94. For an account of how conscription was extended until it became compulsory for all white men in 1967, see G. Callister, "Patriotic Duty or Resented Imposition? Public Reactions to Military Conscription in White South Africa, 1952–1972," *Scientia Militaria. South African Journal of Military History* 35, no. 1 (2007), especially 51–52.

95. Department of Social Welfare and Pensions. Explanatory memorandum on treatment of white alcoholics in work colonies and the retreats for women. 1962. Department of Social Welfare and Pensions Research and Information. Taylor papers. Archive for Contemporary Affairs.

96. Explanatory memorandum on treatment of white alcoholics in work colonies and the retreats for women. Taylor papers. Archive for Contemporary Affairs.

97. Explanatory memorandum on treatment of white alcoholics in work colonies and the retreats for women. Taylor papers. Archive for Contemporary Affairs.

98. The Chief Social Welfare Officer – Secretary, Rand Aid Association, April 1, 1964. VWN 61/9 367. State archive.

99. Luttig interview.

100. Deborah Posel, *The Making of Apartheid: Conflict and Compromise* (Oxford: Clarendon, 1991), 1; 228; 261

101. Beatrice Jauregui, "Shadows of the State, Subalterns of the State: Police, Authority and 'Law and Order' in Postcolonial India" (unpublished PhD diss., University of Chicago, 2008).

9. The End

1. This was not his real name.

2. The prohibition of sex outside of marriage between "Europeans" and "natives" was introduced in the 1927 Immorality Act. This provision was retained in the amended act passed in 1957.

3. E. P. Thompson, *The Making of the English Working Class* (New York: Victor Gollancz, 1963), 12.

4. Alf Lüdtke, "Introduction: What Is the History of Everyday Life and Who Are Its Practitioners?" in *The History of Everyday Life*, ed. Alf Lüdtke (Princeton, NJ: Princeton University Press, 1995), 3–40, esp. 24.

5. A similar point is made by Robert Gellately in his study of the Gestapo in Hamburg during the Nazi years. See Robert Gellately, "The Gestapo and German Society: Political Denunciation in the Gestapo Case Files," *Journal of Modern History* 60, no. 4 (December 1988): 654–94.

BIBLIOGRAPHY

Primary Sources

Unpublished Documentary Sources

Archive for Contemporary Affairs, University of the Free State. Special Collections, South Africana. Professor Geoffrey Cronjé, Curriculum Vitae en Bibliografie; E. G. Jansen papers; C. D. Taylor papers; V. Shearer 194.

Historical Papers, University of the Witwatersrand. L. F. Freed, Report on Homosexuality in Johannesburg, February 23, 1939. A 1212/CK.

Johannesburg Public Library, Strange Collections. An Alcoholic's Story, 178.1 Alk; Report of the Family Congress, April 4–7, 1961, Aula, University of Pretoria, 301.42 Fam; L. F. Freed. "The Social Aspects of Venereal Disease," Address to the Council of the Southern Transvaal Branch of the South African Medical Association, March 15, 1939, Pam 614–547 Fre.

Killie Campbell Africana Collections, University of KwaZulu-Natal. E. G. Malherbe papers; Mabel Palmer papers; Violet Smith papers, Durban Bachelor Girls' Club.

Kweekskool, Stellenbosch. Arbeidskolonie kommissie; Noord Kaapland Sinode; Nederduitse Gereformeerde Kerk, Transvaal.

Roos, Sheila. "A Thing of the Past..." Unpublished memoir, c. 1986. (personal collection).

State archives, Pretoria. A 272 191 15/11; AG 307/06; ARB 907 1000/21/1/1/10 vol. 6; BNS 1/1/506; BNS 248 96/72 vol. 1; BNS 248 99/72; CEN 65 vol. 1; CEN 68 E1/1/1 13; GC 794 13/3051; GG 13/3538; GG 808 13/3538; GG 2148 71/294, vol. 1; GG 2148, vol. 2; GG 2148, vol. 3; GG 2390; LD 1041; MVE 1134 538/84/3/7; NRO 34; NRSN N 1/2/35; PAE E 151 253/2; PSC 99/G/4; PV 55 52/10/1/1/1; RB 86; 87; SDK 2/G/3 vol. 6 "Inland Revenue"; SDK 4896 vol. 1; SW 176/25; SW 17/81/4; SWA 274; TES 1956; TES 4915 F28/428 vol. 1; TES 5175 28/406; TES 8538 131/9/5; VWN 61/9, 367; VWN 61/10 vol. 367; VWN 61/15; VWN 119 SW 486 vol. 1; VWN 119 SW 486 vol. 2; VWN 120; VWN 125 SW 17/18; VWN 125 SW 17/81; VWN 126 SW; VWN 759 17/81/4; VWN 1141 SW 17/63; VWN 1850.

Universiteit van Pretoria. Notule Fakulteit Lettere en Wysbegeerte; Registrateur; Rektor.

Government Reports, Official and Private Sources

Blanke-Vroue, Naturelle Mans en Drank, Johannesburg, Suid-Afrikaanse Vereniging vir Maatskaplike Dienste, 1943.

Carnegie Commission of Investigation on the Poor White Question in South Africa, Stellenbosch, 1932.

Debates of the House of Assembly (Hansard).
First Report of Commission of Inquiry into Grievances of Railway Workers. October 1949, UG 9 of 1950.

Public Service Commission

Thirty-Seventh Annual Report of the Public Service Commission, 1948. UG 33/1949.
Thirty-Eighth Annual Report of the Public Service Commission, 1949. UG 26/1950.
Thirty-Ninth Annual Report of the Public Service Commission, 1950. UG 23/1951.
Fortieth Annual Report of the Public Service Commission, 1951. UG 33/1952.
Forty-First Annual Report of the Public Service Commission, 1952. UG 23/1953.
Forty-Second Annual Report of the Public Service Commission, 1953. UG 28/1954.
Forty-Third Annual Report of the Public Service Commission, 1954. UG 25/1955.
Forty-Fourth Annual Report of the Public Service Commission, 1955. UG 16/1956.
Forty-Fifth Annual Report of the Public Service Commission, 1956. UG 17/1957.
Forty-Sixth Annual Report of the Public Service Commission, 1957. UG 27/1958.
Forty-Seventh Annual Report of the Public Service Commission, 1958. UG 26/1959.
Forty-Eighth Annual Report of the Public Service Commission, 1959. UG 30/1960.
Forty-Ninth Annual Report of the Public Service Commission, 1960. UG 27/1961.
Fiftieth Annual Report of the Public Service Commission, 1961. RP 26/62.
Report of the Commission on Technical and Vocational Education, 1947. UG 65/1948.
Report of the Committee Appointed to Investigate the Employment of Unskilled European Workers in the Railways Service, 1947. UG 29/47.
Truth and Reconciliation Commission of South Africa Report, Volume 4: Institutional and Special Hearings, Cape Town, 1998, 1.

Work Colonies

First Annual Report of the National Work Colonies and Retreats Advisory Board, 1950. UG 25/1951.
National Work Colonies and Retreats Advisory Board Second Annual Report in Terms of the Work Colonies Act, No. 25 of 1949, 1951. UG 35/1952.
National Work Colonies and Retreats Advisory Board. Third Annual Report in Terms of the Work Colonies Act, No. 25 of 1949, 1953. UG 29/1953.
National Work Colonies and Retreats Advisory Board Sixth Annual Report, 1956. UG 53/1958.
National Work Colonies and Retreats Advisory Board Eighth Annual Report, 1958. UG 22/1960.
National Work Colonies and Retreats Advisory Board Eleventh Annual Report in Terms of the Work Colonies Act, No 25 of 1949. RP 60/1962.

Secondary Sources

Abrahamsen, Rita. "African Studies and the Postcolonial Challenge." *African Affairs* 102, no. 407 (April 2003): 195.
Adonis, D. Z. "The Public Service Association's Response to the Changes Brought about by the Public Service Labour Relations Act (Act 102/1993)." Master's of Business Leadership research report, University of South Africa, 2007.
Albertyn, J. R. *Die Stadwaartse Trek van die Afrikanernasie.* Johannesburg: Volkskongres, 1947.
———. *The Poor White and Society.* Stellenbosch: Pro Ecclesia-Drukkery, 1932.
Allen, Theodore W. "On Roediger's 'Wages of Whiteness'" *Cultural Logic* 8 (2001). https://doi.org/10.14288/clogic.v8i0.191856.
Andersson, Axel. "Obscuring Capitalism: Vivek Chibber's Critique of Subaltern Studies." *Los Angeles Review of Books* 6 (November 2013).

Appiah, Kwame Anthony. *In My Father's House: Africa in the Philosophy of Culture*. London: Oxford University Press, 1992.
Arendt, Hannah. *Eichmann in Jerusalem: A Report on the Banality of Evil*. Harmondsworth: Penguin, 1977 [1963].
———. *The Origins of Totalitarianism*. New York: Harcourt, 1966 [1951].
Ashforth, Adam. *The Politics of Official Discourse in Twentieth-Century South Africa*. Oxford: Clarendon, 1990.
Baldwin, James. "On Being 'White'... and Other Lies." In *Black on White: Black Writers on What It Means to Be White*, edited by David Roediger, 177–80. New York: Schocken Books, 1999.
Beinart, William, and Peter Delius. "Introduction." In *Putting a Plough to the Ground: Accumulation and Dispossession in Rural South Africa 1850–1930*, edited by W. Beinart and P. Delius, 1–55. Johannesburg: Ravan, 1986.
Berger, D. "White Poverty and Government Policy in South Africa, 1892–1934." Unpublished PhD diss., Temple University, 1983.
Bhadra, Gautam. "The Mentality of Subalternity: Khantanama or Rajdharma." In *A Subaltern Studies Reader*, edited by Ranajit Guha, 63–100. Minneapolis: University of Minnesota Press, 1997.
Biko, Steve. "Black Souls in White Skins." In *I Write What I Like: Steve Biko, A Selection of His Writings*, edited by Aelred Stubbs, 20–28. Johannesburg: Picador Africa, 2004.
Blignaut, Charl. "From Fund-raising to Freedom Day: The Nature of Women's General Activities in the *Ossewa-Brandwag*." *New Contree* 66 (July 2013): 121–50.
Boner, Kathleen. *Dominican Women: A Time to Speak*. Pietermaritzburg: Cluster, 1998.
Bottomley, John. "The Orange Free State and the Rebellion of 1914: The Influence of Industrialization, Poverty and Poor Whiteism." In *White but Poor: Essays on the History of Poor Whites in Southern Africa, 1880–1940*, edited by Robert Morrell, 29–74. Pretoria: University of South Africa, 1992.
———. "Public Policy and White Rural Poverty in South Africa, 1881–1924." D. Phil., Queen's University, 1990.
Bozzoli, Belinda, ed. *Class, Community and Conflict: South African Perspectives*. Johannesburg: Ravan, 1994.
———, ed. *Labour, Townships and Protest*. Johannesburg: Ravan, 1978.
———, ed. *Town and Countryside in the Transvaal*. Johannesburg: Ravan, 1983.
Bozzoli, Belinda, and Peter Delius. "Radical History and South African Society." *Radical History Review* 46, no. 7 (Winter 1990): 13–45.
Brink, Elsabé. "Man-Made Women: Gender, Class, and the Ideology of the *Volksmoeder*." In *Women and Gender in Southern Africa to 1945*, edited by Cherryl Walker, 273–92. Cape Town: David Philip, 1990.
Browning, Christopher. *Ordinary Men: Reserve Police Battalion 101 and the Final Solution in Poland*. London: Penguin, 2001 [1992].
Bundy, Colin. *The Rise and Fall of the South African Peasantry*. London: Heinemann, 1979.
———. "Vagabond Hollanders and Runaway Englishmen: White Poverty in the Cape Before Poor Whiteism." In *Putting a Plough to the Ground: Accumulation and Dispossession in Rural South Africa, 1850–1930*, edited by William Beinart, Peter Delius, and Stanley Trapido. Johannesburg: Ravan, 1987.
Bunerji, Anurima, and Illaria Distante. "An Intimate Ethnography." *Women and Performance. A Journal of Feminist Theory* 19 (March 2009): 35–60.

Callister, G. "Patriotic Duty or Resented Imposition? Public Reactions to Military Conscription in White South Africa, 1952–1972." *Scientia Militaria, South African Journal of Military History* 35, no. 1 (2007): 46–67.
Chakrabarty, Dipesh. "Invitation to a Dialogue." In *Subaltern Studies IV*, edited by Ranajit Guha, 364–76. Delhi: Oxford University Press, 1985.
———. *Provincializing Europe: Postcolonial Thought and Historical Difference*. Princeton, NJ: Princeton University Press, 2000.
———. "Subaltern Studies and Postcolonial History." *Nepantla: Views from the South* 1, no. 1 (2000): 9–32.
Chatterjee, Partha. "Reflections on 'Can the Subaltern Speak?': Subaltern Studies After Spivak." In *Can the Subaltern Speak?: Reflections on the History of an Idea*, edited by Rosalind Morris, 81–86. New York: Columbia University Press, 2010,
Chibber, Vivek. *Postcolonial Theory and the Specter of Capital*. London: Verso, 2013.
Chipkin, Clive M. *Johannesburg Transitions: Architecture and Society from 1950*. Johannesburg: STE, 2008.
Chipkin, Ivor, and Sarah Meny-Gibert. "Why the Past Matters: Histories of the Public Service in South Africa." Public Affairs Research Institute Short Essays no. 1, May 2011: 1–12. https://pari2.wpenginepowered.com/wp-content/uploads/2017/05/PARI-S-E-1-why-the-past-matters-may2011-web-2.pdf.
Chisholm, L. "Crime, Class and Nationalism: The Criminology of Jacob de Villiers Roos, 1869–1918." *Social Dynamics* 13, no. 2 (1987): 46–59.
Clark, Nancy. "Gendering Production in Wartime South Africa." *American Historical Review* 106, no. 4 (October 2001): 1181–1213.
Clynick, Timothy. "Afrikaner Political Mobilization in the Western Transvaal: Popular Consciousness and the State, 1920–1930." D. Phil, Queen's University, 1996.
Cock, Jacklyn. *Maids and Madams: A Study in the Politics of Exploitation*. Johannesburg: Ravan, 1980.
Coetzee, Abel. *Die Opkoms van die Afrikaanse Kultuurgedagte aan die Rand, 1886–1936*. Johannesburg: Afrikaanse Pers, 1937; Cape Town, 1938.
Coetzee, J. M. *Giving Offense: Essays on Censorship*. Chicago: University of Chicago Press, 1996.
———. "Idleness in South Africa." *Social Dynamics* 8, no. 1 (1982): 1–13.
———. "The Mind of Apartheid: Geoffrey Cronje (1907–)." *Social Dynamics* 17, no. 1 (1991): 1–35.
Cohen, Morris J. "The Epileptic." Unpublished paper presented at the National Conference on Social Work. Empire Exhibition, Johannesburg, 1936.
Comaroff, John. "Dialectical Systems, History and Anthropology: Units of Analysis and Questions of Theory." *Journal of Southern African Studies* 8, no. 2 (1982): 143–72.
———. "Reflections on the Colonial State in South Africa and Elsewhere: Factions, Fragments, Facts and Fictions." *Social Identities* 4, no. 3 (October 1998): 321–61.
Comaroff, John, and Jean Comaroff. *Ethnography and the Historical Imagination*. Boulder, San Francisco, Oxford: Westview, 1992.
———. *Theory from the South: Or, How Euro-America Is Evolving Towards Africa*. Boulder, CO: Paradigm, 2012.
Cooper, Frederick. "Conflict and Connection: Rethinking Colonial African History." *American Historical Review* 99, no. 5 (December 1994): 1516–45.
Court, Anthony. *Hannah Arendt's Response to the Crisis of Her Times*. Pretoria: UNISA; Amsterdam: Rozenberg, 2009.
Cronjé, Geoffrey. *Afrika sonder die Asiaat: Die Blywende Oplossing van Suid Afrika se Asiatevraagstuk*. Johannesburg: Publicite handelsreklamediens, 1946.

———. *'n Tuiste vir die nageslag: die blywende oplossing van Suid Afrika se rassevraagstukke*. Pretoria: Auspiciis Universitatis Pretoriensis, 1945.

———. *Regverdige Rasse-Apartheid*. Stellenbosch: C. S. V. Boekhandel, 1947.

———. *Voogdyskap en apartheid*. Pretoria: J. L. van Schaik, 1948.

Cronjé, Geoffrey, and G. C. van Zyl. *Slagoffers van Drank*. Cape Town: HAUM, 1959.

Crush, Jonathan, and Charles Ambler, eds. *Liquor and Labor in South Africa*. Athens: Ohio University Press, 1992.

Czada, Robert. "Corporativism." In *International Encyclopedia of Political Science*, edited by Bertrand Badie, Dirk Berg-Schlosser, and Leonardo Morlino, 458–63. London: SAGE, 2011.

Davies, Robert. *Capital, State and White Labour in South Africa, 1900–1960: An Historical Materialist Analysis of Class Formation and Class Relations*. Atlantic Highlands, NJ: Humanities, 1979.

Davies, Robert, David Kaplan, Mike Morris, and Dan O'Meara. "Class Struggle and the Periodisation of the State in South Africa." *Review of African Political Economy*, no. 7 (1976): 4–30.

Deacon, Roger. "From Confinement to Attachment: Foucault on the Rise of the School." *The European Legacy* 11, no 2 (2006): 121–38.

De Kiewiet, C. W. *A History of South Africa: Social and Economic*. Oxford: Clarendon, 1941.

De Kock, W. J. *Jacob de Villiers Roos, 1869–1940: lewensket van 'n veelsydige Afrikaner*. Cape Town: A. A. Balkema, 1958.

Devarenne, Nicole. "'In Hell You Hear Only Your Mother Tongue': Afrikaner Nationalist Ideology, Linguistic Subversion and Cultural Renewal in Marlene van Niekerk's *Triomf*." *Research in African Literatures* 37, no. 4 (Winter 2006): 105–20.

De Villiers, René. "Afrikaner Nationalism." In *The Oxford History of South Africa, Volume II*, edited by Monica Wilson and Leonard Thompson, 365–423. New York: Oxford University Press, 1971.

Dick, Archie. *The Hidden Histories of South Africa's Book and Reading Cultures*. Toronto: University of Toronto Press, 2013.

Du Bois, W. E. B. "The Souls of White Folk, 'The Riddle of the Sphinx.'" In *Black on White: Black Writers on What It Means to Be White*, edited by David Roediger, 184–203. New York: Schocken Books, 1999.

———. *The World and Africa: An Inquiry into the Part Which Africa Has Played in World History*. New York: International, 1965.

Dubow, Saul. *Apartheid, 1948–1994*. Oxford: Oxford University Press, 2014.

Dubow, Saul, and Alan Jeeves, eds. *South Africa's 1940s: Worlds of Possibilities*. Cape Town: Double Storey, 2005.

Dugard, John. "Convention on the Suppression and Punishment of the Crime of Apartheid." *Audiovisual Library of International Law*, United Nations, 2008. https://doi.org/10.18356/770ae15b-en-fr.

Du Toit Spies, F. J., and D. H. Heydenrych. *Ad Destinatum II, 1960–1982: 'n Geskiedenis van die Universiteit van Pretoria*. Pretoria: University of Pretoria, 1987.

Edwards, Griffith, E. Jane Marshall, and Christopher C. H. Cook. *The Treatment of Drinking Problems: A Guide for the Helping Professions*. Cambridge: Cambridge University Press, 2003.

Eley, Geoff. *A Crooked Line: From Cultural History to the History of Society*. Ann Arbor: University of Michigan Press, 2005.

Enslin, P. "The Role of Fundamental Pedagogics in the Formulation of Educational Policy in South Africa." In *Apartheid and Education: The Education of Black South Africans*, edited by P. Kallaway, 139–47. Johannesburg: Ravan, 1984.

Evans, Ivan. *Bureaucracy and Race: Native Administration in South Africa.* Berkeley: University of California Press, 1997.
Evans, R. J. "From Hitler to Bismarck: 'Third Reich' and Kaiserreich in Recent Historiography." In *Rethinking German History: Nineteenth Century Germany and the Origins of the Third Reich,* edited by Richard J. Evans, 55–92. London: Allen and Unwin, 1989.
Ewing, Ann. "Administering India: The Indian Civil Service." *History Today* 32, no. 6 (June 1982): 43–48.
Fanon, Frantz. *Black Skin, White Masks.* New York: Grove, 1967.
Finzsch, Norbert, and Robert Jutte. *Institutions of Confinement: Hospitals, Asylums and Prisons in Western Europe and North America, 1500–1950.* Cambridge: Cambridge University Press, 2003.
Freed, L. F. *Crime in South Africa: An Integralistic Approach.* Johannesburg: Juta, 1963.
———. *The Problem of European Prostitution in Johannesburg: A Sociological Survey.* Cape Town: Juta, 1949.
Freund, Bill. *The Making of Contemporary Africa: The Development of African Society since 1800.* 2nd ed. Boulder, CO: Rienner, 1998.
———. "The Poor Whites: A Social Force and a Social Problem in South Africa." In *White but Poor: Essays on the History of Poor Whites in Southern Africa, 1880–1940,* edited by Robert Morrell, xiii–xxiii. Pretoria: UNISA, 1992.
———. "*South Africa's 1940s: Worlds of Possibilities,* by Saul Dubow and Alan Jeeves," *Kronos* 33 (November 2007): 275–79.
Froneman, C. J. J. "Die Nederduitse Gereformeerde Gemeente van Roossenekal op Laersdrif: 'n Rekonstruksie van die geskiedenis van die eerste drie en dertig jaar." Unpublished postgraduate diploma in theology, University of Pretoria, 1981.
Gellately, Robert. "The Gestapo and German Society: Political Denunciation in the Gestapo Case Files." *Journal of Modern History* 60, no. 4 (December 1988): 654–94.
Geyer, Michael. "Introduction: Resistance against the Third Reich as Intercultural Knowledge." In *Resistance against the Third Reich,* edited by Michael Geyer and John Boyer, 1–11. Chicago: University of Chicago Press, 1994.
Gibson, John Linton. "A Critical Study of the Report of the De Villiers Commission on Technical and Vocational Education." Unpublished master's thesis, University of Natal, 1968.
Giliomee, Hermann. *The Afrikaners: Biography of a People.* Cape Town: Tafelberg, 2003.
———. "Cronje, Geoffrey, 1907–1992." In *Dictionary of African Biography,* edited by Emmanuel K. Akyeampong and Henry Louis Gates, Jr. Oxford: Oxford University Press, 2012.
Gines, Kathryn T. "Race Thinking and Racism in Hannah Arendt's *The Origins of Totalitarianism.*" In *Hannah Arendt and the Uses of History: Imperialism, Nation, Race, and Genocide,* edited by Richard H. King and Dan Stone, 38–53. New York: Berghahn Books, 2007.
Glaser, Clive. "Portuguese Immigrant History in South Africa: A Preliminary Overview." *African Historical Review* 42, no. 2 (2010): 61–83.
Goldberg, David Theo. *The Racial State.* Oxford: Wiley, 2002.
———. *Racist Culture: Philosophy and the Politics of Meaning.* Oxford and Cambridge, MA: Wiley, 1993.
Goldhagen, Daniel Jonah. *Hitler's Willing Executioners: Ordinary Germans and the Holocaust.* London: Little, Brown, 1996.
Gordon, Lewis. *Bad Faith and Antiblack Racism.* Atlantic Highlands, NJ: Humanities, 1995.
Gosney, E. S., and Paul Popenoe. *Sterilization for Human Betterment: A Summary of Results of 6,000 Operations in California, 1909–1929.* New York: Macmillan, 1929.
Greenstein, Ran, ed. *Comparative Perspectives on South Africa.* London: Palgrave Macmillan, 1998.

Grimbeek, Mervin Hugo. "Vereniging van Staatsamptenare van Suid Afrika: 'n Ontleding van die Doelwitte en Aktiwiteite Gemik op die Daarstelling van Diens- en Ledevoordele." Unpublished master's thesis, University of South Africa, 1988.

Grundlingh, Albert. "Are We Afrikaners Getting Too Rich? Cornucopia and Change in Afrikanerdom in the 1960s." *Journal of Historical Sociology* 21, no. 2–3 (June 2008): 143–65.

———. "'God het Ons Arm Mense die Houtjies Gegee': Poor White Woodcutters in the Southern Cape Forest Area c.1900–1939." In *White but Poor: Essays on the History of Poor Whites in Southern Africa, 1880–1940*, edited by Robert Morrell, 40–56. Pretoria: University of South Africa, 1992.

———. "Transcending Transitions? The Social History Tradition of Historical Writing in South Africa in the 1990s." Unpublished inaugural lecture, University of South Africa, February 20, 1997.

Hall, Catherine. "Review of *Carnal Knowledge and Imperial Power: Race and the Intimate in Colonial Rule* by Ann Laura Stoler." *Social History* 29, no. 4 (2004): 532–34.

Hamilton, Paula, and Linda Shopes. "Building Partnerships between Oral History and Memory Studies." In *Oral History and Public Memories*, edited by Linda Shopes and Paula Hamilton, vii–xvii. Philadelphia: Temple University Press, 2008.

Hauptfleisch, Eudora. "Kleuterskole van die SAVF in Transvaal," *Vrou en Moeder*, July 1957.

Hexham, Irving. *The Irony of Apartheid: The Struggle for National Independence of Afrikaner Calvinism Against British Imperialism*. New York: Edwin Mellen, 1981.

Hirsch, Steven, and Lucien van der Walt, eds. *Anarchism and Syndicalism in the Colonial and Postcolonial World, 1870–1940: The Praxis of National Liberation, Internationalism, and Social Revolution*. Leiden: Brill, 2010.

Hobart Houghton, D. "Economic Development, 1865–1958." In *The Oxford History of South Africa, Volume II*, edited by Monica Wilson and Leonard Thompson, 1–48. Oxford: Oxford University Press, 1975.

Hook, Derek. *(Post)apartheid Conditions: Pychoanalysis and Social Formation*. Basingstoke: Palgrave Macmillan, 2013.

hooks, bell. "Representations of Whiteness in the Black Imagination." In *Black on White: Black Writers on What It Means to Be White*, edited by David Roediger, 38–53. New York: Schocken Books, 1999.

Hopkins, H. C. *Kakamas – uit die wildernis 'n lushof*. Cape Town: H. C. Hopkins, 1978.

Hyslop, Jonathan. "E. P. Thompson in South Africa: The Practice and Politics of Social History in an Era of Revolt." *International Review of Social History* 61, no. 1 (2016): 95–116.

———. "The Imperial Working Class Makes Itself White: White Laborism in Britain, Australia and South Africa." *Journal of Historical Sociology* 12 (December 1999): 398–421.

———. "Political Corruption: Before and After Apartheid." *Journal of Southern African Studies* 31, no. 4 (Dec. 2005): 773–89.

———. "White Working-Class Women and the Invention of Apartheid: 'Purified' Afrikaner Nationalist Agitation for Legislation Against 'Mixed' Marriages, 1934–9." *Journal of African History* 36, no. 1 (1995): 57–58.

Jackson, Will. *Madness and Marginality: The Lives of Kenya's White Insane*. Manchester: Manchester University Press, 2013.

Jalusic, Vlasta. "Post-Totalitarian Elements and Eichmann's Mentality in the Yugoslav War and Mass Killings." In *Hannah Arendt and the Uses of History: Imperialism, Nation, Race and Genocide*, edited by Richard H. King and Dan Stone, 147–70. New York: Berghahn Books, 2007.

James, C. L. R. *The Black Jacobins*. 2nd ed. New York: Vintage Books, 1989.

Jansen, Jonathan. *Knowledge in the Blood: Confronting Race and the Apartheid Past.* Stanford, CA: Stanford University Press, 2008.
Jauregui, Beatrice. "Shadows of the State, Subalterns of the State. Police, Authority and 'Law and Order' in Postcolonial India." PhD diss., University of Chicago, 2008.
Jessop, Bob. *The Capitalist State.* Oxford: Martin Robinson, 1983.
Johnstone, Frederick. "Class Conflict and Colour Bars in the South African Gold-mining Industry, 1910–1926." Unpublished Institute of Commonwealth Studies seminar paper, 1970.
Kalb, Don, Hans Marks, and Herman Tak. "Historical Anthropology and Anthropological History: Two Distinct Programs." *Fokaal* 26/27 (1996): 183–89.
Kenny, Bridget. "Restructuring, Recognition and Race: The Story of a White Afrikaans Shopworker's Struggle." Paper presented at "The Burden of Race? 'Whiteness' and 'Blackness' in Modern South Africa," University of the Witwatersrand, Johannesburg, 2001.
Khanna, Rajana. "Asylum: Notes towards Alternative Subalternities." Paper presented at "Subaltern Studies: Historical World-making Thirty Years On." Australian National University, Canberra, 2011.
Ki-Zerbo, Joseph, ed. *General History of Africa I: Methodology and African Prehistory.* London: Currey.
Klausen, Susanne. *Abortion under Apartheid: Nationalism, Sexuality and Women's Reproductive Rights in South Africa.* Oxford: Oxford University Press, 2015.
———. *Race, Maternity and the Politics of Birth Control in South Africa, 1910–1939.* Basingstoke: Palgrave Macmillan, 2004.
Krikler, Jeremy. *The Rand Revolt: The 1922 Insurrection and Racial Killing in South Africa.* Johannesburg: Jonathan Ball, 2005.
———. "White Working Class Identity and the Rand Revolt." Paper presented at "The Burden of Race: 'Whiteness' and 'Blackness' in Modern South Africa," University of the Witwatersrand, Johannesburg, 2001.
———. "William Macmillan and the Working Class." Paper presented at "The Making of Class," University of the Witwatersrand, Johannesburg, 1987.
Kynaston, David. *Modernity Britain: Book One—Opening the Box, 1957–1959.* New York: Bloomsbury, 2014.
Lange, Lis. *White, Poor and Angry: White Working Class Families in Johannesburg.* Aldershof: Ashgate, 2003.
Larmer, Miles. *Rethinking African Politics: A History of Opposition in Zambia.* Aldershot: Ashgate, 2011.
Lee, Christopher J. "Race and Bureaucracy Revisited: Hannah Arendt's Recent Reemergence in African Studies." In *Hannah Arendt and the Uses of History: Imperialism, Nation, Race and Genocide,* edited by Richard H. King and Dan Stone, 68–86. New York: Berghahn Books, 2007.
Legassick, Martin. "The Making of South African 'Native Policy' 1903–1923." Unpublished I.C.S. seminar paper, 1973. Societies of Southern Africa seminars at the Institute of Commonwealth Studies, London. https://sas-space.sas.ac.uk/3648/. Accessed 3 June 2016.
Lewis, Jon. *Industrialization and Trade Union Organisation in South Africa, 1924–1955: The Rise and Fall of the South African Trades and Labour Council.* Cambridge: Cambridge University Press, 1984.
Lipkin, Zwia. *Useless to the State: "Social Problems" and Social Engineering in Nationalist Nanjing, 1927–1937.* Cambridge, MA: Harvard University Asia Center, 2006.

Lissoni, Arianna, Noor Nieftagodien, and Shireen Ally. "Introduction: 'Life after Thirty.' A Critical Celebration." *African Studies* 69 (April 2010), 1–12.

Ludden, David. "Introduction: A Brief History of Subalternity." In *Reading Subaltern Studies: Critical History, Contested Meaning and the Globalisation of South Asia*, edited by David Ludden, 1–42. New Delhi: Permanent Black, 2001.

Lüdtke, Alf. "Introduction: What is the History of Everyday Life and Who Are Its Practitioners?" In *The History of Everyday Life*, edited by Alf Lüdtke, 3–40. Princeton, NJ: Princeton University Press, 1995.

MacCrone, I. D. *Race Attitudes in South Africa: Historical, Experimental and Psychological Studies*. London: Oxford University Press, 1937.

Macdonald, Peter D. *The Literature Police: Apartheid Censorship and Its Cultural Consequences*. Oxford: Oxford University Press, 2009.

Macmillan, W. M. *Complex South Africa: An Economic Footnote to History*. London: Faber and Faber, 1930.

———. *The South African Agrarian Problem and Its Historical Development*. Johannesburg: Central News, 1919.

Mager, Ann. *Beer, Sociability and Masculinity in South Africa*. Bloomington: Indiana University Press, 2010.

Maki, Ellen D. "Domestic Service and the Girls' Friendly Society." *Finding Folk: Discovering Ancestors across Time and Place*, March 27, 2016. http://findingfolk.org/2016/03/domestic-service-the-girls-friendly-society/.

Malherbe, Ernst G. *Education in South Africa (1652–1922): A Critical Survey of the Development of Educational Administration in the Cape, Natal, Transvaal and Orange Free State*. Johannesburg: Juta, 1925.

Mamdani, Mahmood. *Citizen and Subject: Contemporary Africa and the Legacy of Late Colonialism*. Princeton, NJ: Princeton University Press, 1996.

Mandela, Nelson. *Long Walk to Freedom: The Autobiography of Nelson Mandela*. Boston: Little, Brown, 1995.

Marks, Monique, Kira Erwin, and Tamlynn Fleetwood. *Voices of Resilience: A Living History of Kenneth Gardens Municipal Housing Estate in Durban*. Pietermaritzburg University of Kwazulu-Natal Press, 2018.

Martin, A. Lynn. *Alcohol, Violence, and Disorder in Traditional Europe*. Kirksville, MO: Truman State University Press, 2009.

Martin, H. J., and Neil Orpen. *South Africa at War*. Cape Town, Johannesburg, and London: Purnell & Sons, 1979.

Martin, Luther H., Huck Gutman, and Patrick H. Hutton. *Technologies of the Self: A Seminar with Michel Foucault*. Amherst: University of Massachusetts Press, 1988.

Marx, Christoph. *Oxwagon Sentinel: Radical Afrikaner Nationalism and the History of the "Ossewa Brandwag."* Pretoria: University of South Africa Press, 2009.

Massaquoi, Hans J. *Destined to Witness: Growing up Black in Nazi Germany*. London: Fusion, 2001.

May, Elaine Tyler. *Homeward Bound. American Families in the Cold War Era*. New York: Basic Books, 1999.

May, Larry, and Jerome Kohn. *Hannah Arendt: Twenty Years Later*. Cambridge, MA: MIT Press, 1997.

Medick, Hans. "'Missionaries in the Row Boat': Ethnological Ways of Knowing as a Challenge to Social History." *Comparative Studies in Society and History* 29 (1987): 76–98.

Meester, Wyle. "Geskiedenis van Kakamas." Unpublished manuscript. Kweekskool – Stellenbosch, [nd].

Memmi, Albert. *The Colonizer and the Colonized*. London: Earthscan, 2003.

Metzl, Jonathan. *Dying of Whiteness: How the Politics of Racial Resentment Is Killing America's Heartland*. New York: Basic Books, 2019.

Moodie, T. Dunbar. *The Rise of Afrikanerdom: Power, Apartheid and the Afrikaner Civil Religion*. Berkeley: University of California Press, 1975 [1980].

Mooney, Katie. "'Ducktails, Flickknives and Pugnacity': Subcultural and Hegemonic Masculinities in South Africa, 1948–1960." *Journal of Southern African Studies* 24, no. 4 (December 1998): 753–74.

———. "Identities in the Ducktail Youth Subculture in Post-World-War-Two South Africa." *Journal of Youth Studies* 8, no. 1 (2005): 41–57.

Morrell, Robert. *From Boys to Gentlemen: Settler Masculinity in Colonial Natal, 1880–1920*. Pretoria: UNISA, 2001.

———. "The Poor Whites of Middelburg, Transvaal 1903–1930: Resistance, Accommodation and Class Struggle." In *White but Poor: Essays on the History of Poor Whites in Southern Africa, 1880–1940*, edited by Robert Morrell, 1–28. Pretoria: University of South Africa Press, 1992.

———, ed. *White but Poor: Essays on the History of Poor Whites in Southern Africa, 1880–1940*. Pretoria: University of South Africa, 1992.

Morris, Polly. "Incest or Survival Strategy: Plebeian Marriage within the Prohibited Degrees in Somerset, 1730–1835." *Journal of the History of Sexuality* 2, no. 2 (October 1991), 235–65.

Naude, Louis. *Dr. A. Hertzog, Die Nasionale Party en die Mynwerker*. Pretoria: Nasionale Raad vir Trustees, 1969.

Ndebele, Njabulo. "Iph'indlela? Finding a Way through Confusion." https://www.njabulondebele.co.za/work/iphindlela-finding-a-way-through-confusion/. Accessed May 31, 2015.

Norval, Aletta J. *Deconstructing Apartheid Discourse*. London: Verso, 1996.

Nyamnjoh, Francis B. "Blinded by Sight: Divining the Future of Anthropology in Africa." *Africa Spectrum* 47 (2012): 63–92.

O'Meara, Dan. *Forty Lost Years: The Apartheid State and the Politics of the National Party, 1948 to 1994*. Athens: Ohio University Press, 1996.

———. "The 1946 African Mineworkers' Strike and the Political Economy of South Africa." *Journal of Commonwealth and Comparative Politics* 13, no. 2 (1975): 146–73.

———. *Volkskapitalisme: Class, Capital and Ideology in the Development of Afrikaner Nationalism, 1934–1948*. Johannesburg: Ravan, 1983.

Painter, Nell Irvin. *Southern History across the Color Line*. Chapel Hill: University of North Carolina Press, 2002.

Pandey, Gyanendra. "In Defence of the Fragment. Writing about Hindu-Muslim Riots in India Today." In *A Subaltern Studies Reader*, edited by Ranajit Guha, 1–33. Minneapolis: University of Minnesota Press, 1997.

———. *Routine Violence: Nations, Fragments, Histories*. Stanford, CA: Stanford University Press, 2005.

Parnell, Susan. "Slums, Segregation and Poor Whites in Johannesburg, 1920–1934." In *White but Poor: Essays on the History of Poor Whites in Southern Africa, 1880–1940*, edited by Robert Morrell, 115–29. Pretoria: University of South Africa Press, 1992.

Parry, Benita. *Postcolonial Studies: A Materialist Critique*. London: Routledge, 2004.

Pauw, S. *Die beroepsarbeid van die Afrikaner in die stad*. Stellenbosch: Pro Ecclesia-Drukkery, 1946.

Pavlich, George. "Administrative Sociology and Apartheid." *Acta Academica* 46, no. 3 (2014): 151–74.

Pieterse, J. E. "Aangehoudenes in werkkolonies: 'n sosiologiese ondersoek." Unpublished D. Phil., University of Pretoria, 1957.

———. *Drank-misbruikers: 'n Sosiologiese Ondersoek van 250 Aangehoudenes in Werkkolonies.* Cape Town: HAUM, 1959.

———. "Die ontstaan en ontwikkeling van werk-kolonies in Suid Afrika." *Tydskrif vir Geesteswetenskappe* 1, no. 4, 1961.

Pieterse, J. E., and G. Cronjé. *Verslag van die jeugondersoek wat die Departement Sosiologie van die Universiteit van Pretoria vir die Naionale Jeugraad onderneem het.* Johannesburg: Voortrekkerpers, 1962.

Pinto, Antonio Costa. "Fascism, Corporatism and the Crafting of Authoritarian Institutions in Inter-War European Dictatorships." In *Rethinking Fascism and Dictatorship in Europe*, edited by A. C. Pinto and A. Kallis, 87–117. London: Palgrave Macmillan, 2014.

Plaatje, Solomon T. *Native Life in South Africa before and since the European War and the Boer Rebellion.* London: Laurence King, 1917. http://www.gutenberg.org/ebooks/1452.

Popenoe, Paul. *Problems of Human Reproduction.* Baltimore, MD: Williams & Wilkins, 1926.

Popenoe, Paul, and Roswell Hill Johnson. *Applied Eugenics.* New York: Macmillan, 1918.

Posel, Deborah. "The Case for a Welfare State: Poverty and the Politics of the Urban African Family in South Africa in the 1930s and 1940s." Paper presented at a workshop on South Africa in the 1940s, Southern African Research Centre, Queen's University, Kingston, September 2003.

———. *The Making of Apartheid: Conflict and Compromise.* Oxford: Clarendon, 1991.

———. "Social History and the Wits History Workshop." *African Studies* 69 (April 2010): 29–40.

———. "Whiteness and Power in the South African Civil Service: Paradoxes of the Apartheid State." *Journal of Southern African Studies* 25, no. 1 (March 1999): 99–119.

Potter, David C. "The Last of the Indian Civil Service." *South Asia: Journal of South Asian Studies* 2, no. 1–2 (1979): 19–29.

Prinsloo, M. J. M. *Blanke vroue-arbeid in die Unie van Suid Afrika.* Cape Town: Nasionale Boekhandel, 1957.

Ranger, Terence. "White Presence and Power in Africa." *Journal of African History* 29 (1979): 463–69.

Rassool, Ciraj, and Leslie Witz. "The 1952 Jan van Riebeeck Tercentenary Festival: Constructing and Contesting Public National History in South Africa." *Journal of African History* 34 (1993): 447–68.

Rautenbach, C. H., ed. *Ad Destinatum: Gedenkboek van die Universiteit van Pretoria.* Johannesburg: Voortrekkerpers, 1960.

Reich, Walter. "The Men Who Pulled the Triggers." *New York Times*, April 12, 1992.

Rive, Richard. *Buckingham Palace, District Six, A Novel of Cape Town.* Johannesburg: D. Philip, 1986.

Rodriguez, Ileana. "A New Debate on Subaltern Studies." LASA Forum, Latin American Studies Association, XXXIII, 2002.

Roediger, David R., ed. *Black on White: Black Writers on What It Means to Be White.* New York: Schocken Books, 1999.

———. "Critical Studies of Whiteness, USA: Origins and Arguments." *Theoria* 98 (December 2001): 72–98.

———. *The Wages of Whiteness: Race and the Making of the American Working Class.* New York: Verso, 1991.

Roizen, Ron. "How Does the Nation's 'Alcohol Problem' Change from Era to Era? Stalking the Social Logic of Problem-definition Transformations since Repeal." In *Altering the Amer-*

ican Consciousness: Essays on the History of Alcohol and Drug Use in the USA, 1800–2000, edited by Sarah Tracy and Caroline Acker, 61–87. Amherst: University of Massachusetts Press, 2004.

Roos, Neil. "The Army Education Scheme and the 'Discipline' of the White Poor in South Africa." *The History of Education* 32, no. 6 (November 2003): 645–59.

———. *Ordinary Springboks: Ordinary Servicemen and Social Justice in South Africa, 1939–1961.* Aldershot: Ashgate, 2005.

———. "Subaltern Historiography and South African History: Some Ideas for a Radical History of White Folk." *International Review of Social History* 61, no. 1 (2016): 117–50.

———. "The Torch Commando, the 'Natal Stand' and the Politics of Inclusion and Exclusion." In *Natal in the Union Period*, edited by Paul Thompson. Pietermaritzburg: University of Natal Press, 1988.

———. "Work Colonies for White Men and the Historiography of Apartheid." *Social History* 36, no. 1 (February 2011): 54–76.

Rosenhaft, Eve. "Review Article on Geoff Eley and William H. Sewell Jnr." *Social History* 34, no. 1 (February 2009): 74–79.

Rossouw, A. E., and M. L. Spies. *Ons Onthou 74 Jaar: Die C en N Meisieskool Oranje Bloemfontein*. Bloemfontein: Sendingpers, 1982.

Roux, Edward. *Time Longer than Rope: The Black Man's Struggle for Freedom in South Africa*, 2nd ed., Madison: University of Wisconsin Press, 1978 [1964].

Rubin, Don, Ousmane Diakhate, and Hansel Ndumbe Eyoh. *The World Encyclopedia of Contemporary Theatre: Africa*. London: Routledge, 1997.

Sanders, Mark. "Undesirable Publications: J. M. Coetzee on Censorship and Apartheid." *Law and Literature* 18, no. 1 (2006): 101–14.

Sarkar, Sumit. "The Decline of the Subaltern in Subaltern Studies." In *Reading Subaltern Studies: Critical History, Contested Meaning and the Globalisation of South Asia*, edited by David Ludden, 400–29. New Delhi: Permanent Black, 2001.

———. *Writing Social History*. Delhi: Oxford University Press, 1997.

Scholtz, G. D. *Het die Afrikaanse Volk 'n Toekoms?* Johannesburg: Voortrekkerpers, 1954.

Sewell, William H., Jr. *Logics of History: Social Theory and Social Transformation*. Chicago: University of Chicago Press, 2005.

Shephard, Ben. *A War of Nerves: Soldiers and Psychiatrists in the Twentieth Century*. Cambridge, MA: Harvard University Press, 2003.

Silverstone, Roger. "Complicity and Collusion in the Mediation of Everyday Life." *New Literary History* 33, no. 4 (2002): 761–80.

Smith, Ken. *The Changing Past: Trends in African Historical Writing*. Athens: Ohio University Press, 1988.

Snyman, Dana. *Op die Agterpaaie*. Cape Town: Tafelberg, 2011.

Soudien, Crain. "A Praetorian Sensibility? The Social Sciences and Humanities in Pretoria." Unpublished ASSAf Humanities lecture and Human Sciences Research Council (HSRC) 50-90-100 Commemoration. University of Pretoria, August 14, 2019.

Sparrow, James. *Warfare State: World War II and the Age of Big Government*. Oxford: Oxford University Press, 2011.

Spivak, Gayatri Chakravorty. "Can the Subaltern Speak? Speculations on Widow Sacrifice." In *Marxism and the Interpretation of Culture*, edited by Gary Nelson and Lawrence Grossberg. Urbana: University of Illinois Press, 1988.

Stedman Jones, Gareth. "The Deterministic Fix: Some Obstacles to the Further Development of the Linguistic Approach to History in the 1990s." *History Workshop Journal* 42 (1996): 19–35.

Stoler, Ann Laura. *Along the Archival Grain: Epistemic Anxieties and Colonial Common Sense.* Princeton, NJ: Princeton University Press, 2009.
———. *Carnal Knowledge and Imperial Power: Race and the Intimate in Colonial Rule.* Berkeley: University of California Press, 2002.
———. *Race and The Education Of Desire: Foucault's History of Sexuality and the Colonial Order of Things.* Durham: Duke University Press, 1995.
Stoler, Ann, and Frederick Cooper. "Between Metropole and Colony: Rethinking a Research Agenda." In *Tensions of Empire: Colonial Cultures in a Bourgeois World,* edited by Frederick Cooper and Ann Stoler, 1–56. Berkeley: University of California Press, 1997.
Taillon, Paul. "'What We Want Is Good, Sober Men': Masculinity, Respectability, and Temperance in Railroad Brotherhoods, c. 1870–1910." *Journal of Social History* 36 (2002): 319–38.
Taussig, Michael. *Defacement: Public Secret and the Labor of the Negative.* Palo Alto, CA: Stanford University Press, 1999.
Thompson, E. P. *The Making of the English Working Class.* New York: Victor Gollancz, 1963.
———. *The Poverty of Theory: Or an Orrery of Errors.* London: Merlin, 1978.
Thompson, Leonard. *The Political Mythology of Apartheid.* New Haven and London: Yale University Press, 1985.
Trapido, Stanley. "South Africa in a Comparative Analysis of Industrialization." *Journal of Development Studies* 7, no. 3 (1971): 309–20.
Turner, Frederick Jackson. *The Frontier in American History.* New York: H. Holt, 1935.
Van den Berghe, Pierre L. "Miscegenation in South Africa." *Cahiers d'études africaines* 1, no. 4 (1960): 68–84.
Van den Heever, C. M. *Laat Vrugte.* Bloemfontein: Nasionale Pers., 1939.
Van der Walt, Lucien, and Michael Schmidt. *Black Flame: The Revolutionary Class Politics of Anarchism and Syndicalism.* Edinburgh: AK, 2009.
Van Onselen, Charles. *New Babylon, New Ninevah: Everyday Life on the Witwatersrand, 1886–1914.* Johannesburg: Ravan, 1982.
Van Rooyen, E. *Met 'n siekspens: Jeugherinneringe.* Cape Town: Tafelberg, 1994.
Vincent, Louise. "Bread and Honour: White Working Class Women and Afrikaner Nationalism in the 1930s." *Journal of Southern African Studies* 26, no. 1 (March 2000): 61–78.
———. "A Cake of Soap: The *Volksmoeder* Ideology and Afrikaner Women's Campaign for the Vote." *International Journal of African Historical Studies* 32, no. 1 (1999): 1–17.
Visser, C. B. "Die Vereniging van Staatsbeampte en die Totstandkoming van die Wet op Arbeidsverhoudinge vir die Staatsdiens, 1993 (102/1993)." Master's thesis, Potchefstroom University for Christian Higher Education, 1997.
Visser, George Cloete. *OB: Traitors or Patriots?* Johannesburg: Macmillan, 1977.
Wagner, O. J. M. *Social Work in Cape Town.* Cape Town: Maskew Miller, 1938.
Webster, Eddie. *Cast in a Racial Mould: Labour Process and Trade Unionism in the Foundries.* Johannesburg: Ravan, 1985.
Weiner, Lynn Y. *From Working Girl to Working Mother: The Female Labor Force in the United States, 1820–1980.* Chapel Hill: University of North Carolina Press, 1984.
Welsh, David. "The Growth of Towns." In *The Oxford History of South Africa, Volume II,* edited by Monica Wilson and Leonard Thompson, 172–244. Oxford: Oxford University Press, 1975.
Wessels, Albert. *Farmboy and Industrialist.* Johannesburg: Perskor, 1987.
White, W. B. "Apartheid: The U. P. Reaction." Paper presented at "Structure and Experience in the Making of Apartheid," University of the Witwatersrand, Johannesburg, 1990.
Williamson, Peter J. *Varieties of Corporatism: A Conceptual Discussion.* Cambridge: Cambridge University Press, 1985.

Wilson, Francis. "Farming." In *The Oxford History of South Africa, Volume II*, edited by Monica Wilson and Leonard Thompson, 104–71. Oxford: Oxford University Press, 1975.

Wolf, Arthur P., and William H. Durham. *Inbreeding, Incest and the Incest Taboo: The State of Knowledge at the Turn of the Century*. Stanford, CA: Stanford University Press, 2004.

Wolpe, Harold. "The 'White Working Class' in South Africa." *Economy and Society* 5, no. 2 (1976): 197–240.

Wright, Harrison. *The Burden of the Present: The Liberal-Radical Controversy in Southern African History*. Cape Town: David Philip, 1977.

Wright, John. "Probing the Predicaments of Academic History in Contemporary South Africa." Paper presented at the South African Historical Society Conference, University of the Western Cape, July 11–14, 1999.

Young, Robert J. C. *Postcolonialism: An Historical Introduction*. Oxford: Blackwell, 2001.

Yudelman, David. *The Emergence of Modern South Africa: State, Capital and the Incorporation of Organized Labour on the South African Gold Fields, 1902–1939*. Westport, CT: Greenwood, 1983.

Zijderveld, Anton C. "History and Recent Development of Dutch Sociological Thought." *Social Research* 33, no. 1 (Spring 1966): 115–31.

INDEX

administrative division, of public service, 77, 84, 88, 94, 108, 117
Africa, precolonial, 10
African American studies of race, 11–15, 23–24
African historiography, Marxist, 21, 24–26, 30–31, 33, 134
African National Congress, 7, 24, 192n12
African nationalists, 70
African studies, 10
African women, as domestic workers: employment of, by working-class whites in 1950s, 126–27; infantilization/de-sexualization of, 127; only permitted close contact with the woman of the house, 127; as sexual threat, 127
Africanist scholarship, whites in, 9–13
Afrikaans theater, 73–74. *See also* Cronjé, Geoffrey
Afrikaans: Afrikaner nationalism and, 56, 124–26; loss of, in Roos family, 52, 56; recognition of, as official language, 195n8; use of, in staatsdiens, 89
Afrikaner femininity, 17, 108–15, 128–29. *See also volksmoeder*
Afrikaner nationalism: ideal of family in 54, 61, 67, 69, 115, 120–22, 124–25, 136, 166, 173, 178, 180; ideology of, 12, 28, 30, 73, 87, 94–96, 108, 112–15, 124–25, 128–29, 133–34, 154, 160, 170; in the Cape, 66, 69, 198n12; in the Transvaal, 66, 198n12
Afrikaner nationalist women's movements. *See* Suid-Afrikaanse Vrouefederasie (SAVF)
Afrikaner *volk*, concept of: perceived threats to, 56–57, 64, 66, 106–7, 121; role of family in, 61, 67, 106–11, 115, 121–22, 173, 176; role of religion in, 73, 86, 97, 122, 133, 176;
Afrikanerization, of Public Service (*staatsdiens*), 16, 78, 83–89, 103, 135–36

agency: available to public service *beamptes*, 80, 97, 99, 101–4; of the subaltern, 29, 31–34, 189; of work colony detainees, 180–81
Albertyn, Dominee J. R., 46–47, 196n27. *See also* Carnegie Commission of Investigation on the Poor White Question in South Africa
alcohol panic, 161–62, 183–84
alcohol use: fears of race mixing and, 47, 66–67; urbanization and, 163, 178
alcoholic women, 163–66, 182–83
Alcoholics Anonymous, 163, 167, 169–70, 182
alcoholism: as illness, 163–70; as moral failing, 47–48, 66–69, 163–164, 167–69, 175–77, 182–84
Andersson, Axel, 31
Anglican church, 39, 207n85
Anglo-Boer War, 7, 9, 21, 39, 41, 106, 109
anthropological turn, 33, 194n32
anti-colonial movements global rise of, after Second World War; 62
anti-colonial scholarship, 10–11, 192n16
Antisemitism, 142, 199n36, 208n44. *See also* Hoggenheimer, Jews
apartheid, armed resistance to, 182, 185; declared a "crime against humanity", 5, 191n4; early, 3, 31, 57–58, 75, 80, 83, 95, 116, 120, 125, 135, 140, 162, 165, 173, 178; systematic implementation of, 7–8, 66, 137–38
apologia, history of whites and, 28, 37, 188
appliances, household, as credit purchase, 144, 146
archival evidence, methodological approach to, 18, 33–34, 194n37
Arendt, Hannah; 15, 26–29, 187, 194n19; *Eichmann in Jerusalem: A Report on the Banality of Evil*; 15, 27–29, 194n19
Ashforth, Adam, 68

231

Asian, as racial category under Population Registration Act, 101
aspiration: cultivation of, by state, 88, 132–33; middle-class; 137–38, 140, 142, 146–47
authoritarian societies: complicity and, 5–7, 19, 26; study of everyday life in, 3, 5, 7, 9, 13, 20, 26–27, 33, 37
autobiography, in *Ordinary Whites*, methodological notes on, 13–15, 33, 35–37

Baldwin, James, 24
Ballinger, Margaret, 94
Bambatha Rebellion, 43
"banality of evil," apartheid and, 13, 27–28, 99, 171–72
banks, and poor Afrikaners, 142–43, 208n43
banned books, 70–71, 200n53. *See also* censorship, regime of
Basson, J.H., 78
Baviaanspoort-Boerederykolonie en-Dronkaardgestig (agricultural colony and alcoholics' retreat for idlers/loiterers/loafers): failures of, 48; as first work colony, 48
Bhadra, Gautam, 32
Biko, Steve, 24–25
bilingualism, Afrikaans/English, in Public Service, 89
birth rates, decline in, among Afrikaners, 106–7, 122
Black Consciousness Movement, 24
Black French citizens, 11
Black poor, historical relation to white poor, 15, 20–21, 40–41, 50
Black South African critical commentary, 24
Black workers, in segregated labor market, 21, 44, 50, 133, 135
Blignaut, Charl, 114
bloedsap, Karel/Charles Roos as, 40, 53
bloedvermenging (blood mixing): Cronjés concern regarding, 63–65; as distinct from miscegenation, 199n2
Board of Censors, 70–71
book-burning, 72
boom gate, Durban, 131–32, 159
Bouman, P. J., 106–7
Brink, Elsabé, study of *volksmoeder* concept, 108–9
British Public Service traditions, and *staatsdiens*, 79
building societies, as distinct from buy aid societies, 137, 142

Bureau of Female Labour, 107, 128
bureaucracy, relation of, to authoritarian society, 10, 19, 26–28, 49, 59, 99, 188
buy aid societies: as distinct from building societies, 142; loans offered to members by, 142–43; motor vehicle purchase and, 143–44; public servants and, 142–43. *See also* consumer credit
bywoners, 39, 44

Calvinist moral reasoning, 42, 47, 66–67, 196n16
Cape liberalism, 24
Cape Nationalists, 66, 69, 142
Cape Town Home for Friendless Girls, 46. *See also* unmarried mothers
Carnegie Commission of Investigation on the Poor White Question in South Africa, 46, 110, 113, 166, 196n17
Catholic nuns, as heads of Anglophone nursery schools, 125
censorship, regime of, 70–72
central planning, 59, 67, 137
centralization, in public service, 28, 85, 90, 92, 97
Ceylon (Sri Lanka), 40
Chakrabarty, Dipesh, 33, 36, 194n23, 195n43, 202n66
Chibber, Vivek, 30
children, care of, 17, 60–61, 107, 123–26, 139
Chipkin, Clive, 208n27
Christian social work, 61–62, 164, 211n15
Christian, apartheid state as, 61–62, 134
Cillié, Piet, 69, 156
civilized labor policy, 49–52, 94, 131, 135, 140–41
Clark, Nancy, 113–14
Clark, W. Marshall, 82
Clarkson, C. F., 77–78
class analysis, relationship of, to cultural analysis, 30–31. *See also* Chibber, Vivek
clergy: involvement of, in poor whiteism, 40; involvement of, in rehabilitation of alcoholics, 180, 184. See also *dominees*
clerical division, of public service: women in, 84–85, 90, 115–17
clothing, advertisements for, 146–47
Coetzee, John M.: scholarship on Cronjé by, 57–58, 63–64, 72, 199n26
Cold War, 134
colonial subjects in India, 29–32, 84–85, 203n99

color bars, workplace, 7, 50, 100, 187, 197n42
colored, racial category under Population Registration Act, 8, 91, 101, 110, 163, 191n9
Coloured Peoples' Congress, 192n12
Comaroff, Jean, 192n16
Comaroff, John, 192n16
Commission of Enquiry into Protected Work, 95
Commission of Inquiry into Family Life, 165–66
Commission of Inquiry into the Structure of the Public Service, 119
Commission of Inquiry into Undesirable Publications (or Cronjé commission), 70–72
commissions of inquiry, Conjés involvement with, 16, 68, 161
Committee on Alcoholism, 70
communism, Afrikaner nationalist rhetoric about, 8, 63, 111, 137
Communist Party of South Africa's Central Committee, 110; Afrikaner women in, 110
complicity, 5–7, 15, 19, 26, 28, 36, 104, 129, 133, 178, 188
Comrades Marathon, The, 5, 191n3
Congress of Democrats; 28, 192n12
Congress of the People, 8
conscription. *See* military conscription, expansion of
consumer credit, rise of, 142–47
consumer culture, 153–54, 156. *See also* consumption
consumption: Afrikaner middle class and, 17, 135, 137–39, 142–45; as threat to Afrikaner nationalist ideals, 47, 133–34, 142–60; global circuits of, 17, 147, 160; trends in, 142, 146–47, 152, 156
Cooper, Frederick, 34
Cornelius, Johanna, 110–12
corporativism, 59, 62, 78, 90, 97
cost of living allowances, for public servants, 77–78, 119, 206n45
Cottesloe House, 169
Court, Anthony, 194n19
Cradock conference, 1916, 48. *See also* poor whiteism
credit blacklisting, 133, 147
credit companies, Afrikaner, 143
credit purchases, most common, 146–47
credit relationships, as transgressing apartheid principles, 36, 143–44
criminology: 31, 58–59, 61–62, 153, 159–60

Cronjé, Geoffrey, 15–16, 28, 30, 33, 56, 57–76, 78, 82, 105, 107, 133, 154, 161–62, 164–66, 168–70, 172, 175–78, 181–84, 198n5–7, 199n26, 200n57, 210n4, 213n70; as authoritarian, 59, 62–63; as bureaucrat, 15–16, 28, 61, 64–65, 68–72, 75, 82, 161, 165, 170, 183–84; dramatology and, 72–75, 154; published works of, 62; social engineering and, 15–16, 58–61, 67, 72, 76, 162, 172, 182, 184; view of alcohol, 61, 65–70, 161–70, 175–78, 181–84; view of white poor, 15–16, 56–57, 66, 68, 71–72
Customs Management Act, 1913, 70

dagga (marijuana), 152, 179, 185
Davies, Robert, 68, 134–35
De Kiewiet, C.W., 15, 20–21, 44, 132, 193n6
Deacon, Roger, 201n14, 212n44
Defiance Campaign against Unjust Law (1952), 8, 143–44
desire, apartheid regime as attack on, 63–64, 72, 175–76. *See also* Coetzee, John M
Dick, Archie, 71–72
Diederichs, Nico, 34; 144–45
disability grants, provision of, 43. *See also* poor whiteism
disabled whites, employment for, 95. *See also* sheltered employment
dispossession, rural, 39, 41, 61, 106, 195n6
divorce: rise in rates of, during war, 121–22; as sign of social degeneration, 58–59, 69, 107
dominees, 12, 49, 180, 184
Donges, T.E., 100–1, 112, 162
dramatology, 92–95, 174
Du Bois, W. E. B., 11–13, 15, 24, 195n41
Du Toit, J. D., development of volksmoeder mythology and, 109
Du Toit, Marie, critique of volksmoeder mythology, 109
ducktail subculture, 73, 152–54, 156, 158
Durban Bachelor Girls' Club, 129–30; 188
Durban: as English-speaking, 1, 22, 38, 52; housing in, 136–37, 139–41
Dutch colonialism, 7
Dutch Reformed churches, 12, 41–42, 48–49, 52, 69–70, 144, 199n29, 205n28

Eastern mysticism, popularized for whites in 1950s, 154
economic growth, in 1950s, 132–35, 156
Eersterivier work colony, 49, 173, 175–76
Eichmann, Adolf, 27, 29
Eiselen, Werner "Max", 69, 82

Index   233

Ekonomiese Volkskongres (National Economic Congress), 142
elderly women, wartime employment of, 113
Eley, Geoff, 11, 13, 26, 32, 80
enfranchisement, of white women, 111, 191n9
English-speaking whites, 1, 3, 17, 21–22, 39, 82, 86, 88–89, 125, 132, 138, 158–59, 207n1, 208n43
Entertainment (Censorship) Act, 70
epilepsy, 46, 156
Eskom (the electricity supply corporation), 51
ethnography, as historiographic lens in *Ordinary Whites*, 3, 13–19, 30, 33–37
Eudora Hauptfleisch school, 125. See also *kleuterskole*
eugenics, 76, 122
everyday life, white, 13, 16, 20, 26, 28–29, 32, 37, 58, 65, 74, 162, 184, 187
eviction. See dispossession, rural

family history, author's, 1–3, 13–15, 22–23, 26–28, 35–41, 52–57, 60, 105, 120, 131–32, 170–71, 180–81, 188
family, as counter to "disorder," 61, 66–67, 139
Fanon, Frantz, 94, 192n22
farm schools, 58, 198n4
fascism, Afrikaner nationalism and, 59
Federasie van Afrikaanse Kultuurverenigings [Federation of Afrikaner Cultural Organizations] (FAK), 65, 73, 142–143, 154, 156, 199n34
Finzsch, Norbert, 201n14
First World War, 20, 59, 115, 129, 211n15
floriculture, as occupation for white men with epilepsy, 46
foster care, 65, 177
Foucault, Michel: concept of power formulated by, 31, 34; technologies of the self, 204n3
"the fragment" (small historical vignette), value of, 19, 34–36, 161–62, 210n2. See also subaltern studies; Pandey, Gyanendra
Fraser, Gael, 164, 183
Freed, Louis, 33, 153–54, 162, 210n4
Freedom Charter, 8
furniture, as credit purchase, 14, 36, 143, 146

gardening, social value of, 45, 121
Garment Workers' Union (GWU), 110–12
Gellately, Robert, 215n5
general division, of public service, 84–85, 201n29; black workers in, 201n29
"generative mistakes", 36–37. See also autobiography; Chakrabarty, Dipesh; ethnography; subaltern studies

Genovese, Eugene, 24
Gerhart, A. E., 80–81
German historiography, 7, 27–28, 189, 191nn7–8, 210n3
Gestapo, 215n5
Geyer, Michael, 191n7
Giliomee, Herman, 132, 198n12
Girls' Friendly Society, 130, 207n85
Glatt, Dr. Max, 210n14
Goldberg, David, 207n82
Good Hope Model Village, 45
Gramsci, Antonio, 30–31
"grand apartheid", 1–2, 8, 26
Grandfather L, 13–14, 38–39
Grandmother Roos, 15, 52–54, 120, 121
Great Depression, 5, 40, 57, 60, 90, 140, 142
Great Trek centenary celebrations, 1938, 111–12, 114, 160, 199n36; women in, 111–12, 114
Group Areas Act, 1950, 138, 144, 160
Grundlingh, Albert, 132–33, 142, 158; "Are we Afrikaners Getting Too Rich?," 132
Guha, Ranajit, 30–31, 36; *Elementary Aspects*, 36
gun culture, 159

halfgeskooldes (semi-educated people), sheltered work for, 95–96, 102, 175–76, 181
hard labor, as corrective, 49, 176. See also "labour therapy"
Hartwell, Dulcie, 110
Harvey, Ian, 147. See also homosexuality: scandals surrounding
Hauptfleisch, Eudora, 125–26
Herenigde NP (Reunited National Party), 66, 199n36
Hertzog, J.B.M., 40, 111
hire purchase (or layaway): as "future saving," 145; as distinct from "extravagant" credit-fueled consumption, 144–45
Hire Purchase Bill, 1954, 144
histories across the color line, 23–24, 35, 144, 160, 188
history from below, 13, 29–30, 33
Hobsbawm, Eric, 24
Hoggenheimer, 142, 208n44
home ownership: as aspirational, 140; as bastion against communism, 137; as stabilizing influence; 137
home visits / *huisbesoek*, to working-class homes, 17, 124, 129, 140
"homelands," ten ethnic, 8, 191n10, 205n24
homosexuality: as pathology, 153, 178; scandals surrounding, 147

homosexuals, assaults on, 52, 152
hooks, bell, 23–24
Hoovervilles, 40
hostels: as alternative to hospitals for treating alcoholics, 169; as housing for young working men and women, 45, 114, 116, 129–30, 141
household-scale economies, changes to, 135–36
housing, cultural significance of, 136–38
housing, subsidized, 2, 46, 101, 136–42, 142, 146
human resource management, in public service, 16, 93–94
Hyslop, Jonathan, 111, 128, 204n111

Ibadan school, 192n14
idleness: among ducktails, 153; as social ill, 3, 47–49, 165, 167, 1210n5
Immorality Act (1927), 8–9, 40, 214n
Immorality Act (1957), 186–87
Immorality Amendment Act (1950), 68, 127
incest, among poor whites, 63–64, 199nn29, 31
India: colonial, 29–30, 84–85, 203n99; postcolonial, 30
Indian Civil Service, as influence on Public Service / *staatsdiens* 83–85, 203n99
Indian historiography, 29–32
individualism, as dangerous, 106, 127–28, 158
induction training, in public service, 96, 100, 119
Industrial Conciliation Act (1924), 50
industrial psychology, 16, 94
industrialists, South African, 90
industrialization, 63, 163
infrastructure, 44, 133
insluiper, the, 56, 63, 65, 68, 72, 75–76, 175–76, 183; indifference and, 63, 67–68
interracial sex: fear of, 44, 71, 111, 126–27, 153; legal prohibition of, 8–9, 40, 66, 68, 126–27, 178–79, 184, 186–87
Iscor (the Iron and Steel Corporation), 51

Jackson, Will, 94
Jansen, Jonathan, 12
Japanese industry, 16, 90
Johannesburg, crime and street life in, 162. *See also* Freed, Louis
Jooste, J. L., 98

Kakamas, 42
KaNgwane, 191n10
kappie kommandos [bonnet brigades], 112. *See also* Great Trek centenery celebrations, 1938: women in

Kenneth Gardens, 139, 208n32
Kinsey Report, 212n54
Klausen, Susanne, 204n12
kleuterskole (nursery schools), 125–26, 129, 206n68–69; as alternative to Black women servants as childcare providers, 126; funding of, by SAVF, 125; instruction in Afrikaans at, 125; as provider of childcare for working mothers, 125–26
Koophulpvereniging vir Staatsdiensamptenare [Buying aid society for civil servants], 143
Koopkrag, 143, 209n46
Kuyper, Abraham, 198n7
KwaZulu-Natal, 35–36, 143, 157, 186, 191n3,
Kynaston, David, 147

"labour therapy" (in rehabilitation), 170, 176
land evictions. *See* dispossession, rural
landlopers (hoboes), use of work colonies for seasonal shelter by, 181
language testing, in public service, 88–89
leeglopers (idlers/tramps/loiterers/loafers/beggars), assignment of, to work colonies, 48, 162–63
leisure activities: state surveillance of / intervention in, 76, 99, 133, 158; at work colonies, 176–77
lesbians, highlighting of, in Freed's "Report on [white] homosexuality," 153
Liberal Party, 28
liberal whites, 24, 62, 70, 72, 129
librarians, pre-emptive destruction of books by, 72, 188
Lloyd George, David, 203n99
LM radio, 158. *See also* rock and roll music
loans: for housing, 136–37; personal, from buy aid societies, 143, 208n43
local studies, methodological complexities of, 33–36; 195n42
"locations", native. *See* native "locations"
Louw, Eric, 34, 144; opposition to work colonies, 169, 182, 185
Lüdtke, Alf, 188

Macdonald, Peter D., 71
Macmillan, W. M., 15, 20–21
maid (*meid*), as insult/racial slur, 112, 118, 122, 205n14
Malan, D.F., 7, 66, 70, 111, 132, 164, 211
Malherbe, Ernst G., 196n19–21
management bands, of public service, 84, 87–88, 117; entry of women into, 117

Index   235

Mandela, Nelson; 7, 24, 197n48; inauguration of; 197n48, *Long Walk to Freedom*, 24
manual labor, racial implications of, 21, 42, 44, 84, 94
manufacturing sector, women in, 110, 112, 115
Maree, W. A., 136–37
married women, wage labor among, 90, 118, 123, 128
Marxist historiography, 11–12, 21, 24–26, 30–33, 134, 1970s
masculinity, macho, 159
masturbation, as pathology, 175–76, 212–13n54
materialism, as danger to *volk*, 122–23
"Mauritians," 101–2
McLachlan, R., 69
mechanization, 93, 135; effects of, on racial capitalism, 135
meid. See maid
memory studies, 37
mental hospitals, treatment of alcoholics in, 167
merit assessment system, 90–94, 142. See also quality control
middle class, 3–4, 17, 39, 56, 66, 109, 111, 135, 137–39, 142, 145–46, 152
military conscription, expansion of, 160, 182, 214n94
mineral revolution, 20, 41
miscreants, as category of subordinate whites, 18–19, 56, 64, 75, 164, 172–74, 178–80
Mixed Marriages Act, 1949, 68
moederkunde ["crafts of motherhood"], as formal curriculum, 123–24, 129
Mooney, Katie, 152–53
moral inversion, 27–28, 187. See also Arendt, Hannah
Morrell, R., 195n3
motherhood, Afrikaner nationalist notions of, 120–24
motor vehicles, as credit purchase, 143–45, 147

Natal sugar belt, 38–39, 187; company towns in, 39, 187; white anglophone society in, 39
National Conference on Alcoholism, 1952, 166–70; broadening of scope of surveillance by, 170
National Party (NP), position of, regarding credit, 144–45; role of Public Service for, 79, 81–82, 92, 97; wages of whiteness and, 2, 132–35, 141, 160; white poverty as early focus of, 17, 46, 66, 132, 138, 140–41

nationalism, Afrikaner. See Afrikaner nationalism
nationalism, broad white South African (South Africanism), 21
Native (Urban Areas) Act of 1923, 44–45. See also pass laws
native "locations", 44–45
Nazi Germany: historiography of, 7, 27–28, 189, 191n7, 210n3, 215n5; South African support for, in Second World War, 80–81, 114
Nederduits Hervormde Kerk (NHK), 42
Nederduitse Gereformeerde Kerk (NGK), 41–42, 48–49, 52
Neethling-Pohl, Anna, 74–75
Njamnjoh, Francis, 37
North Africa, Second World War in, 5, 54–56

occult, interest in, among middle-class whites, 134
occupational adjustment, 94, 103
O'Meara, Dan, 66, 68, 79–82, 134–35, 143, 199n36, 208n44
oral history, 35–37
ordentlikheid (respectability), 3, 17 132, 136, 182
order and disorder, principles of, in Afrikaner nationalism, 61
Organization and Methods Study (O&M) on training of officers, 93
Ossewa Brandwag (OB), 66, 114–15, 121, 199n36, Emergency Fund of, 114; *volksmoeder* ideology and, 114–15, 121; Women's Division of, 114–15, 121

Paarl Boys' High School, 58
Painter, Nell Irvin, *Southern History Across the Color Line*, 13, 23
Pandey, Gyanendra, 32, 34–35, 210n2. See also "the fragment"
parastatals: Afrikanerization of, 135; growth of, 68, 73, 134–35, 207n11
Pass laws, 44–45, 127
passive resistance, 8
Pavlich, George, 198n7
piano, aspirational value of, 148, 151
Pietermaritzburg, 52, 191n3
Pieterse, Jannie, 30, 33, 65, 73, 133, 154, 180, 197n38
Plaatje, Solomon T., 24–25
platteland (countryside), 41, 84, 89, 141, 198n4
Police force, expansion of, 159–60
Pollack, Hansi, 110

poor whiteism, 9, 40–48, 56, 61, 71, 90, 132–33, 140, 195n6; end of, through Public Service expansion, 90, 132–33
Popenoe, Paul, 122. *See also* eugenics
Posel, Deborah, 86, 99, 117, 184, 201n12
postapartheid South Africa, history-writing in, 12, 26, 37
Postma, Willem: *Die Boervrou: Moeder van Haar Volk* (The Boer Woman: Mother of Her Nation), 109–10
poststructuralist scholarship, 34
post-traumatic stress disorder, 171
postwar economic growth, 134–38
prepublication censorship, 70
Presbyterian Church, 52
Prinsloo, Dr. Maria J., 105–8, 115, 120, 127–29, 133; *Blanke vroue-arbeid in die Unie van Suid-Afrika*, 105–8, 115, 120,
private sector: growth in, 86–87, 132–33, 135, 202n43
proletarianization, 63, 140
prostitution, as threat to white family life, 4, 69–70
public servants, agency of, 16, 80, 97, 99–103; control of leisure time of, 99; as disrespected social group; 86, 102; management of; 76, 88, 91–94, 96–98, 103, 129, 142, 158–59
Public Servants' Association (PSA), 88, 98–100, 116–19, 145–46
Public Servants' Association Women's Section, 117–19; concessions obtained from PSC by, 119; and respectability of working women, 118
Public Service Act, 1923, 84, 93
Public Service Commission (PSC): annual reports of, 80, 85, 119; executive government and, 82–83; recruiting measures used by, 22, 51, 78, 83–90, 102, 113, 116–18, 138; response to rise in female employment 84–85, 90, 107–8, 115–20, 128
Public Service Commission of Enquiry, 116–17
Public Service Competitive Examination, 84–85
public service: Afrikanerization of, 16, 78, 83–90, 103, 135–36; and Afrikaner nationalism, 16–17, 81–82, 87, 89–90, 96, 103, 107–8; age limits for entry into, 84, 117; and corporativism, 78, 90, 97; dress codes in, 98; and formation of middle class, 4, 17, 68, 87, 135–38, 142; gendered hierarchies in, 16, 79, 84, 90–91, 108, 115–119; job re-grading in, 68; postwar condition of, 77–78, 80–83; scientific management used in, 16, 90–97, 103
Publications Control Board, 70–71
Public Servant, The, 88, 145–51; advertisements in, 88, 146–51, 154–56; advice on aesthetics and taste in, 146

quality control principles, applied to public service, 16, 90–93

Rabie, Victor / "Die Wit Yogi" [The White Yogi], services advertised in *The Public Servant*, 154–56
racial capitalism, 9, 20, 134
racial violence, as preserve of the state / institutionalized, 102, 153
racialized sexual discourse / anxieties, 8–9, 44, 71, 126–27, 179; Black domestic workers as targets of, 126–27
radical history, 11–13, 20, 26, 31–32, 35–37, 80
railway workers, 22, 36, 51, 100, 116, 139–41, 143–44, 146, 168; racial wage gap among, 51, 94, 135
Rand Aid Society, 164, 166, 183
Rand Revolt, 1922, 50, 197n41
reformers, social, of 1920s, 64, 121, 125, 154
rehabilitation of alcoholics: community-based approaches to, 168; medical approaches to, 162–63, 168–70; religious approaches to, 69, 168, 170; welfarist approaches to, 18, 67, 162, 168, 170, 182
repatriation of Indian South Africans, Cronjés advocacy for, 62–63
representation, historiographic significance of, 31–34. *See also* subaltern studies
republicanism, Afrikaner nationalist, 26, 62
respectability, and working women, 17, 108, 112, 118, 124, 129
Riebeeck, Jan van; 156–59, 209n77
rinderpest epidemic of 1896, 41, 195n7
road camps, 141
Robben Island, prison, 24
rock and roll music, 73, 158
Roediger, David, 23–24, 133; *The Wages of Whiteness*, 132–35
Roos Committee, 61
Roos, Charles. *See* Roos, Karel/Charles
Roos, Dick, 3–4, 14–15, 28–29, 36, 54–57, 60, 131–32, 159, 170–71, 177, 180–81
Roos, grandmother. *See* Grandmother Roos
Roos, Jacob de Villiers, (Director of Prisons), 48

Index 237

Roos, Karel/Charles, 15, 39–41, 44–45, 52–54, 56–57, 60, 63, 114, 131, 171, 188
Roos, Neil, 1–3, 5, 22, 35–37, 38–39, 53–54, 86, 105, 131, 186–87, 192n13; *Ordinary Springboks*, 22, 197n51
Roos, Sheila, 1–4, 14–15, 22–23, 26–28, 31, 35–36, 38–39, 105, 120
Roos, Vic, 3, 54, 56–57, 60, 170–71, 177, 180–81
Rothmann, M. E., report on poor white women, 110
Roux, Eddie, 50
rural dispossession. *See* dispossession, rural
rural poverty, 20–21, 25

Sachs, Solly, 110–11
sacred history, 73, 97, 133
Said, Edward, 31
salary parity, in public service, 118–19
Samba, 142–43. *See also* buy aid societies
sheltered employment (for disadvantaged whites), 69, 95, 175
slums, multi-racial, 44–47; welfare work in, 45–47, 60
Smuts, General Jan, 39–40, 50, 52–53, 197n42 39–40, 50, 52–53, 190
social engineering, 16, 59–60, 67, 71–72, 76, 103, 162, 166–67, 181–82, 184
social history, 11–13, 15, 20, 22, 24–26, 29–31, 34, 46, 58, 79, 99
social work: amateur/voluntary, 124, 166; Afrikaner nationalist women's groups and, 60–61, 121, 124, 166; professional, 166; Cronjé's approach to, 33, 58, 60–62, 64–65, 76, 162, 166, 168; "scientific" approaches to, 166
soft loans, for white male veterans, 136
Sonderwater (work colony), 171–72, 174–79, 181
Sonnenberg, Fritz, 158
sound, in popular culture, 74, 147
South African mint: employment of women by 113; working conditions at, 113
South African National Council on Alcoholism (SANCA), 170
South African Native National Congress (later African National Congress), 24
South African Party (SAP), 40, 42–43, 48–50, 53, 130
Sparrow, James, 198n10
Spivak, Gayatri Chakravorty, 34
Springbok Legion, 28, 208n33
Springbok rugby, 186

squatter settlements, 41, 109. *See also* poor whiteism
staatsdiens. *See* public service
state-making, 19, 97–98, 100, 103, 160, 162, 204n111
statism, 134–35
Stellenbosch University, 58, 73, 110, 192n13
Steyn, D. J. C., 83. *See also* Public Service Commission: executive government and
Stoler, Ann Laura, 193n4, 194n37; *Along the Archival Grain: Epistemic Anxieties and Colonial Common Sense*, 194n37; *Carnal Knowledge and Imperial Power: Race and the Intimate in Colonial Rule*, 193n4
Strijdom, J.G. 66
strikes: by Black gold miners (1946), 8; in public service, 99–100; by white gold miners around color bar (1907, 1913, 1914, 1922), 50
subaltern studies, 28–37, 194n23, 210n2
subeconomic housing estates, 139–40; distaste for among SAVF; 139–40; as indication of erosion of family life, 140; lack of strict enforcement of apartheid principles in, 140
subordination, and subalternity, 29–30, 32, 53
suicide, 19, 180, 186–88
Suid-Afrikaanse Vereniging vir Maatskaplike Dienste (South African Association for Social Services), *Blanke-Vroue, Naturelle-Mans en Drank* (White women, native men and alcohol), 163
Suid-Afrikaanse Vrouefederasie (SAVF): program of *huisbesoek* (home visits), 17, 124–25, 129, 140; on childcare, 17, 60–61, 123–26, 139; class character of, 114–15, 121, 124–25, 129, 138–40; views of, on working women, 17, 120–29. *See also Vrou en Moeder, moederkunde, kleuterskole*
Suppression of Communism Act, 1950, repression allowed by, 8, 71
surveillance: expansion of, by state, 160, 182, 197n38; in public service, 91, 102, 142; subjection of white subalterns to, 3–4, 8–9, 31–33, 35, 56; work colonies and, 172, 180, 184; of working-class women by SAVF, 124–25, 129–30, 140
Swart, C. R., 34
Swartfontein (work colony), 49, 173, 175–76

taste, middle-class trends / influences on, 17, 88, 133, 142, 146
Taylor, Frederick, principles of scientific management, 90
Te Water, Dr. Maria, 60

technology of the self, 204n3. *See also* Foucault, Michel
Teddy Boys, 152
"theory from the south," 10–11, 192n16
Theron, Erika, 110
Thompson, E. P., 24, 31, 188
Thompson, Leonard, 192n20
Toc H, Women's Section, 164, 211n15
Totius. *See* du Toit, J. D.
Toyota Motor Corporation, 90
trade unionism, 23, 50, 110–13
Transkei; independence of, 191n10
Treason Trial (1956), 8
Trump, Donald, 11
Truth and Reconciliation Commission of South Africa (TRC), 6–7
typists, in Public Service, 85, 116, 118–19, 145; salaries of; 116–19; schools for (*tikskole*), 116, 118

Umzinto, 143–44, 160, 209n48
unemployment, among whites, 9, 21–22, 25, 30, 46, 49–51, 61, 64, 67, 72, 76, 109, 134, 139
Union of South Africa, formation of; 7–9, 21, 24, 43, 47, 95
United Party (UP), 40, 53, 77, 111, 136, 171
United States: advancements in treatment of alcoholism from, 163–64; scientific management in, 93; youth subcultures from, 147,
University of Pretoria, 33, 60, 62, 69, 72, 74–75, 159, 162, 170, 197n38, 198n7, 198n13, 210n4
University of the Witwatersrand, 25, 153
unmarried mothers, 46, 69, 124–25
upward social mobility, for Afrikaners, 33, 68, 73, 87, 102, 146, 159, 165
urban planning, state involvement in, 137–38
urbanization, social tensions sparked by, 9, 20, 44–45, 61, 63–64, 109, 163;
US-American South, 23

van den Bergh, Pierre L., 40
Van Riebeeck tercentenary, 156–59
Venda, independence of, 191n10
Venter, H. J., 159
Verwoerd, Henrik; as academic supervisor, 110; assassination of, 75; implementation of separate development 7, 9
Vincent, Louise, 110–12
volk. *See* Afrikaner *volk*
volkskapitalisme ("people's capitalism"), Afrikaner nationalist, 142–47
Volkskongres (People's Congress), 1947, 66

volksmoeder, Afrikaner nationalist ideal of: and Ossewa Brandwag, 114–15, 121; characteristics of, 54, 108–12, 114–15, 120–25, 128; Grandmother Roos as, 54; importance for populist rhetoric of, 111, 128; origins of, 108–9; rebuttals of, by female fesearchers, 109–10; working-class women and, 110–12, 114, 121. *See also* Suid-Afrikaanse Vrouefederasie (SAVF)
Vorster, (B.) John, 75, 143
Vrije Universiteit Amsterdam, 58, 198n7
Vrou en Moeder, 72, 121–23, 126–27, 138, 141; racialized sexual discourse in, 126–27; and working women, 122–23, 127. *See also* Suid-Afrikaanse Vrouefederasie (SAVF)
Vrouemonument (Women's Memorial), 109

wage gap, racial, 133
"wages of whiteness" under apartheid: as cause for disruptive cultural shifts, 133–34, 143–45, 154–56, 160; in housing, 136–37; in labor market, 134–35; psychological and social, 133
Wagner, O. J. M., 45–46
Wakkerstroom by-election, 1952, political street fights surrounding, 53, 193n3
war veterans, demobilization of, from Union Defence Force: housing shortage and, 136, 208n33; neighborhoods built for, 136; reintegration into postwar society, 54, 56, 81, 171
War Veterans' Torch Commando, 53, 197n51
wartime production, gender and, 112–14
Wessels, Albert, 90, 97
western popular culture, influence on apartheid whiteness, 73, 147, 162, 154, 158
white drinking: anxieties surrounding, 18, 161–70, 183–84; effects of urbanization on, 63, 178; prewar state response to, 162–63
white femininity, policing of: by non-nationalist Bachelor Girls' Club; 129–30; by SAVF, 121–23, 128–29
white women, as traitors to white nation, 111, 163, 204n12
white women's work: as "race suicide," 106–7, 122; as threat to Afrikaner nationalist ideology, 16–17, 47, 105–8, 110–15, 120–23, 127–29. *See also* eugenics
whiteness, apartheid-era: characteristics of, 79, 87, 115, 120; relationship to Afrikaner nationalism in state cohesion, 132–34, 158–60,
whiteness: Black perspectives on, 12–13, 23–25; construction of, 3, 5, 11, 75, 164, 188; dehumanizing effects of, 12–13; essentialized, 5, 36, 104; ethnographic contemplation of, 37

Index 239

Willemse, W.A., 61

Wits History Workshop, 24–25

work colonies: active leisure activities at, 176–77; as absent from historical literature, 18, 174; as places of reeducation, 172, 177, 182, 184; closure of, 3, 19, 178, 181–82; fear of, as surveilling influence, 8, 172, 180, 182, 184; *halfgeskooldes* as sub-wardens in, 95–96, 175–76; occlusion of, from middle class imagination, 180; official regime of, 176; reorganization of, by Cronjé, 18, 162, 173–77

Work Colonies Act of 1927, 49, 173

Work Colonies Act of 1949: increase in capacity to monitor population, 172–73, 212n44; introduction of probation, 173; shift of control from Ministry of Justice to Ministry of Social Welfare, 67–68, 165–66, 182

Work Colonies Advisory Board, 67–68, 172, 175–76, 180–81

work colony detainees: agency of, 180–81; desertion by, 35, 180–82, 185; regulations imposed upon following release, 18, 173, 177–78, 183; Dick and Vic Roos as, 3, 28–29, 54, 56, 170–71, 177, 180–81; surveillance of families of, 49, 177, 180

working-class white women, political allegiances of, 110–12

Yale University, Center for Alcohol Research at, 163, 170

youth crime / juvenile delinquency, 45–47, 61, 69, 107, 159–62

youth culture, as threat to social order, 73–74, 147, 152–54, 159, 160

Neil Roos is author of *Ordinary Springboks: White Servicemen and Social Justice in South Africa, 1939–1961*. He is currently Dean of Social Sciences and Humanities and Professor of History at the University of Fort Hare, South Africa. He is also co-implementer of the South African Department of Higher Education and Training's Future Professors Programme.

FOR INDIANA UNIVERSITY PRESS

Tony Brewer, *Artist and Book Designer*
Brian Carroll, *Rights Manager*
Gary Dunham, *Acquisitions Editor and Director*
Anna Francis, *Assistant Acquisitions Editor*
Brenna Hosman, *Production Coordinator*
Katie Huggins, *Production Manager*
Nancy Lightfoot, *Project Editor and Manager*
Dan Pyle, *Online Publishing Manager*
Leyla Salamova, *Senior Artist and Book Designer*
Stephen Williams, *Marketing and Publicity Manager*